A Handbook on

GUADALUPE

Franciscan Friars of the Immaculate

Our Lady's Chapel, New Bedford, MA, USA

Imprimatur: ✠ Most Rev. Sean Patrick O'Malley, O.F.M. Cap.
Bishop of Fall River, Massachusetts, USA
The Feast of the Assumption of Mary into
Heaven
August 15,1996

ISBN: #0-9652044-2-1

Picture Credits: Frank Smoczynski, front cover, pages, VI (top), 3, 9, 153, 155, 156, 178, 195, 197, 199, 200, 204, 219; Merle Watchter, page 40; Franciscan Herald Press, page 43; Basilica Museum, pages 50, 92; World Monument Fund page 25 (left); Carolyn Brown, page 25 (right); Janet Barber, pages 53, 71, 79, 187, 188

Park Press, Inc. - P.O. Box 475, 355 6th Ave. N., Waite Park, MN 56387

Acknowledgments

Besides acknowledging the contributions of a number of people, mentioned in the Forward of this book, special thanks are due to several of the authors, Fr. Christopher Rengers O.F.M.Cap., Fr. Martinus Cawley, O.C.S.O., Dan Lynch and Janet Barber who contributed many valuable suggestions, besides their articles. To the latter we are especially indebted for the latest developments on Guadalupana. We were especially pleased and honored to have our Bishop Sean O'Malley, O.F.M. Cap. write the inspiring preface to the book, which summarizes so well its purpose and direction. To the other authors who contributed to this book our profound thanks.

The typists who keyboarded the many articles were, Patricia Correia, Phillip Spindola, Mildred Duff and Diane Poiters and her daughter, Michelle. Diane Poiters, also proof read and offered many suggestions in the editing of articles. All of these lay people belong to, or are affiliated with the Secular Franciscan community here in New Bedford, at Our Lady's Chapel. Our thanks to all of these Third Order members of our Franciscan family. And we must not forget the members of the Franciscan Second Order, the Poor Clares, and all others whom we asked for prayers for the success of the *Handbook*.

Thanks too to our First Order Franciscans here at Our Lady's Chapel and at Marytown in Libertyville, IL, who by their example and words of encouragement helped immeasurably in making *A Handbook on Guadalupe* a reality. We were pleased to make more corrections after Bro. Charles Madden, O.F.M. Conv., the expert proofreader from Marytown, volunteered his help. Special mention to the Father Guardian of the Franciscan Friars of the Immaculate here in New Bedford, Father Francis Mary, F.F.I., who gave his permission and encouragement to the whole project. To Fr. Peter Fehlner, F.F.I., house theologian and retreat director here in New Bedford, goes the credit for checking the theology and historic soundness of the *Handbook*, besides contributing the article on Franciscanism and Guadalupe, Fr. Paul Marx, O.S.B., of "Human Life International" not only contributed at the last minute his excellent article (see page 147), but offered to publicize the *Handbook* and suggested a printer, a former student of his. To James and Dorothy Blommer of Park Press, Inc., Waite Park, MN, we give credit for the early printing of this *Handbook*. They cooperated in every way and we are very grateful to them.

And of course, we are forever indebted to the Immaculate Virgin, Mother of the True God, who ever inspired us to persevere in the production of this hymn of praise in her honor, for the glory of her Divine Son. It was she who inspired, directed and brought together all the above people, without whom the *Handbook* would never have materialized. To all of the contributors to the *Handbook*, our profound thanks. May she reward them as she did Juan Diego.

To her Sorrowful and Immaculate Heart we dedicate this work.

The Editor

v

The holy Image is mounted on a paneled wood wall behind the main altar. Below the sanctuary floor in an open well, pilgrims are able to view the Image close up from four moving treadways.

Contents

Foreword

"The accomplishments of our present times are like a dwarf sitting on the shoulders of the past," as the saying goes. We forget too often that the great strides which man is making in the present would have been impossible were it not for the many accomplishments of humanity in the past. In a sense, the same could be said about *A Handbook on Guadalupe*, which has a lengthy and checkered history going back to 1962, when a Special Issue on Guadalupe of IMMACULATA magazine was published by the Franciscan Friars of Marytown. Editorially speaking, it was made possible through the help of the monks at the Trappist Abbey of Our Lady of Guadalupe in Lafayette, Oregon, in particular, Abbot Dom Columban Hawkins O.C.S.O.

In addition to the Trappists, Bill Queen, a journalist and Franciscan tertiary from San Francisco, rendered invaluable help with his articles and advice. Other contributors were Coley Taylor and Helen Behrens. Fourteen years later, a paperback, *A Handbook on Guadalupe* was published by Marytown.

Dr. Charles Wahlig, an optometrist, and one of the foremost English-speaking authorities on Guadalupe, who had already written a biography on Juan Diego, was able to supply material for articles, amounting to better than half the contents of the 160-page *Handbook*. The attractive Guadalupe paperback was quickly sold out, necessitating a second and third printing. As new developments arose, a Guadalupan authority, Fr. Ernest Burrus, S.J., who had spent years researching Guadalupe in Mexico City, was enlisted to check the *Handbook* for accuracy. He carefully studied it and offered a number of corrections and suggestions. His valuable comments were carefully noted and incorporated in this *Handbook*.

Around 1990, contacts were made with outstanding Guadalupan authorities who had extensive experience in researching and writing on many subjects pertaining to Guadalupe. The first was Fr. Martinus Cawley, O.C.S.O., from the same Guadalupe Abbey as Abbot Hawkins. Fr. Martinus had studied the Aztec language, Nahuatl, so he could translate the original account into English. Along with this translation, which he made in 1968, he has done much research on

Guadalupe and composed other Guadalupan literature that has made him a valuable resource for the *Handbook*.

Another authority on Guadalupe, Janet Barber, I.H.M., who has been a devotee of Our Lady of Guadalupe since 1952 and been to the shrine numerous times, has a Doctorate in Spanish, which enables her to gather firsthand information from the experts in Mexico. It is she who translated into English the *Nican Mopohua* from the Spanish of the eminent Guadalupan scholar, Fr. Mario Rojas Sánchez who translated the original Nahuatl work into Spanish. Janet Barber, along with the late Dr. Charles Wahlig and Fr. Christopher Rengers, O.F.M. Cap., are substantially represented in *A Handbook on Guadalupe*. Frank Smoczynski, a businessman from Chicago, President of the "Queen of the Americas Guild," which has yearly conferences on Mary of Guadalupe in various parts of the country, and Martin Kelly, an attorney from Phoenix, who has done much in promoting Mary of Guadalupe's place in the arts and culture, rounded out the editing and production team.

All agreed that there was a great need for an updated, accurate and popular *Handbook*. Interest on Guadalupe is at an all-time high. A number of organizations and apostolates have taken her as their special patron, not least of which is the pro-life movement. One question remained: who would pull the loose ends together, edit and make the necessary contacts for printing the *Handbook*? The Franciscan Friars of the Immaculate in New Bedford, Massachusetts were pleased to accept the honor of being the publishers. This young Franciscan community whose first house in the United States was dedicated to Our Lady of Guadalupe has a beautiful shrine to her, with a life-sized reproduction of the sacred Image in their chapel. Moreover, in the Franciscan tradition, they are deeply committed to promoting devotion to Our Lady in her Immaculate Conception, which is how she appeared at Tepeyac (article on page 158). In addition to the traditional three vows of poverty, chastity and obedience, these Franciscans take a fourth vow, of giving one's self totally to Mary Immaculate. This was introduced into the Franciscan Order by St. Maximilian Kolbe, the hero of Auschwitz, while he was in Japan.

All that was needed now, was an unquestioning trust in Our Lady, since it was she who undoubtedly brought together all the necessary people and circumstances that made *A Handbook on Guadalupe* possible at this time. Moreover, her timing has proven to be perfect. An American historian has recently written a book questioning the historicity of the early Guadalupe account, thus putting the whole Guadalupe apparition under a cloud of doubt. The *Handbook* gives the facts and should contribute much in refuting his arguments and others that question the authenticity of Guadalupe. It will not only be an effective means of setting the record straight, but it will serve to reinforce belief in and devotion to Holy Mary of Guadalupe, Mother of the Americas.

We are confident that even as Our Lady of Guadalupe has put together all the contacts and providential circumstances to make the *Handbook* possible, she will supply the necessary help in publishing and propagating it. To sum it up, we know from personal experience that Our Lady does great things with the most unlikely instruments. The key word in all this is TRUST! As she said to Juan Diego, "Trust in me, am I not your Mother?" – a lesson which we must all learn and continually put into practice.—*Bro. Francis Mary Kalvelage, F.I., The Editor.*

Preface

One hundred and fifty years ago in 1846, twenty-two bishops of the United States unanimously petitioned Rome to have Mary, under her title of the Immaculate Conception, declared the official patroness of our country. I am pleased to read in the *Handbook* of the close connection between the Immaculate Conception and Our Lady of Guadalupe. It is universally believed that Mary appeared on Tepeyac Hill as the Immaculate Conception and there is also clear evidence that she is "with child." That is the second reason I am pleased to recommend this book which has devoted so much space to Mary as the patroness of the pro-life movement in the United States. This book demonstrates that we must seek her motherly protection, and imitate her virginal purity and total giving of herself to God. From the time of the Annunciation to the Crucifixion, where Mary stood at the foot of the cross, she gave herself totally to God, no matter what the cost. Mary is always saying "yes" to life, and "yes" to the Cross.

It is only in recent times that the close relationship between Mary of Guadalupe with the Immaculate Conception has become recognized in the United States. It is hard to believe that the Miracle of Tepeyac and the sacred Image were practically unknown north of the border between Mexico and the United States for over four centuries. One-hundred and fifty years ago when the United States bishops convened for the Sixth Provincial Council in Baltimore, little was known of Guadalupe in our country. Yet in the sacred Image of Mary of Guadalupe we have the only self-portrait of Mary, our National Patroness.

Today is much different. There are numerous organizations, the pro-life movement in particular, that are involved in propagating her Image and the message of Mary of Guadalupe. There are concerted efforts of national organizations, such as the Knights of Columbus, to disseminate reproductions of the miraculous Image to increase knowledge of the Empress of the Americas and venerate her. There is a beautiful chapel dedicated to Our Lady of Guadalupe in the National Shrine of the Immaculate Conception in our nation's capital. Even as one sees many Images of Our Lady of Guadalupe everywhere in Mexico, so too in our country she has become more and more visible through her Missionary Images touring the country, images on holy cards, medals, flyers promoting the pro-life cause, and reproductions enshrined in our churches, etc.

There is no need to explain the pro-life imagery of Our Lady on the tilma of Juan Diego, that is clearly covered in the section of the *Handbook* dealing with the tilma and the apostolates. I would add that life is always at the center of the great struggle between light and darkness. In the last book of the Bible, the Apocalypse, we read about the woman about to bring forth a male child and of another portent which appeared in the sky, "a huge red dragon." The dragon represents Satan, the personal power of evil, as well as all the powers of evil at work in history and opposing the mission of Christ and His Church. Satan is waiting to destroy the Child.

That Child is also a symbol of every child, especially every helpless baby whose life is threatened. The Holy Father says that the rejection of a human life is really a rejection of Christ. It was the Holy Father who described well our modern society as a "culture of death." She who was responsible for the conversion of millions of Indians, who were involved in sacrificing thousands of victims to their false gods, is certainly capable of stopping the anti-life juggernaut, but she is waiting for our participation in this all out battle, not only for human life but the souls of, yes, even the abortionists.

In the apparitions of Our Lady of Guadalupe, in her tender, intimate conversation with Juan Diego we find everything that would show her motherly care and inspire trust in her wayward children. Moreover, she is especially the "mother of all who dwell in these lands." We need that trust and abandon to the Will of our heavenly Father in these crucial times. She has come to show her love, her compassion, her help and protection. On our part we are expected to respond to such total love by our "yes," as Mary did at the Annunciation and beneath the Cross when the Church was born out of the pierced side of Her Son. We were all born into the Church when Mary said "yes" to God. We are her children. With her help, we too shall say "fiat" - "yes" to life, "yes" to the Cross, "yes" to love.

✠ Sean O'Malley, O.F.M., Cap.
Bishop of Fall River

PART I

Introduction to America's Mother

---

1. Mother of the Americas
Fr. Christopher Rengers, O.F.M. Cap.

2. Mary Asks, Mary Promises, Mary Affirms
Motherhood of Mary
Msgr. Angel Garibay

Of all the apparitions of Our Lady, Guadalupe in Mexico is the most unique and specially directed for our times. Nowhere else does Mary give us a tangible "relic" of her visit as in the miraculous Image on the tilma of Juan Diego; nowhere else has she shown such tender, motherly affection.

Pen and ink drawings on this page and following introductory pages by Lloyd Ostendorf.

Mother of the Americas

Fr. Christopher Rengers, O.F.M. Cap.

*M*ost paintings have the artist's signature in the lower corner. The unusual $4^{1}/_{2}$-century-old image of the Blessed Virgin hanging high in the modern-day Basilica of Our Lady of Guadalupe at the north end of Mexico City, in an area called the Villa de Guadalupe, has no such artist's name. There is no evidence that any mortal being painted this picture. On the contrary, the evidence is that no one on earth could have painted it. As far as history can establish and science can investigate, Mary herself gave us this marvel. Long tradition, Church approval and enduring evidence point to this image as a directly visible proof of Mary's love, brought by her from heaven to the inhabitants of the Americas on the morning of Dec. 12, 1531. As far as history and modern science can discern, it was Mary herself who gave us this marvel as a proof of her love of the inhabitants of the Americas.

The Image of Our Lady of Guadalupe, for that is the name by which she is known, represents Mary standing on a crescent, her long flowing garments held up by the arms of an angel; her eyes are looking down with an expression of compassion and humility, apparently at someone on a lower level. She is standing in a glowing halo as though before the sun. There are stars on her mantle and a moon at her feet. (This showed the Aztecs that the sun, the moon, and the stars are not gods to be worshipped). Her dress is that of a Middle Eastern maiden at the time of Christ as can be seen even today in the women inhabiting that land. Artists have vied with one another in trying to paint a duplicate of Our Lady of Guadalupe, but all have failed. She is seen in full color on the front cover. An article on the Iconography of the Image is on page 63.

The story of Holy Mary of Guadalupe, her inexpressibly tender words to Juan Diego and the symbolic Image are not as well known in the United States as are the stories and messages of Lourdes and Fatima, though more people come to her shrine than any other Marian shrine. Yet, Holy Mary of Guadalupe belongs to the United States in a special way, since the Patroness of the U.S. is the Immaculate Conception. In a broader sense she belongs to the whole continent since there were no national boundaries when she came to Mexico City in 1531. The sweep of her compassionate eyes took in the two great continents both north and south as well as central America. She stood at the center of the New World, and deserves to be called the Mother of the Americas. It was less than 40 years after Columbus' discovery

when she said: "I am a merciful Mother to you and to all your fellow peoples on this earth who love me and trust me and invoke my help. I listen to their lamentations and solace all their sorrows and their sufferings."

The first apparition of the Virgin of Guadalupe was on the Feast of the Immaculate Conception, which was celebrated at that time throughout the Spanish Empire on December 9. There were two appearances on December 9, one on December 10, and two on December 12. These four appearances were to Juan Diego. The fifth was to Juan Bernadino, Juan Diego's uncle, and it was to cure him. The recipient of Mary's message was a humble Indian who had recently lost his beloved wife. Perhaps in these latter centuries adults have lost their simplicity; and that is why the Blessed Virgin gave her confidences at Lourdes and Fatima and other modern-day apparitions to children. But in 1531, her choice was a man already past the prime of life, who lived only another sixteen and a half years.

The conversation between this humble man and the Blessed Virgin has a directness and a gracious charm which are inexpressibly captivating. It was while on his way to the special Saturday Blessed Virgin Mass early on December 9, 1531, that Juan Diego first heard heavenly music, and then the music of a sweet voice calling his name affectionately, using the diminutive: "Juanito, Juan Dieguito!" He approached unafraid and bowed. She asked him: "Listen, my dearest and youngest son, Juan. Where are your going?" He responded "My Lady, my Queen, my dearest girl, I am going as far as your little house in Tlatelolco (now a part of Mexico City), to follow the things of God (everything that makes God be God), that are given to us, that are taught to us by the ones who are the images of Our Lord, our priests."

The place of this meeting was Tepeyac Hill, then a few miles outside Mexico City, and at that time open country, (and the former temple site of the snake-mother goddess, devourer of children). The charming Lady identified herself:

"Know for sure, my dearest and lowliest son, that I am the perfect, ever Virgin, Holy Mother of the One great God of truth Who gives us life, the Inventor and Creator of people, the owner and Lord of what is around us and what is touching us or very close to us, the Owner and Lord of the sky, the Owner of the earth. I want very much, I desire very much that they build my sacred little house here, in which I will show Him. I will exalt Him in making Him manifest: I will give Him to the people, in my compassionate gaze, in my help, in my salvation, because I am truly your compassionate Mother. . . . Go to the residence of the Bishop of Mexico and you will tell him how I am sending you, so that you may reveal to him that I very much want him to build me a house here. . . ."

Only with much difficulty did he gain admittance into the Bishop's presence. The servants of the household of Bishop-elect Fray Juan de Zumárraga viewed the extremely early arrival and lowly-looking Indian as an unwelcome visitor. As might be expected, the Bishop (who was not consecrated yet, but exercising episcopal jurisdiction) withheld judgment. He had in fact been praying to Our Lady to unite the two races and to avert an impending massacre by the restive Indians who outnumbered the Europeans one thousand to one. Juan returned crestfallen to see the Lady on Tepeyac. She was waiting for him.

"Send Someone Well-Known...."

When he arrived, he hastened to explain: "My dear little Mistress, Lady, Queen, my littlest Daughter, my dear little One, I did go to where you sent me to carry out your breath, your dear word; although I entered with difficulty. . . . He received me kindly and listened to it perfectly, but from the way he answered me, it's as if he didn't understand it; he doesn't think it's true. . . . I beg you, my Lady, Queen, my Little One, to have one of the nobles who are held in esteem, one who is known, respected, honored, (have him) carry, take your breath, your dear word, so that he will believe. . . ."

The Lady looked on him with compassion but did not heed this well-meant advice. So Juan Diego had to continue his unaccustomed and embarrassing role as gate crasher for Our Lady. Twice more he would have to force his way past the Bishop's overly protective household. The last time, on December 12, Juan would have the sign which was to turn out to be much greater than he or the Bishop had expected.

Juan Diego missed his appointment with the Blessed Mother on Tepeyac Hill on December 11, since all that day he had been caring for his sick uncle, Juan Bernardino. On the morning of December 12, as he was hurrying to find a priest to administer the last rites to his uncle, he approached Tepeyac and remembered his broken appointment. Fearing reproach and delay, he changed his course by going around the east side of the hill. But the Lady was not to be denied. She came over to his side of the hill and asked: "What is the matter? Where are you going?"

Somewhat like a schoolboy caught going home early, Juan made an attempt to be pleasant and nonchalant. "How did the morning find you?" he asked. "I hope that you are well." But the thought of his most serious errand almost immediately forced him to beg to be excused while he went to get the priest for his uncle. But he added: "After I succeed in doing this duty, I will return here later to go and deliver your message. Forgive me, my Lady and my Child. Be patient with me for the moment. I am not deceiving you, my daughter. Tomorrow I will come early."

In her turn, the Lady assured him that his uncle was already cured and told him not to worry, but to go to gather the flowers at the top of the hill. So Juan went to the frozen, barren hilltop and found and gathered a variety of flowers including beautiful Castilian roses (which had not yet been introduced to this continent at the time by the Europeans). He came back to the Blessed Virgin and *she arranged them* in his tilma with her own hands.

Hurrying happily to the episcopal residence, Juan still took the time now and then to look at the roses and to enjoy their fragrance. He endured even more than the usual difficulties from the servants who tried to snatch the roses which they saw he was carrying. Juan was finally admitted to Bishop Zumárraga's presence and flung open his cloak to let the heaven-sent bouquet of fragrant flowers cascade to the floor. But now he was suddenly alarmed. The precious roses seemed to make little impression on the Bishop. He appeared to be looking more intently at Juan himself! The poor Indian's perplexity grew as the Bishop came to kneel before him. It was only then that Juan Diego looked down, and saw that the exact image of the Lady of Tepeyac Hill had appeared in bright colors on his tilma.

The Care and Compassion of a Mother

Now, more than four and a half centuries later, men are still dropping to their knees before the Image of Our Lady on the tilma of Juan Diego. An average of 15,000 a day come to the Basilica in Mexico City. For the first hundred years and more the tilma was exposed to the elements and to the eager handling and kissing of the people. Today the holy Image is mounted on the plain, paneled wooden wall behind the main altar of the New Basilica built in 1976. Four moving treadways below the sanctuary floor carry the nearly endless streams of pilgrims before the Image of the Madonna. Below her Image are the words of her message in Spanish. They begin with the question: "Am I not here who am your Mother?" Along the wall to the left are the flags of all of the countries of the New World.

Like other great Marian places of pilgrimage, the shrine has become a center of Eucharistic devotion. The Holy Sacrifice is offered throughout the day till 8:00 p.m. at the main altar, while other Masses are also celebrated in the crypts, the San Jose Chapel, and at the altars on the balcony. Like all mothers, Mary says: "Come and see my Child." She leads her children by grace to the Child of her womb. The tilma, made of frail cactus fiber, which should have crumbled long ago, bears the same clear Image as it did in 1531. It is the very same shawl-like garment worn by Juan Diego on that memorable day in December when it received the image of our Blessed Mother. The coarse weave of the tilma contains no sizing which would be absolutely necessary to paint such a delicate image of Mary. Nevertheless it has no equal in beauty and simplicity.

A long seam runs the length of the tilma near the center, neatly missing the face, and holding the two pieces of cloth together by a slender tread. Professor Camps-Ribera, an artist from Barcelona, and later a resident of Mexico, examined the tilma in May, 1954 and again in March, 1963. He measured the fabric as 66 x 41 inches in size, the image of Mary being 56 inches high. He noted with surprise that it appears much larger at a distance. In his written statement he also noted that the colors which at close range, and especially under a magnifying glass, seem faded, are vigorous and fresh when viewed at a distance. (For further description of the tilma of Our Lady see page 56).

Pope John XXIII declared a Marian Year dedicated to Our Lady of Guadalupe, which ran from October 12, 1960 - October 12, 1961. At the conclusion of that year he gave an address naming Our Lady "Mother of the Americas." President and Mrs. John F. Kennedy attended Sunday Mass in the Old Basilica on July 1, 1962. They inscribed the guest book: "Our prayers for peace." Pope Paul

The Blessed Sacrament chapel in the Basilica, with its large tabernacle and the beautiful mural of the Trinity.

VI sent a golden rose to Guadalupe on March 25, 1966. It may be viewed in the museum attached to the rear of the Old Basilica. Pope John Paul II made the first papal visit to Guadalupe on January 27, 1979. He celebrated Mass in the New Basilica with 300 Latin-American cardinals and bishops. He returned in May, 1990 to beatify Blessed Juan Diego and four other Americans, three of whom were children martyrs.

Pilgrims who see Mary's Guadalupan Image in Mexico City also feel her gracious motherly presence. Those who do not go in person can easily obtain beautiful reproductions of the Image to honor her in their homes. Mary's words to Juan Diego when she reassured him about the cure of his uncle's illness are worth copying and remembering, since they express the care and compassion the Mother of the Americas has for each one of us who approach her with the simplicity of a child:

"Listen, put it into your heart, my youngest and dearest son, that the thing that frightens you, the thing that afflicts you, is nothing: do not let it disturb you; do not fear this sickness, nor any other sickness, nor any sharp and hurtful thing. Am I not here, I, who am your Mother? Are you not under my shadow and protection? Am I not the source of your joy? Are you not in the hollow of my mantle, in the crossing of my arms? Do you need something more? Let nothing else worry you, disturb you; do not let your uncle's illness pressure you with grief, because he will not die of it now. You may be certain that he is already well."

The Spiritual Motherhood of Mary

By Monsignor Angel M. Garibay K.

*T*he first apparition of Mary (Our Lady of Guadalupe) is on the frosty morning of December 9, 1531, Juan Diego, the Indian, is passing at the foot of Tepeyac Hill. Suddenly the hill is enveloped in rays of light. The air is filled with song and music. He halts in his steps, he looks, he listens, and hears an order from above to climb up. He sees Mary and Mary tells him:

"Know for certain, littlest of my sons, that I am the perfect and perpetual Virgin Mary, Mother of the True God through

Symbolic painting by Jorge Sánchez Hernández showing Our Lady of Guadalupe's role of sheltering Juan Diego and all of her children under her mantle.

Whom everything lives, the Lord of all things near and far, the Master of heaven and earth."
This is the first part of Mary's declaration. She spoke in Juan Diego's language and her words sounded like music.

"Maxicmatti, ma huel yuh ye in moyollo, noxocoyouh: Ca nehuatl in nicenquizcacemicac ixpochtli Santa Maria, in inantzin in huel nelli teotl Dios, in ipalnemohuani, in teyocoyani, in tloque nahuaque, in ilhuicahua, in tlalticpaque."
In this manner she introduced herself to the Indian as the Mother of God. In the second part she tells him what she wants:
"I wish and intensely desire that in this place my sanctuary be erected. Here, I will demonstrate, I will exhibit, I will give all my love, my compassion, my help and my protection to the people. I am your merciful Mother. The merciful Mother of all of you who live united in this land, and of all mankind, of all those who love me. Here I will hear their weeping, their sorrow, and will remedy, and alleviate all their multiple sufferings, necessities and misfortunes."

It is necessary to make an analysis of each word, of each sentence. The Mexican (Aztec) language in its abundant ancient literary productions manifests two styles. One has a trend towards parallelism; a surprising parallelism because of its similarity to Hebrew poetry. It is a phenomenon that we find in the ancient poetry of all parts of the world from that of the Hindus to that of the Finns. The other literary phenomenon is the abundance and profusion of expressions to elaborate one single thought.

The first act of the Guadalupan revelation consists of three parts: Mary asks, Mary promises, Mary affirms. With insistence she pleads for a sanctuary: *"Huel nicnequi, cenca niquelehuia."* The purpose of the sanctuary was not to be entirely for veneration; it was also to have a social function. The promises of what she will do in that sanctuary she makes known in three short sentences: She will show, she will make apparent, or literally speaking, raise to the surface and give. *"In oncan nicnextiz, nicpentlazaz, nictemacaz."*

Give what? She proceeds according to the Mexican custom using a series of words that reveal the meaning of these verbs:
"My love to the people: notetlazotlaliz."
"My compassion: noteicnoittaliz."
"My help: notepalehuiliz."
"My protection: notemanahuiliz."

Four activities essentially maternal: to love, to have compassion, to aid, to defend. Can anything more be added to the offices of a mother? If she promises to give these things, it means that she is promising to be a mother and show herself a mother. She says it with precision. Then comes the affirmative part of Mary's words which are the most important:

I. *"I am your merciful Mother."* It is a solemn declaration of motherhood. Much more is contained in the Nahuatl words than we quote. In accordance with the general belief that Mary is the Mother of Mercy, we find in the text of the history of the revelations on Tepeyac the confirmation that Mary is "Mater misericordiae, Virgo clemens," according to the teaching of the Church. The mercies of a mother, the clemency of a virgin, the two glories which gird the forehead of the daughters of Eve, never united in harmonious assembly except in Mary.

II. Then she points out to whom she wants to show herself a Mother. Yours, that is to say, Juan Diego's. He comes first, not for his merits but because of his election by Mary. Like St. John on Calvary, John on Tepeyac represents humanity.

"Of all those who live united in this land." The Nahuatl phrase is adamantine in its expression. *"In ixquichtin in ic nican tlalpan ancepantlaca."* It is impossible to translate it into its fine tones and shades. But by stretching the English language we would say: "as many as are here in this land." She includes all the inhabitants of the land to whom she intends to show her clemency. In the third place, she includes the rest: all humanity, all the various kinds of people.

III. The conditions which she sets forth are really a series of norms of Christian life in its highest spirituality:

They must love her: notetlazotlacahuan.
They must cry to her: notech motzatzilia.
They must seek her: nechtemoa.
They must have confidence in her: notech motemachilia.

To love, to call upon, to seek and to confide. Is there any other way for man to show his appreciation for Mary, and is there any other way for a mother to express her love for her children?

IV. In the fourth place comes the promise of what she wants to do: To listen to their cries of sorrow and distress: *Niquincaquiliz in inchoquiz, in intlaocol.* Remedy their sufferings: *nicyectiliznicyectliliz nicpatiz.* Two verbs which in Nahuatl style express the two phases of a helpful activity: first by rectifying, then by curing or remedying.

V. That which is to be cured and which is to be remedied is expressed in the exuberant manner of the language in three terms: the need for something: *in netoliniliz;* anguish or affliction: *intonehuiz;* the burn, literally, or the cautery of pain, *chichinaquiliz*. This is the content, in compressed terms, of the first part of the message of Tepeyac. In it is expressed:

The person who exercises the office.

The personal object to whom she extends her services.

The matter in which she manifests herself.

The evils she wishes to remedy.

The expression, all of it, speaks of the functions of a mother for all, to remedy all kinds of misfortune. It is in a different form, a kind of commentary on the supplication of a child's love for the mother.

Solve vincla reis, - Loose the bonds of the condemned

Profer lumen caecis - Give light to the blind

Mala nostra pelle, - Ward off our evils

Bona cuncta posce.- Ask for us of every good [for us].

I will make only one more reflection before closing this part of my study. It could be extended much more. The person who wrote the narrative in the language of the Indians with such a harmony of style and expression yet with such deep theological meaning, would have had to be a genius. That was impossible for the people of the sixteenth century, Indian or Spanish. The precision of terms, the arrangement of the themes, the perfect inclusion of all the aspects presupposes that the person who spoke these words so that they would be put into writing, knew what he was saying. It is another proof that they were not invented, but transcribed. It is another indication that the one who is speaking is she who could well be called teacher par excellence of the deepest theology. . . . If any Spaniard or Indian of the sixteenth century had reached such dogmatic heights, his name would have become famous. But if we can not find such a brilliant theologian, we may be sure that it was Mary who spoke these words and revealed herself to us in this way.

The second text which I am going to analyze is the one we find in the narrative of the final apparition. It was the twelfth of December, 1531. Juan Diego was hurrying to bring a confessor to his uncle who was dying. He tried to hide from Mary and took a new path, sure that the Blessed Virgin would not see him. But she came to meet him and asked him why he was going that way. He excused himself, and filled with the sorrow of his uncle's suffering he entreated her to permit him to proceed on his way to bring a confessor to his relative. This is when she made a new declaration in which we find the content of the message in its greatest precision. I will translate it literally into our language:

"Hear and let it penetrate into your heart, my dear little son; let nothing discourage you, nothing depress you. Let nothing alter your heart, or your countenance. Am I not here who am your Mother? Are you not under my shadow and protection? Am I not your fountain of life? Are you not in the folds of my mantle? In the crossing of my arms? Is there anything else that you need? Do not fear any illness or vexation, anxiety or pain. Let not the illness of your uncle afflict you, because he is not going to die now of what he has in himself. Be sure that he will get well."

The text sounds like a poem. It is beautiful and perfect conformity with the poetic style of the Mexican language of the prehispanic period. But its content is much richer than its poetic beauty. We will analyse each statement point by point, in order to discover the hidden lessons which they enclose. After an introductory phrase, Mary takes three steps in her declaration. The solemn insistence that the Indian fix his mind on what she is saying indicates the seriousness of what she is about to say:

He must fear nothing, he must let nothing discourage him, he is not alone in the world nor without help. Of whatever evils there are he must fear none. Then she tells him why his soul must be free from fear. This is the most important part of the whole message.

She expounds a theme, she unrolls it in three metaphors, each more brilliant and precise than the preceeding one. It is the exalted style we find in hundreds of poems and speeches in the Mexican language. Let us scrutinize this statement:

(a). A complete affirmation of her Motherhood. *"Cuix amo nican; nicah nimonantzin." "Am I not here? I am your Mother."*

(b). *"Cuix amo nocehuallotitlan necauhyotitlan in ticah?"* "You are under my shadow, under my protection."

In the imagery of the Nahuas, the chief, the prince, the father, were like the ahuehuete tree (cypress) or like the ceiba (silk cotton tree). *"In Pochotl in Ahuehuetl"* is the phrase we find constantly in the speeches of the Aztecs which were made before their kings and rulers. It is a shade that refreshes. It is a shelter and protection.

Mary compares herself to a tree with luxuriant foliage that protects from the heat of the sun or from rain and gives shelter and joy to whoever takes refuge under its branches. It is an affirmation that she, as a Mother, gives what mothers give: protection, tenderness and kindness that is never exhausted.

(c). *"Cuix amo nehuatl in nimopaccayeliz."* *"I am your fountain of life."*

These words must be analysed further. The Nahua roots of the principal word contain a concept of well-being, contentment and happiness almost to the letter. *"Pacc"* stands for tranquil, peaceful and *"yel"* contains the concept of existence, of living in some place. It affirms that the fountain, cause or origin of the good existence, of persistence and being in peace, is Mary. Mary is the fountain of our life in the sense that we all know: Mother of the One Who is life and Who condescended to take His human form from her. He is the fountain of grace, which is the communication of Divine Life to the soul. The purely abstract concept of this supernatural reality in the imaginative phrase becomes concrete, it becomes palpable. Mary affirms that she is the life of the soul in all its joyous perfection.

(d). The third picture is obviously the sweetest and the most profound. *"Cuix amo nocuexanco, no mamalhuazco in ticah?"* *"Are you not in the fold of my mantle, in the crossing of my arms?"*

This is a perfect picture from the family life with which the Indian was familiar, and which we continue to see even today. It is the best expression of motherhood in its complex and varied reality. *Cuexantli* means the fold made in the shawl or mantle of a woman, or in a man's tilma or ayate when it is wrapped around them to hold something. In this fold or hollow is carried whatever is most cherished or precious. In the hollow of their mantles women carry their youngest; it is a portable crib. A Mexican mother carries her baby in the warm hollow of her *reboso*.

The other picture is even more beautiful. *Mamalhuaztli* was the instrument for striking fire. Two sticks were crossed and rubbed against each other. They produced the spark that ignited the flame. From this, the Aztecs derived the most suggestive symbol, the *nahui olin*: the cross which has confused some historians and which is only the symbol of new born life, as fire is created from the friction of two pieces of wood. But it also signifies the manner in which a mother crosses her arms when she presses her child to her heart.

Mary declared that Juan Diego and all who are personified in him, lie in the warm cavity of her mantle and in the crossing of her arms.

To shelter and protect! Is there any better way of expressing the functions of a mother? In this form, with these examples, part poetical and part metaphysical, the Queen of Heaven told Juan Diego, the Mexican nation, the world, that she is the one who protects and assists; that it is she who gives peace and life; that it is she who with motherly tenderness carries the child in her arms, presses it to her heart and quiets and defends it. Greater precision is impossible; greater beauty cannot be conceived.

We will make a short summary in which we will define the meaning of Mary's words in accordance with the historical narrative.

(1). Mary declares that she is the Mother of all humanity as she is the Mother of God. The mention of both functions and of both dignities, one after the other, demonstrates the importance which she gives to her words.

(2). She states that she is the Universal Mother and she enumerates the various categories of persons whom she includes in her sphere of action without excluding anyone.

(3). She makes known what is the object of her maternal activity: to remove bad things and to bring the good things nearer.

(4). With brilliant examples, both poetic and instructive, she informs us that she is our shelter, our fountain of grace, tenderness and maternal compassion.

At any time and on any day the Mexican pilgrims inspire admiration by their faith and penances.

(5). She makes it known definitively that she is the Universal Mother who gives life, the true life that her Divine Son brought into the world.

In conclusion, we may positively say that Mary in her manifestations at Tepeyac declared herself Mother of Grace for the entire world, fountain of supernatural health, and help in the things of this world.

Nothing is more appropriate, in order to conclude my reflections, than to insert the final part of the short narrative to which I referred in the beginning of this article, especially since it is almost unknown. I will give it in our language as literally as possible: "This is the Image of the Queen." *In tlatocacihuapilli.* Through a miracle it was stamped on the mantle of the humble man; and her Image remains until today (16th century). All the inhabitants of the neighborhood come to venerate her and to pray, and that Mother, with her great mercy aids them and gives them what they ask for. *Auh in yehuantzin in ica ihuey tetlaocoliliz Nanyotzin oncan quinmopalehuilia, quinmomaquilia in tlein quimitlanililia.*

Truly, to those who invoke her as advocate, who have devotion to her, she makes herself a refuge, she, the Mother of God. "She truly helps and shows compassion to all who love her, as if they were under her shadow and under her protection. . . ."

The author of this scholarly chapter, the late Monsignor Angel M. Garibay, was one of the Canons of the Basilica of Our Lady of Guadalupe in Mexico City. He was also a Guadalupan historian and a Professor of Nahuatl at the University of Mexico. This translation is a part of the original study in Spanish which first appeared in a quarterly newsletter of the Apostolate of Our Lady of Guadalupe, Mother of the Americas Inc., P.O. Box 17634, El Paso, TX 79917

PART II

Historical Roots of Guadalupe

---

1. Evangelization of the New World and Spain's Role

Bro. Francis Mary, F.F.I.

2. Spain's Guadalupe Shrine

3. The Culture and Life of the Preconquest . . .

Aztec Civilization

Dr. Charles Wahlig

4. Cortés and . . .

. . . the Conquest of the "Valiant Ladies"
Diana Cary

Catholic Spain of the 16th Century, the conquest and fall of the Aztec Empire, were the necessary preamble to the appearance of Our Lady in 1531. This ushered in the evangelization of the natives and established the Church in Latin America. Her presence in the Sacred Image is now helping to renew the Faith in America.

The Three Cultures Plaza in Mexico City: the base of a former Aztec pyramid which was surmounted by a sacrificial temple, a colonial church with the first college in the New World, and modern apartment and office buildings.

Catholic Spain in the Evangelization of the New World

Bro. Francis Mary, F.F.I.

*H*ow providential it was that Catholic Spain and Portugal were the prime instruments used by God in the evangelization of the New World, in particular South and Central America! Today Latin American countries have the greatest concentration of Catholics in the world. If Spain had been torn by religious dissension and division, as in England and Germany at the time of the Protestant revolt, this would not have been possible. It was Spain, the country vitally linked to the Catholic Faith, that God used to instruct and evangelize the natives of the New World, through her Franciscan, Dominican and Augustinian missionaries. The Spain of the sixteenth century was a united Catholic country deeply rooted in devotion to the Mother of God. It is inconceivable that Our Lady would have ever appeared, as she did in Mexico in 1531, through a country separated from the center of unity, the Catholic Church and the Papacy. Mary is ever the litmus test of Catholicity.

Besides the fact Spain was thoroughly Catholic and thus Marian; the political and economic climate of the country had to be stable and unified. This came about through the union of the two kingdoms of Aragon under Ferdinand II and Castile, under the great Catholic Queen, Isabel. Prior to this union and Isabel's ascension to the throne, both countries had been in a state of virtual anarchy. Spain remained relatively religious while the rest of Europe became more and more secularized in politics, culture and economics. Moreover, the political concept of the Divine Right of Kings was progressively separating Catholic monarchies from the influence of the Church and the Papacy.

As a result of the weakening of the Church's moral force in individual countries, greed and envy, the underpinnings of laissez-faire capitalism and of socialism took on the guise of virtues. Abandonment of the traditional teachings against usury and the concentration of vast power in central governments set the stage for the powerful modern secular states. Spain was not immune to these influences. Nonetheless, thirty years of religious and social reform at home won the allegiance of the people and set the stage for the discovery of America. The discovery provided the opportunity for the evangelization of millions and the lasting establishment of the Catholic Church in Latin America.

Spain, unlike other colonizers of that time, England and Holland in particular, was unaffected by the "new theology." Thus she was used effectively by God to evangelize Spain's new discoveries around the world. That is not to say that Spain did not have problems with a few ruthless, greedy colonizers who brutally suppressed the native population. But these abuses were never sanctioned by the Spanish government of the 16th century. The primary aim of the crown was the evangelization of the natives in the areas of the world which came under Spanish rule. Economic considerations were secondary. Yet, the providential discovery of America with its vast riches, helped immeasurably to bolster Spain as the leading European power of the 16th century.

When Christopher Columbus approached Queen Isabel and her court seeking help to fit out ships for an unchartered exploration of the vast stretch of ocean to the west, the time was right. Spain had just liberated Granada, the last part of her country under Moorish domination, and so was free to give Columbus' bold venture prayerful consideration. Both Isabel and Columbus were deeply committed to the Faith and seemed to have a special calling from the Almighty to seek out new worlds to win for Christ. Through measures, thought to be harsh at least by twentieth century standards, Isabel was able to keep religious peace in her country, which was hardly the case in the rest of Europe which was ravaged by religious war.* As historian Warren Carroll points out in his history book series, "The Glory of Christendom" (vol. 3), "Whenever there was a dispute involving accusations of heresy or occult practices, the Inquisition was available to settle it, and it did, before it

Columbus and his followers upon landing, kissed the ground, erected a crucifix and according to the engraver, J. Knight's, interpretation, participated in Benediction. (Courtesy Knights of Columbus Headquarters Museum).

became a threat to the Church or to the country." What Isabel had accomplished in uniting Spain, through just rule, constant vigilance and love of God and her people, made it possible for the Almighty to work out His providential plans for mankind in the discovery of the New World by Christopher Columbus.

Columbus and Isabel were similar in many ways. Both were Franciscan tertiaries. Both had a strong devotion to the Blessed Mother. Both were bold leaders who believed strongly in Divine Providence and relied totally on God for the ultimate success of their plans. As a Third Order Franciscan, Isabel placed great trust in the Franciscans, especially in their reform movement in the 15th century which helped to renew the Faith in Spain (See article on page 158).

When Columbus' plan of sailing west to find the Indies was turned down by the Portuguese, Columbus turned his attention to Spain and the court of Isabel. As he passed by the Franciscan monastery of Rabida on his way to the Spanish court he stopped there to pray to Our Lady for the success of his proposal. Providentially, the friars there had a lively interest in navigation and astronomy and were able to give him valuable information and advice. Of even greater import, the guardian of the friary had been the Queen's confessor. He provided Columbus with papers introducing him to the Royal Court.

Columbus immediately struck it off with the devout Queen, by relating how in the Bible he had come across a reading in Isaiah, which had convinced him that it was God's inspiration that he carry the Catholic Faith to distant lands and nations through his exploration. This passage reads: "*I will send fugitives to the nations, . . . to the distant coastlands that have never heard of my name, or seen my glory, and shall proclaim my glory among the nations.*" He added, "There is no question that the inspiration was from the Holy Spirit, because He comforted me with rays of marvelous illumination." He then sought and found many other references in the Bible that urged him on in his "divine" mission. On hearing him, Isabel became convinced that this prophetic figure before her had inspiration from on high and that she dare not turn a deaf ear. The necessary aid was given him and the rest is history.

During the time that Columbus was outfitting his ships and hiring their crews, Queen Isabel and her husband Ferdinand spent two weeks at the shrine of Our Lady of Guadalupe in Extremadura, no doubt praying for the success of the bold venture. Columbus also visited the Spanish Guadalupe shrine on a number of occasions. He was an ardent devotee of Our Lady, so much so that he wove her initials into his signature and requested to be buried in her Guadalupe chapel dedicated to the Immaculate Conception.

As is well known, the flag ship "Santa Maria" was named after Our Lady. Continuing the tradition of Catholic mariners in that age of faith, the whole crew gathered each evening to sing the "Salve Regina," in honor of Our Lady. They recognized how precarious their sea journeys were and prayed ardently to Mary, Star of the Sea, for a safe voyage. It would seem that this voyage under her banner and captained by a devotee of hers had her special protection. Toward the end of the voyage the Santa Maria's crew were on the verge of mutiny, when the ships were stalled in a calm that unnerved them. A strong west wind suddenly blew up, after Columbus had reprimanded the crew for their lack of faith and they had prayed to Our Lady. The next day the scene was repeated. This time the sea became rough, and strong winds drove the ships on to the great destiny preordained by God. Columbus did not hesitate to write in the ship's log that this "miracle" was similar to Moses leading the Jews out of captivity.

The New World discovery by Columbus was almost lost on the return journey, when the Niña was caught in so violent a storm in the north Atlantic. When the situation worsened and waves were breaking over the frail ship, Columbus called his crew together, vowing to make a pilgrimage to the Guadalupe shrine in Spain if their lives were spared. He personally fulfilled that vow, barefoot and in sackcloth, after making his report to the Queen.

In summary, the providential plans of God were realized for the evangelization of the New World through two great and charismatic figures, Isabel, the devout Catholic Queen of Spain, and Christopher Columbus, the Catholic mariner who trusted in that inner voice urging him on to seek new lands inhabited by souls who had never had the Gospel preached to them. But it was not until thirty-nine years later that the total plan of evangelization of the New World was revealed on a hill outside of Mexico City, by the Star of Evangelization, Mary herself. Even as Mary of Nazareth brought Jesus in her womb to her cousin Elizabeth two thousand years ago, she has ever been the principal and essential instrument over the centuries in bringing souls to Christ, her Divine Son. Similarly, she used her devotee the "Christ Bearer" (Christopher) to plant the standard of the Cross in new lands, ripe for the harvest.

*The Inquisition and the expulsion of the Moslems and Jews from Spain in our history books is, for the most part written from an Anglo-American point of view. The Jews and Moslems were the intellectuals and entrepreneur class at that time in Spain. It was with great economic loss that the Spanish crown expelled them, but it was necessary to preserve the Faith. Many modern historians seem to be more fair and even-handed in writing about the Inquisition, and admitting that there were abuses on both sides

Guadalupe in Spain

*W*hen Our Lady used an Aztec name in identifying herself to Juan Bernardino which sounded like the title of the famous shrine of *Guadalupe,* in Extremadura, Spain (see page 179) it was no accident. It was our heavenly Mother's way of appealing to both her Spanish and Indian children. When the Spanish heard the name Guadalupe, they immediately associated it with their shrine in Spain. They understood from this that she was not the exclusive property of the Aztecs. It is interesting to note that there is a little known statue of the Immaculate Conception (not to be confused with the highly venerated statue there) in the choir of the Spanish shrine which is very similar to the miraculous Image (see page 160). Other than that, similarities are few.

Whereas the Miraculous Portrait of Mary in Mexico was not painted by human hands, the image of Our Lady of Guadalupe in Extremadura is a statue of the Madonna with Child, said to have been carved by St. Luke. The one in Mexico, of supernatural origin, is a masterpiece which far surpasses any work ever done by a master-painter. The other is of little artistic value, dressed in very elaborate royal robes, it is very much a part of Spanish history and clearly links the nation with the Faith.

One cannot completely understand the history and culture of Spain and other Catholic countries which have devotion to Mary, apart from their love of her. Each country has its own national Madonna. Whether it be Knock in Ireland, Czestochowa in Poland, or in the case of the Orthodox Church, Our Lady of Kazan in Russia, it is in these shrines that one finds an identity and common bond that unites these peoples in good times as well as in times of persecution. The following is the story of the first Guadalupe shrine in Extremadura, Spain.

Tradition has it that Pope St. Gregory the Great (590-604) gave the statue to St. Leander, Bishop of Seville. When the Moslems took possession of most of the Spanish peninsula in 711, they imposed the Moslem religion in territories under their domination. They defeated Roderick, the last of the Visigoth kings of Spain, and by 719 had pressed on as far as the Pyrenees. As the Christian forces

The Basilica of Our Lady of Guadalupe in Extremadura, Spain, and the statue venerated there for many centuries.

retreated, they took with them the small statue of Mary, later to be known as Our Lady of Guadalupe, to the mountains of Asturias. Threatened with annihilation, they placed the statue in an iron casket and buried it in an unmarked place in the province of Extremadura, where it remained hidden for many centuries.

During the reconquest, in the mid-thirteenth century, while Alfonso was king, the statue was miraculously discovered and restored to public veneration. At that time a certain cowherd named Gil was tending his cattle when the Blessed Mother appeared to him and directed him to dig in a certain spot where he would find her statue. He was then to have a chapel built there where she was to be venerated. He reported this apparition to the ecclesiastical authorities, who came to the little village of Guadalupe and dug up the casket which contained a note confirming its identity. A chapel was built, and as more and more pilgrims came to Guadalupe, funds became available to build a larger chapel. By 1340, the kings of Spain were coming to the shrine to give thanks for victories over the Moslems. A monastery was built later, which was under the care of the Hermits of St. Jerome. Kings and Queens, peasants and nobles, sinners and saints came to the shrine with their petitions and thanksgiving offerings for favors received. Among the most famous of these was the saintly Queen Isabel, who went to the shrine in critical times to pray. She chose the shrine as the repository of her last will and testament. King Ferdinand II, her husband, who along with Queen Isabel brought about the unity of Spain, visited the shrine a number of times. During the period of Spain's great exploration and expansion many of the conquistadors also prayed at the shrine of Guadalupe. The two most notable are Christopher Columbus and Hernando Cortés, both devout Catholics. During Columbus' return trip to Spain when his ship was near sinking during a violent storm and all seemed to be lost, he had recourse to Our Lady of Guadalupe in Extremadura, promising a pilgrimage on foot to her mountain shrine if the ship and their lives were spared. She answered his prayers and he fulfilled his promise.

The bold conqueror of the Aztec Empire, Cortés, was born near the shrine in Medellín, Extremadura, about 50 miles down the valley from Guadalupe. He was known to have turned to Our Lady many times in the crises and trials he experienced in the New World. When outnumbered as much as a thousand to one in pitched battle with the warlike Aztecs, he turned to Spain's special national Madonna for victory. As soon as he prevailed over the enemy he would tear down their pagan statues and replace them with a statue of Our Lady. Bishop Juan de Zumárraga, the first Bishop of Mexico also prayed at the Old World Guadalupe shrine before setting out for the New World. It was he who received the "sign," the miraculous Image of Our Lady on the tilma of Juan Diego, in the Episcopal residence on December 12, 1531.

Over the years, the shrine of Our Lady of Guadalupe has been perhaps the most popular shrine to Our Lady in Spain after that of Our Lady of the Pillar. However, it fell onto hard times during the nineteenth century when a wave of anticlericalism swept over Spain, culminating in the bloody persecution of the Church during the Spanish Civil War in the 1930's. The Franciscans, who restored the shrine in 1908, are the present custodians. But its fame in modern times falls very much under the shadow of the much more world renowned shrine of Guadalupe in Mexico City. That is not to say that the Spaniards love their Guadalupe Lady less, for after all it is the same Mary, Mother of the True God, who appeared at both shrines. -B.F.M.

This article is based on the article by Dr. Charles Wahlig, "The Original Guadalupe Shrine in Spain," which appeared in the <u>Guadalupe Handbook</u> and the unpublished article, "Guadalupe in Spain," by Fr. Martinus Cawley, O.C.S.O.

The Aztec Empire and Civilization

By Dr. Charles Wahlig

*T*he history of Mexico's past is so unique and novel that it has gained the attention of some of the highest ranking scholars and writers of the past 400 years. Many famous experts like Bernal Diaz del Castillo, Fray Bernardino de Sahagún, Bartolomé de las Casas, Baron Von Humboldt, Dr. Robertson, Lord Kingsborough, Samuel Prescott, William Bancroft, Frances Parkinson Keyes, Jacques Soustelle, Dr. Warren Carroll and many others, have researched and written extensively on pre-Columbian, Colonial and modern phases of the history of Mexico.

The heart of the Aztec empire was centered around the Zocalo or great square. On the side where the Metropolitan Cathedral is now situated were located the great twin pyramids. The magnificent 300 room palace of the emperor was on the east side of the Zocalo, where the Adminstration Building now stands. The palaces of the great nobles, now the site of the state department and the city hall buildings of Mexico City, were on the other two sides. The city was divided into sectors, each with its own temple, market, schools and residential area. The palaces of the nobles were majestic structures resembling the ancient Egyptian palaces, whereas the homes of the middle class and the poorer people were all constructed of dried brick faced with cement, plaster, or adobe and painted beautiful pastel colors. At the time, there were about 60,000 edifices of all kinds.

So beautiful was the city, that when the Spaniards came over the mountains for their first glimpse of it glistening in the sunlight, they said they must have come upon the enchanted city of Amadis, a fabulous place in a popular romance of the time. The shores of Lake Texcoco were lined with many towns, the greatest being the

The Aztec capital, Tenochtitlan (now Mexico City), as Cortés found it in 1519.

city-state of Texcoco. The kings of Texcoco had shared the rule of the empire with the Aztecs from early times. The Aztecs, headed by the emperor, controlled the armed forces and ruled the empire, while the kings of Texcoco regulated the judicial and economic life of the empire.

JUDICIAL SYSTEM. The judicial system of the Mexican (Aztec) Empire was remarkably like our own. However, a supreme judge had the final say, which not even the Emperor could overrule. Under him, was a tribunal of three, who headed the judicial system in each of the kingdoms, then finally, there were local judges and magistrates. Since there were no lawyers to represent the clients, there were court attendants whose duty it was to see that the litigants and their witnesses had their cases prepared and were on time for the trial. There was a high degree of integrity in the courts, since taking bribes was punishable by death.

LEGISLATIVE SYSTEM. The supreme law-making power rested with the emperor. The laws were registered and published to the people in hieroglyphic codices. They displayed a high regard for both property and personal protection; all major crimes against society were punishable by death, including the murder of a slave. Adulterers were stoned to death. Stealing was punishable by slavery or death (they had no locks on their doors) and there were other offenses which we would consider minor, which were punishable by the death penalty. The laws were indeed puritanical in their severity. This allowed the citizens a high degree of personal liberty, which still persists in Mexico up to the present day. This personal freedom also extended to social practices. There was no prohibition against individuals of one class associating with those of another. Juan Diego, with his lofty spiritual nature, may have had occasion to associate with Valeriano, the Lords of Texcoco, and others.

SCIENCE AND THE FINE ARTS. Mexico abounds today in temples, pyramids, palaces and artifacts constructed by the ancient inhabitants. They had skillfully developed the use of plants and herbs to make hundreds of medicines. They had hospitals and surgeons which the Spanish considered as good as any European ones. They knew the importance of clean water and built aqueducts to bring it into the city from the mountains. Their writing had progressed to a phonetic form, and almost to an alphabetic form. They kept all kinds of records, but mainly on legal matters, their mythology, rituals and history. They wrote on several types of surfaces, including a fine grade of paper made from the maguey cactus, on sections about 10 inches square, attached so that they would fold like a folding screen. Many of these "codices" may be seen at the National Museum of Anthropology and History in Mexico City.

The Mexicans excelled in astronomy. The Mayans had calculated the most accurate calendar produced up to that time; and the Aztecs devised a version of it that is circular in form. The greatest example of this is the 26 ton Calendar Stone, which is in the Archeological Museum in Mexico City. Their solar year was divided into 18 months of 20 days each. The extra five days of the year belonged to no month and were put in at the end of the year. Other extra hours were adjusted in the completion of their time cycle, which was a period of 52 years. The Mexican mind associated each cycle's end as possibly the end of the world. As a consequence of this, great religious ceremonies were performed anticipating death as each cycle came to a close. When they found they were still alive as the new era began, they celebrated with ceremonies of great joy. The year of Acatl, or end of a 52-year cycle, occured in 1507.

AGRICULTURE AND THE MECHANICAL ARTS. The huge maguey plant, a type of cactus, was the marvel of Mexico. Its cluster of flowers, shooting above a thick growth of enormous dark leaves, could be seen growing on all the plains of Mexico, and the same plant is even more widely cultivated today. They made a pulp from the pounded fibers from which paper was manufactured. Its center is like a receptacle filled with a fluid which is fermented into an intoxicating beverage called pulque. Its fleshy "leaves" are used for impermeable thatched roofs for the more humble homes. The thread of the tilma that Juan Diego wore was made from maguey fibers. Pins and needles were made from the thorns which grow at the ends of its leaves. Strong cords were made from maguey fibers. The roots and "leaves" when properly cooked, make a very nutritious food. The maguey plant was to the Mexicans what the papyrus was to the Egyptians, and much more.

Before the coming of the Spaniards, although the Mexicans did not have a great variety of meats, they did have many fruits and vegetables. They took their produce to market by a well organized system so that it could be sold while fresh. Their money consisted of cocoa beans, small silver coins in the form of a T, and quills filled with different amounts of gold dust. Most of the trade was by barter. Gold was used mostly for jewelry and ornamentation instead of money, which is why it was so hard for them to understand the Spaniards' obsession for gold. They also worked tin, copper, gold and silver into jewelry, utensils, ornaments and accouterments for their religious ceremonies, etc. Their pottery art was very advanced, and beautifully painted pottery, then as now, was used for the adornment of the household and for cooking utensels.

The textile industry was well developed and clothing, bedding, costumes, banners etc. were made of cotton. They were very clever at making vegetable dyes like cochineal which they used to dye fabrics in beautiful colors and designs. The Mexicans have always been very skilled and ingenious in making hand-crafted objects. Although Mexico is now highly industrialized, an enormous amount of quality goods are still made in homes. Juan Diego wove mats, called "petates," at which he must have been skilled and industrious, since he was quite successful.

The Mexicans of today are the same sociable, hospitable kind of people as they were described in the days of Montezuma. All family affairs and religious feast days were celebrated with festivals, banquets, processions, entertainment by musicians, clowns, jugglers and theatrical performances.

RELIGION. Religion in the Aztec Empire was an intermingling of dedication to exalted spiritual concepts, idolatry and human sacrifices. This last abomination had been imposed on the rest of the nation by the Aztec rulers who taught that Huitzilopochtle, their god of war, demanded human sacrifice. The prisoners the Aztecs took in their "Flower Wars" were offered to these bloodthirsty gods. In early times, the culture hero Quetzalcóatl had taught the Toltecs of the existence of a Supreme Being, the Creator of all things, Whose help and blessings they were to seek through worship and adoration that did not involve human sacrifice. His teaching about the true God was revived by the king of Texcoco, Nezahualcóyotl, in the middle of the fifteenth century. However, the struggle to maintain life and deal with the powerful forces of nature gradually caused them to seek relief in deifying the elements, which they thought they could placate to the advantage of a better life.

The name "Quetzalcóatl," which means both "Precious Twin" and "Feathered Serpent" was given to a god; to a succession of Toltec rulers, the most important one of whom was the cultural hero mentioned above; and eventually to a series of Aztec priests. Around 890 A.D., Quetzlcóatl, the historical culture-hero-king of Toltec, was forced to leave his throne. He went through Cholula on his way to the Gulf, where legend says he sailed east promising to return in the year Ce Acatl (1519), to rule Mexico again. The Aztec Lords dreaded having to surrender their power to him. This tradition helped to pave the way for the outstanding success of the Spaniards in conquering the Aztec nation and Montezuma's ambivalent attitude towards Cortés. As great and brave a man as he was, he no longer had the courage to do anything else but surrender to the inevitable.

The Aztecs had many practices resembling the Catholic religion. They had a form of infant baptism, performed by the midwife right after birth. Marriages were officiated over by their priests, and divorce was very difficult to obtain, requiring long and expensive court action. There was even a form of confession, which was usually resorted to when a person was quite on in years, because it could only be availed of once in a lifetime. The individual could never be punished by the civil authorities for the sins he confessed, the only penalty being the penance that the priest gave him. There were feast and fast days, litanies, processions and services for almost every day in the year. Some historians have expressed the thought that with all the religious activities, it is a wonder that the Aztecs ever had any time to do any work. (There is further exposition of the Aztec social structure and its educational system in the article, "Juan Diego, Ambassador of the Queen of Heaven" on page 42). This short description of the civilization of the Aztecs gives an orientation to the milieu in which Juan Diego lived.

He was a man of modest attainment, successful in his work and financially well off. His "poverty" was basically a spiritual one, as counseled in the Gospels. Like all the saints, he achieved union with God in the measure he practiced this evangelical poverty. Because he was actively involved in the evangelization of his fellow

*Aztecs adoring one of their many gods. The miraculous
Image and words of Our Lady of Guadalupe pointed to the
true God, and stamped out their false worship, which
included human sacrifice.*

Indians at Tepeyac, he is an ideal patron for the lay apostle (see article on page 130). He was one with all of us: a real-life person who attained holiness in the world by working for the salvation of other souls. As instruments of Our Lady, we would all do well to emulate his example.

The above article is an adaptation from a chapter in the book, "Juan Diego," by the late Dr. Charles Wahlig. We are grateful to Janet Barber for her comments and input to this article.

✝   ✝   ✝   ✝   ✝

An Editor's Conversion through Guadalupe Research

With good reason, Mr. Coley Taylor, co-author of an anthology on Guadalupe: "The Dark Virgin," has a special place in his heart for Guadalupe. It was through his translation of material on Guadalupe that he began to reexamine the state of his "beliefs and disbeliefs," which ultimately led to his embracing the Catholic Faith. He first went to Mexico in 1953, and was struck by the omnipresent Image of Our Lady of Guadalupe, "in taxicabs, in business offices, in stores, in homes, wherever I went." The veteran editor was in Mexico to promote a cultural interchange with the Mexicans, especially in the field of creative writing. Mr. Donald Demarest, an assistant director of the Writing Center, suggested that they prepare a book on Guadalupe. "He agreed to gather up all the documents relating to the apparitions, and I was to do most of the translating," Mr. Taylor said.

As he pored over the story of how Our Lady had appeared to Juan Diego, leaving to this day the tangible evidence of her appearance in the Miraculous Image, he found himself examining the sixteenth-century Aztec's story with the standards of a twentieth-century New York editor and publisher. "The fact that Juan Diego completely forgot his appointment with the Blessed Virgin on December 11, and that when he did remember it the next day, on his way to get a priest for his dying uncle, he tried to dodge her - this is charming and quite natural, and couldn't have been invented."

Equally convincing, were Juan Diego's confused attempts at small talk when the Virgin intercepted him. "He asked how she felt, if she had slept well." This couldn't have been inserted by some devout writer. An editor can spot what's phony in a narrative. He also recalled that when Juan Diego discovered the Castilian roses and brought them to the Virgin, she took them out of his tilma and "rearranged them." "This is very authentic," observed Mr. Taylor. "Here she showed her human nature and did what every woman would have done." Mary also displayed "a marvelous sense of humor" he said, "to put her portrait on that thin, sleazy material. No artist would ever have chosen such material. . . ."

Extracted from an interview with Coley Taylor, co-author of the "Dark Virgin," an Anthology on Guadalupe

Cortés and the Valiant "Little Ladies"

Diana Cary

*W*hen the fleet of eleven caravels arrived carrying six hundred men, sixteen horses, ten cannons, and Capt. Hernando Cortés from Cuba to Vera Cruz, Mexico, in February of 1519, it was loaded with historic dynamite. But the most explosive cargo aboard were several small, wooden statues of the Virgin, which could rightly be called the "Madonnas of Cortés." These statues proved to be the real dynamite, judging from the events that followed. They escaped the inventory only because they were undoubtedly the personal possessions of the friars and soldiers. But from the outset, these stowaways managed to get right into the thick of things, going down in history as valiant "little ladies."

After the expedition had landed on the southern coast of Mexico, Cortés was quick to sense the political climate of the new land. He had a genius for understanding the entire scope of any given situation, and the situation in Mexico at the time of his arrival was very simple. Through interpreters, Cortés learned that the smaller Indian nations were ruled by the Aztec emperor, Montezuma, whose grandfather had built an empire largely through the "Flower Wars" in which he had suppressed the neighboring tribes. The captives from these wars were offered as human sacrifices to the Aztecs' gods. Like enslaved people in any era or time, they hated the tyrant but lacked a strong leader to unite them against his rule.

They were eager to put an end to decades of heavy taxation and bloody tribute, purportedly well over 25,000 human sacrifices offered to their gods in a single year!

They Understood and Respected Courage

But conquering these smaller tribes was not simply a matter of overawing their warriors with superior weapons and modern European tactics. Like most warlike peoples, the Mexican Indians understood and respected only courage and leadership on the battlefield. Even though Cortés offered them peace negotiations and an exchange of envoys, they initially had no means of evaluating the Spaniards as men. They demanded the test of battle, and despite their small numbers, the Spaniards were ready to meet the challenge, even though they faced armies of warriors that often outnumbered them five hundred to one!

Against such odds as these, the Spaniards fought their first battle in Mexico, on what they termed "Our Lady's Day," March 25, the present feast day of the Annunciation. They named the first town they established on this site *Our Lady of Victory*. The Indians, who were fierce and experienced fighters, were deeply impressed by the cool courage and tactics of their white enemies. The encounters were brief, usually one or two day clashes, from which the Indians invariably withdrew chastened and even baffled, but with a high respect and admiration for the invaders. With considerable shrewd political self-interest on both sides, Cortés dealt with the *caciques*, or official rulers, as lawful administrators, and as far as religion and culture permitted, as equals. Notaries drew up legal forms, and the rulers, swore their allegiance as a nation to the King of Spain, whose loyal, peaceful subjects, and worthy allies they intended to be.

Religion Was a Vital Part of Their Lives

To Cortés and the men who fought with him, religion was as much a part of the practical side of living as breathing. Though they were sinners, they knew themselves to be what they were. There were good Christians and bad ones, but they all held the same truths whether they lived up to them or not. The Spaniards were appalled at what they found. In each of the towns there were temples, or pyramids made of stone, topped with small wooden apartments which housed the hideous idols of the Indians' bloodthirsty gods. Since so little revenge was possible against their powerful Aztec lords, the subjected tribes made the most of things whenever they were lucky enough to capture an Aztec prisoner of war.

Cortés found many such Aztec captives being fattened in little wooden cages for the next local feast day and he immediately ordered their release. He had the temples cleansed, the images cast down, and a crucifix and a Madonna placed on an altar atop each pyramid. The idols quickly went to pieces when kicked off their pedestals, since they were made of clay and corn meal mixed with vegetables and dried human blood. What did not break up so easily was the deepseated hold which the diabolical beliefs had upon the people.

With thousands of these Indian-allies marching behind him either as carriers of baggage or as fellow warriors, Cortés and his men now turned toward the great city of Mexico, Montezuma's capital, which was set like a jewel in the center of a sapphire lake. Montezuma had tried for months to keep the newcomers at bay by peaceful gifts and by lies, for the fatalistic emperor had read his own doom in the prophecy of the fall of the Aztec empire. Montezuma did things in a lordly manner, even when his sumptuous hospitality may have been a cloak for the uneasy fear that prompted it. Things seemed peaceful, but for the Spaniards it was like living on top of the volcano Popocatépetl. Cortés noticed that the lake was threaded with silver, as slim Aztec canoes shot back and forth on secret errands, weaving a web of death for the intruders. His Indian allies told him the priests and rulers were planning to drive them out. To secure his foothold in the city, which up to this hour had been maintained without the exchange of even an angry word, Cortés made the bold decision to make the spider who was spinning the web his prisoner. He placed Montezuma under house-arrest, and held him hostage.

It was then that Cortés ordered a carpenter to set up an altar in his apartments on which he placed a statue of the Madonna. Because it was destined to play the key role in the conquest of Mexico, this little Madonna statue is today, of all those who sailed with it, the most renowned. It belonged to one of Cortés' captains, Rodrigues Villafuerte. Carved of wood, it measures just a little over a foot in height, and represents Our Lady carrying the Infant Christ on her left arm, with a tiny scepter in her right hand. The image resembles the famous Lady of Guadalupe in Extremadura, Spain, to whom Cortés and many of his captains had a special devotion.

The Fathomless Cruelty of Pagan Religion

Cortés introduced Montezuma to the Mother of God by means of this little Madonna, and by means of her, tried to explain the Christian Faith to him and persuade him to abandon his demon gods. When Montezuma seemed unmoved, Cortés asked to be taken to the central temple in the main square of the city. He was struck to the heart at the sight of the fifty clay images, the hideous priests, their hair smeared with human blood, the altar curtains hung with tiny bells whose very chiming in the breeze sounded like the voice of evil incarnate. Overcome by the fathomless cruelty of which these otherwise noble people were capable under the influence of superstition and fear, Cortés spoke out fearlessly in the presence of the idols and their high priests. Montezuma warned the Spaniard not to speak against their gods, and the priests paled at the outrage; but Cortés seized that moment which was perhaps the very pinnacle of his life, and told the onlookers he would prove the Christian God would render their demons impotent. He struck the mighty Huitzilopochtli statue between its emerald-studded eyes, and hurled it down the blood-stained steps. He ordered the Madonna to be brought from his own apartment to replace the pagan deity.

That altar was the most dangerous spot the little Madonna had ever been placed. Flaming hatred blazed in the coal-like eyes of the Aztec priests. Montezuma, prisoner though he was, roared like a wounded lion. Even Huitzilopochtli himself seemed to be furious, for later that day the high priest reported to Montezuma that the outraged deity was planning to walk out on the whole Aztec Empire. The second most powerful god, Tlàloc, and all the lesser gods with him, would not stay in the same place where they had been treated so cruelly, and where the Christians had dared set up the image of a woman and a child in their place! The top of a *teocalli* was hardly a safe place for Captain Villafuerte's treasured Lady. But in the flickering light of a candle, the statue inspired courage in the worried Spaniards until the storm finally broke, and the fury of the gods poured like a torrent of blood over the Spanish company.

Having needlessly provoked an attack while Cortés was out of the city, the Spaniards barricaded themselves in one of the palaces. When Cortés reached them he found his men besieged and isolated in a sea of hostile Aztecs. The Spanish fought their way out of the city, but first Cortés and Captain Villafuerte cut their way to the top of the hundred steps of the central *teocalli* to rescue the Madonna and the crucifix. It was hand-to-hand fighting from the bottom to the top, every step slick with the blood of wounded or dying men. Cortés snatched the Madonna from its altar, Villafuerte seized the cross, and together they made their descent through a forest of obsidian swords, showered with stones thrown by warriors from nearby rooftops.

The flight from the capital was frightful beyond description, for the city of Mexico sat in the midst of Lake Texcoco and was linked to the mainland by narrow causeways over which no more than four horsemen could ride abreast. Not only were the few hundred Spaniards fleeing along these swarming causeways, but nearly ten thousand Indian allies as well. Men and horses were shot down, cut to pieces, or drowned as they lost their precarious footing. Warriors in canoes picked up the wounded prisoners, and soon the Spaniards had to endure the agony of hearing the screams of their fellow soldiers who were being sacrificed alive on the same stone altar where the Madonna had reigned so briefly. Rest and safety came at last when the scattered survivors regrouped about eleven miles from the capital. Cortés and his men, kneeling before the Madonna, thanked her for their miraculous deliverance.

An answer to prayers was the discovery that their Indian allies had remained loyal despite the catastrophe which had befallen them. Towns welcomed them back, *caciques* loyally promised food and supplies and even warriors for another try at the impregnable city, which was eventually retaken, an epic in itself. After the conquest, the new city of Mexico began to rise from the ruins of the old pagan capital. A church was built near the sight of a razed Aztec *teocalli*. Our Lady of Remedies was given a church of her own. Even in the lifetime of Bernal Diaz, the old Spanish soldier who had fought beside Cortés and Villafuerte, and to whom historians owe nearly all of what is known of the conquest from the Spanish perspective, this church of Our Lady of Remedies was already a famous shrine and a favorite place of pilgrimage.

Nuestra Senora de los Remedios still remains the second Lady of the land, after Our Lady of Guadalupe. A gracious and modest Queen who came with the Great Conquistador Cortés and who remembers what it was to overthrow the mighty god Huitzilopochtli and put her own Son as King and Lord in his place.

The above adapted and condensed article first appeared in the <u>Marianist</u> magazine.

By foot, or on horseback, by carriage or automobile millions of Mexican pilgrims have come to Guadalupe to venerate and seek help from she who speaks of herself as our merciful mother. The old basilica in the background housed the sacred Image for over two and a half centuries.

PART III

Main Characters in Guadalupe

1. Juan Diego
Ambassador of the Queen of Heaven
Dr. Charles Wahlig

2. Bishop Zumárraga,
The Defender of the Indians
Sr. Amatora, O.S.F.

3. Antonio Valeriano,
Author of Historic Account on Guadalupe
Dr. Charles Wahlig

The two Juans cooperated in heaven's plan, and their generous response to Mary of Guadalupe's bidding brought tremendous graces to all of the Americas. It may well have an even greater impact in the future as more and more people become aware of Mary of Guadalupe, whom the Popes designate "Empress of the Americas."

Juan Diego
Ambassador of the Queen of Heaven

Dr. Charles Wahlig

*I*n the year 1503, Montezuma was chosen from among the four nephews of the late emperor Ahuitzotl to be the new Aztec emperor. His capital, Tenochtitlan (Mexico City), was at that time one of the world's largest cities with a population of 360,000. His empire stretched from the Atlantic to the Pacific and collected tribute from states all the way from what is now New Mexico, to the border of Guatemala. Tenochtitlan was situated on an island in the center of Lake Texcoco, a large body of water which filled the center of the Valley of Mexico at that time. During the succeeding centuries, the water was drained off until today there are only vestiges of the lake remaining. It was well laid out with wide straight paved streets, many of which had canals on its sides like Venice. Among the numerous towns in the Valley of Mexico was Cuauhtitlan (the Place of the Eagle). It is about 14 miles from the capital. Its inhabitants, including Juan Diego, were not Aztecs as is commonly believed. They were Chichimecas, members of one of the groups which had arrived in the Valley of Mexico from the north, years before the Aztecs arrived toward the end of the 1200's.

When Montezuma became emperor, no one would have thought that this well-liked, mild-mannered young 29-year-old Juan Diego, as he came to be known, would some day be the human agency in an event which would determine much of the course of civilization in the western hemisphere. To establish the proper status of the famous-to-be individual, it will be necessary to briefly review the nature of society at the apogee of the renowned Aztec empire. The highest authority was the emperor, then the kings of the 29 larger states, and the high nobles came next. They commanded

Juan Diego on his way to give Mary of Guadalupe's message to the Bishop.

the armed forces, while the lower nobles were mostly civil administrators. The priests, merchants and the large middle class, *macehuales*, to which Juan Diego belonged, made up the rest of society who were considered important. Below these were the laboring and servant class, *tlamaitl*; occupying the lowest class were the slaves. All historians agree that Juan Diego and his family were macehuales. He had a good deal of property, some he inherited, and the rest came from a successful mat making business. In the past he was thought to be poor, but in recent years, historians agree that his was a voluntary poverty that he freely embraced

Juan Diego, being a *macehual*, was a full-fledged citizen. He was obliged to vote in the elections of officials since he was a landowner. He was educated, since under the empire schooling was compulsory. The boys had to go to chool until they were old enough to go to work, and the girls until they were old enough to get married. He was liable for military service, but there is no record of his being conscripted. Under the Aztec rule he had a fairly large measure of freedom. Tradition tells us that after his marriage, he farmed the land next to his house in Cuauhtitlan, growing corn, beans and assorted vegetables. Along with the meat supplied from his hunting turkey and deer, he and his wife ate well. He evidently was of an ingenious and industrious nature and eventually worked up quite a business making mats and furniture from reeds growing along the shores of Lake Texcoco.

The testimony of friends and neighbors described Juan Diego in his mature years as a reflective person, given more and more to meditation and speculation on matters philosophical and spiritual, to which his growing prosperity permitted him to devote more time. The caste system of the Aztec empire operated mainly in the civil and economic phases of daily life. The laws were quite severe, but all the Mexicans above the slave class had the benefit of a high degree of personal freedom. There were no barriers to members of the various classes associating with each other in their social or intellectual pursuits. Revelations are generally made to persons fitted to receive them. We must assume that Juan Diego's intellectual capacities were equal to the stupendous task which God had assigned to him, that of leading his fellow countrymen to embrace the Catholic religion.

The true God had already made his existence known to Nezahualcoyotl, King of Texcoco, in 1464. This king was *the* educated man of his time, and he gathered the intellectuals of that area in his court. Netzahualcoyotl was himself very intelligent, well versed in philosophy, astronomy, literature, etc. - the "humanities" of his day. He reasoned that there had to be some Superior Intelligence responsible for the order in all creation. He abandoned the pagan religion and built temples in which he worshipped the true God, praying before altars containing offerings of flowers and incense. Just before his death Nezahualcoyotl made a great speech ending with these words, "How deeply I regret that I am not able to understand the will of the great God, but I believe the time will come when he will be known and adored by all the inhabitants of this land." No doubt Juan Diego studied what was earlier known about the true God, as Cuauhtitlan had been part of the Acolhua (Texcocan) empire before its conquest by the Aztecs in 1439.

Nezahualcoyotl's son Nezahualpilli who succeeded him was the very image of his father. His devotion to the true God was rewarded by the general acknowledgment that he was the wisest man of his era. Just before he died in 1515, he terrified the emperor Montezuma by telling him he had a dream a few days before in which it was made known to him that Montezuma was soon to lose his throne to invaders from across the sea who were going to bring the True Religion. It was in part occurrences such as these, which intensified the prophecies already made known to him by his sister, Princess Papantzin, which induced Montezuma to surrender his huge Aztec empire to Cortés in 1520. The Aztec leader was subsequently stoned to death by his fellow countrymen, after which the Aztecs drove the Spaniards out of the city. Later, when Cortés attacked from ships he launched on Lake Texcoco, the Aztecs resisted the Spaniards to the point of starving to death, since Cortés had effectively blockaded the city.

Juan Diego and his family must have been associated with the participants in these events and have been profoundly impressed by them. From the time of his conversion, he was imbued with a powerful urge to acquire every bit of knowledge of the True Faith, which he embraced with great fervor. Upon the arrival of the first group of missionaries in 1524, he, his wife and uncle were among the first adults to be baptized in the Catholic Faith, some time before 1528. At that time, they all took Christian names — Juan Diego, Maria Lucia and Juan Bernardino. Juan Diego and Maria Lucia continued to live on in Cuauhtitlan. They received instructions in the Faith from the visiting missionaries and cheerfully walked the 14 miles to Tlaltelolco to attend Mass every Sunday and receive Communion. The Franciscans also had Mass on Saturdays along with their catechetical instructions. The Spaniards had leveled the temple dedicated to Huitzilopochtli and Tlaloc, and the colonial churches of Santiago de Tlalteloco were built on the site of the temple, where the third, begun in 1573, stands to this day.

Juan Diego continued to work hard. He and Maria Lucia were leading a very happy home life and derived much contentment from the practice of their religion. Their happy married life was not to last. In 1529, Maria Lucia took sick and died. In his sorrow and loneliness, Juan turned more and more to his uncle, Juan Bernardino, of whom he was very fond, as his only remaining close relative. Juan Bernardino was at that time living in the village of Tolpetlac. Juan Diego built a rather commodious house not far from his uncle's house, on a large piece of property he already owned, and left Cuauhtitlan to take up his abode in Tolpetlac.

Juan's grief over the death of his wife was assuaged no doubt by his intense devotion to the Blessed Virgin. This can be deduced from his habit of rising very early every Saturday morning to attend the Mass in honor of the Blessed Virgin, in addition to his regular Sunday Mass. Tolpetlac was 9 miles from Tlaltelolco, but it was nothing for him to cover this distance even at his age. All natives of that region were accustomed from early childhood to walk and trot long distances. There is no need to repeat here the details of Juan Diego's participation in the Miracle of Guadalupe. This is nobly done in the account known as the *Nican Mopohua* written by another famous Mexican, Don Antonio Valeriano, an intimate of Juan Diego, and reproduced in another part of this book (see page 193).

On December 26th, only two weeks after the Sacred Icon appeared on Juan Diego's tilma, Spaniards and the Mexicans, working shoulder to shoulder, completed a chapel at the foot of Tepeyac Hill to house the Sacred Image. Fray Juan de Zumárraga, Bishop of Mexico, put Juan Diego in complete charge of the chapel and the Sacred Image. We can imagine that the bishop was confident that there was no more capable and worthy a person than Juan Diego to remain guardian of the world's greatest treasure.

A one-room addition was added onto the east wall of the chapel to serve as living quarters for Juan Diego, and this is where he spent the rest of his life. His uncle, Juan Bernardino, pleaded with him to enlarge it to accommodate both of them. Juan told his uncle to return to Tolpetlac to take over the property there, as well

This portrait of Juan Diego, the original of which is in the Guadalupan Sanctuary of Guadalajara, Jalisco, Mexico, is considered the most authentic likeness of him. It is a faithful copy of the original which Don Lorenzo Boturini Benaduci had, of which he makes mention of in his book on the history of the Americas. It was Andrés Islas who painted it in Mexico in 1774. His career as a painter flourished between the years 1750 to 1775.

as his property in Cuauhtitlan. Juan Diego devoted the last 17 years of his life to the Mother of God. How tired he must have been at the end of each day after continually relating to the thousands of people who came to see the Sacred Image, how Mary had appeared to him and the message she had conveyed to all men through him.

Juan Diego, already learned in Nahuatl and Christian doctrine, recognized immediately the significance and symbolism contained in the Sacred Image and had no difficulty in explaining it to his fellow countrymen. Knowing that this Image was a picture-writing, or visual codex that came from Heaven, and explained much as an icon (see page 63), the natives eagerly embraced the Christian Faith in large numbers. In this manner, 8 million Mexicans were converted to Christianity in the next 7 years. During the years Juan Diego spent in intimate spiritual communion with his Lady from Heaven and caring for her Image, a great change came over him which was not overlooked by his countrymen.

While retaining his essential humility, his face and bearing seemed to take on a new dignity. His frugality and disciplined life revealed the refinement of an ascetic. He had come to be revered as a man of great culture and lofty thinking, as befits a man who leads a holy life. In 1548, at the age of 74, he passed from this life into the eternal presence of God. We may assume he was met by her who placed such great confidence in him to do her bidding. He was buried in the chapel which he had cared for so well.

Adapted from the article with the same title by Dr. Charles Wahlig, from the original Guadalupe Handbook.

Bishop Zumárraga
Defender of the Indians

Sister Mary Amatora, O.S.F.

*I*n announcing herself and her mission to all peoples on this new continent, it was appropriate that the Indian [Juan Diego], native of the land, and the Basque [Bishop Zumárraga], who came to Christianize the Indian, be the principal figures employed by Our Lady in manifesting her merciful love to the peoples of the Americas. . . . Because of the numerous and serious difficulties between the Indians and the Spaniards in the New World, Emperor Charles V was asked by Cortés to send them a bishop, a prelate who would be invested with both ecclesiastical and civil power. He wanted someone who would be a protector to the Indians, and an apostle for their Christianization.

No one was better fitted for this task than Fray Juan de Zumárraga, who was both an outstanding scholar and a zealous religious. Although he declined the honor, the Church authorities realized that his excuses came from his sincere and profound humility. They knew the zeal with which he labored for souls. They recognized his great learning. They were acquainted with the austerity and poverty which he practised in his personal life. Hence, his superiors prevailed upon him to accept the appointment, that he might guide the flock of the Church in the New World in the service of God and country.

Though raised by God to the high dignity of Bishop, Fray Juan de Zumárraga continued to live the austere life of the Friars Minor. He rose in the middle of the night for Matins, observed all the fasts of the Order, and traveled barefoot. To their edification, both priests and people saw in him a perfect, living copy of his spiritual father, St. Francis. Such was the man who came to America in 1528, just three years before the time of the apparitions.

Before, and at the time of Our Lady's coming to America, bloody conflict was going on in the land. Although it was then ten years since the Spaniards had subjugated the Indians and colonized the area, sporadic warfare continued. It would seem that the Virgin chose to come to put an end to this bloodshed and to establish peace. Many of the Spaniards, defying Cortés, were far more interested in personal aggrandizement than in carrying out the policies of the King of Spain. The members of the first audiencia, or governing council of New Spain, were bloodthirsty gluttons of power. Nuno de Guzmán, its leader, took advantage of his position to confiscate the lands of both Indians and conquistadors. He was one of the bitterest foes of the missionaries.

The only powers that stood between Guzmán and his cohorts on the one side, and the Indians on the other, were Cortés, and the Bishop with his companions. Yet, defying both God and King, this cruel tyrant set up a blockade between Mexico City and the only port, Vera Cruz, enforced a strict censorship, and forbade both Indians and Spaniards to bring any complaints to the bishop. Even the personal messages of the bishop to the king were confiscated, as were many of those from Cortés.

In his official capacity as designated by the King, Bishop Zumárraga was "Protector of the Indians." Yet, he could send no direct reports to the King to whom he was responsible in civil matters. Finally, with the aid of a sailor, he succeeded in sending a message hidden in a roll of bacon in a keg of oil. Another was smuggled out of the country inserted in a carved-out crucifix.

In the new land, roads were nonexistent and distances were great. With such a lack of communication, it was easier for the Spaniards to carry out their cruelties against the Indians. Sometimes they burned whole villages, killing the men without cause, or on the pretext of stopping an epidemic. In addition, they would impose such heavy taxes as to force the Indians to sell their women and children into slavery. It is no wonder that conversions to the faith were slow in getting under way.

While the Spanish priests, instructed the Indians about the love of God and neighbor, teaching them to observe the Ten Commandments and to live in peace and harmony - other Spaniards, the soldiers, stole their possessions, burned their homes and killed their people. Was it any wonder that, in the face of such atrocities, the Indians wanted no part of the "new religion," nor wished to go to the "Christian's heaven"?

Though appointed Bishop of Mexico City, Fray Juan de Zumárraga continued to live the austere life of the Friars Minor. He rose in the middle of the night for the Office of Readings, observed all the fasts of the Order and traveled on foot, even barefoot. The people saw in him a living copy of St. Francis. This was the holy friar to whom Our Lady sent Juan Diego to have a chapel built at Tepeyac.

Things became so bad that, in 1529, two years before the apparitions, Cortés was recalled to Spain. Guzmán and his friends had blamed all the troubles on Cortés, hoping to get rid of him so they could act without restraint. About a year later, a second audiencia was established, and matters improved. Cortés returned and was cleared of all charges. Guzmán was ordered back to Spain and the enslavement of the Indians was stopped. However, the general attitude did not change much, and Bishop Zumárraga and his missionaries had to continue the fight for the rights of the Indians against bitter opposition, with their very lives threatened. Such were the conditions in the New World, when heaven came to the rescue, when Christ sent His own Blessed Mother to intervene, to let her children in the western hemisphere know that she would be a mother to all who would come to her in this new land.

The above article is excerpted and adapted from Chapter One of Part II of the book, "The Queen's Portrait: The Story of Guadalupe," published by the Exposition Press, New York.

First Author of Historic Account on Guadalupe
Don Antonio Valeriano

Dr. Charles Wahlig

*T*he original authentic history of the Miracle of Guadalupe was written by an Aztec nobleman who had been given the Spanish Christian name in baptism of Antonio Valeriano. He wrote his history in Nahuatl, the language of the Aztecs. It is known as the "Nican Mopohua" from the first two words of the title, *"Nican Mopohua Moctepana Inquenin Yancuican Hueit-lamahuizoltica Monexiti Inzequisca Santa Maria Dio Ynantzin Tozihuapillatocatzin, In Oncan Tepeyacac Motenehua Guadalupe."* English translation: "Herein is related in order and arrangement the manner in which the ever Virgin Mary Mother of God recently and marvelously appeared in Tepeyac, which is called Guadalupe." Historians have determined that he wrote it sometime between 1548 and 1560.

Valeriano was eminently and singularly fitted for this task. The late historian Padre Mariano Cuevas says he was the nephew of the Emperor Montezuma, and was born in 1520 in Azcapotzalco, a community not far from Tepeyac. He entered the College of the Holy Cross, which would be comparable to our high school, at Tlaltelolco at the age of 16. This was the first college in the western hemisphere, and was founded by Fray Juan de Zumárraga, the first Bishop of Mexico. When it began to function in 1536, Don Antonio was a member of the first class. He was the first graduate to take honors in Latin and Greek, and was kept on as a teacher of these subjects. He advanced to the post of professor of philosophy and was Dean of the college for 20 years. He was the most valued assistant of Friar Bernardine de Sahagún, the first ethnologist of the

New World.

As a young man, Don Antonio married the daughter of one of the Lords of Tenochtitlan (Mexico City). Concomitant with his academic career, he entered public service. He was a judge for some years, and became Governor of the Indians of the City of Mexico, a post he held for more than 30 years. He proved to be just as brilliant an administrator as he was as a scholar, and was very popular with both the Spaniards and the Mexicans. In later life, his talents came to the attention of Philip II, King of Spain, who wrote him a very laudatory letter.

To most readers, something that took place a very long time ago may seem unworthy of mentioning. An incident occurred in 1973, however, which in a sense bridges the gap of exactly 400 years, making it seem as though it could all have taken place much more recently. A most precious document written in Nahuatl was discovered in the National Library of Mexico: a petition drawn up by a group of citizens and presented to Don Antonio Valeriano, the contents of which are validated by his signature as Governor. The document also bears the signature of the scribe and of the notary, and bears the date of January 11, 1573 on the reverse side. A translation of it into Spanish made by the historian of the College of St. Gregory in 1586 was bound with it in the same volume. The petition asks that the members of the chorus of the College of St. Gregory be permitted to enter that institution as students. The other item asks Valeriano to use his authority to make the poor send their children to the schools established and endowed by the king for their education, pointing out that the poor were neither serving their God nor their King by their delinquency.

Valeriano was an intimate friend of all the principal characters in the miracle of Guadalupe: Bishop Zumárraga, Juan Gonzalez, Juan Bernardino, and Juan Diego. According to tradition, he was especially friendly with Juan Diego, and often went to visit him at the chapel in Tepeyac where the Sacred Image of Our Lady was venerated. Most of the historians agree that Valeriano carefully and accurately wrote down the conversations between Juan Diego and the Blessed Virgin, and all the other essential details of the great event as well. It is said that Valeriano enjoyed reciting the story of the miracle whenever he had an audience, which left a strong oral tradition of the miracle.

He died in 1605. Individuals of his stature and accomplish-

Left: "The oldest known portrait of Juan Diego," a copper engraving by Antonio Castro, first printed in 1669 and bearing a close likeness to his image in Codex 1548 (see Historicity article, pg. 184). Lower left: Engraving attributed to Antonio Castro, first published in Mexico in 1675. Instead of a glyph of Valeriano in the lower right corner, as in Codex 1548, it shows a church. Juan Diego's features are Spanish. Lower right: Indian representation of Judge Antonio Valeriano. A similar glyph and inscription occurs in Codex 1548.

ments were not uncommon in the race that produced Montezuma I and II. Having no heirs, Valeriano willed all his documents, including the "Nican Mopohua," to a distant cousin-in-law, Don Fernando de Alba Ixtlilxochitl, the great-great grandson of the last King of Texcoco. He in turn left everything to his son, Don Juan. When he died in 1682, and left no descendants, Don Carlos de Siguenza y Gongora, Canon of the Metropolitan Cathedral inherited the books and documents.

According to Don Antonio Pompa y Pompa, director of the

National Museum of Archeology and Anthropology, and official historian of Guadalupe, Siguenza y Gongora willed all his books and documents, including the "Nican Mopohua" and 29 volumes he had written himself, to the Jesuit College of St. Peter and St. Paul when he died in 1700. When the Jesuits were expelled from the Spanish domains in 1767, his whole library went to the library of the University of Mexico. The books and documents of Siguenza y Gongora, including the "Nican Mopohua" disappeared in the middle of the nineteenth century. No doubt, after passing through several intermediary hands, the New York City Public Library acquired the "Nican Mopohua" at an auction in 1880.

It is very edifying for the human race to have in its midst a perpetual miracle brought from the unseen world into the world of physical reality, but what is its purpose and meaning? That is the vital part, so we must be very certain about the words spoken by Our Lady to Juan Diego and Juan Bernardino. In a certain sense these, together with the message in the Sacred Image itself, are for Guadalupe what the Bible is to the foundations of Christianity.

The more one thinks about it, the clearer it becomes that the Blessed Virgin could hardly have selected two men more suitable for her purposes: Juan Diego, the virtuous one, worthy to receive her message, and Don Antonio Valeriano, the Mexican of great intellect and gifted writing talent for transmitting her words to posterity.

The Lady Is Modest

Another thing we have all noticed is that her face seems "poorly lighted." It isn't. I think she keeps it shadowed a little, perhaps out of modesty; no lady likes to be stared at. And this, too, is another reversal. Her face is clearer in detail up close, but veiled in shadow even when one stares at it from the foot of the altar. It is altogether a paradox, and a delight beyond words. And it is this gentle presence, this vivacious graciousness, this radiance, which no artist, nor any reproduction can capture. In some mysterious, supernatural way, she is still here at Tepeyac, a part of that sacred Image. This may be bad theology for all I know, but it is what one feels as a definite mystical experience.

From a letter by Coley Taylor to Rt. Rev. Columban Hawkins, O.C.S.O.

PART IV

The Tilma
of Juan Diego

The Aztecs originally recorded their documents in picture form since they did not have an alphabet. When Our Lady gave her Image to Juan Diego and the natives, it was in picture writing, or "codex," that explained everything. New and exciting discoveries on the Tilma are continually being found in our day.

The Tilma and Its Miraculous Image

Janet Barber, I.H.M.

*B*lessed Juan Diego's ancient, but ever new tilma, with its divinely beautiful Image is a life-giving source which from the very moment of the Image's miraculous appearance has been gradually revealing its meanings. The *Nican Mopohua* tells us that as the different kinds of precious flowers fell to the floor in the Bishop's house, the Image of the Perfect Virgin, Holy Mary, Mother of God, "suddenly appeared" on the Indian's tilma. Quirozz says of that moment, "Time fell on its knees before the Indian's tilma." Weeping, Bishop-elect Fray Juan Zumárraga and his companions also fell to their knees on that thrilling morning of December 12, 1531.

And every day of the Miracle's continuance has also been mysterious and thrilling, as an examination of the known facts easily shows. The tilma itself had been woven of maguey fibers, on a back-strap loom in two separate panels which were sewn loosely together with maguey thread. The seam goes down the left side of Our Lady's head, barely touching her skin where her mantle, tunic, and neck meet. It touches the cotton cuffs of her left sleeve, neatly goes down the middle of the mantle-fold under her arm, and proceeds straight down through the flowers. That the seam divides the Image in half without affecting the centered portrait in any important way, is in human terms a *tour de force*. On unretouched photographs, the loss of pigment along the seam on the side of her head is very noticeable.

The Image hung for 116 years without any glass to protect it from the strong nitrous fumes given off by Lake Texcoco and from the swords, medals, rosaries, pictures, lips and hands which were constantly touched to it, to say nothing of the soot and heat from

The faithful full length image of Our Lady of Guadalupe as she appeared to Juan Diego on Tepeyac Hill, near Mexico City. No reproduction can do justice to the original.

the many candles that burned at all hours! The glass was sometimes removed for long periods for a more direct veneration by those who loved her. The two pairs of horizontal lines crossing the Image at the level of her tunic cuffs and below her knees are the result of crosspieces of the wooden frame which held the Image for several hundred years.

Humans Try Their Hand at It

In an experiment in the 1780s, Dr. Jose Ignacio Bartolache had copies made on maguey-fiber tilmas woven by the finest Indian weavers and painted by the leading copyists of the day. They were then placed in various buildings at Tepeyac, so as to be subject to the same climatic conditions as the Image itself had been. After seven years, their colors had changed and deteriorated; the paint and gold work were falling off, and the maguey fibers were disintegrating. The almost perfect preservation for 465 years of Juan Diego's fragile tilma and the coloring on it, is clearly miraculous. The original size of the tilma is a matter of question, because toward 1770 it was cut to make it fit into the frame preceding the present one. The height of Our Lady herself, from her mantle to the tip of her right slipper, is some four feet nine inches.

Add-ons or Touch-ups

The university professors who examined the Image in 1666, reported that silver had been added to the original moon. It has turned black and is flaking off. The sash seems to have been repainted and possibly elaborated upon, because it too is flaking, and the tunic beneath it is visible at those points. In the first written description we have of the Image, the sash and the moon were reported to be, in Nahuatl, *camo paltic,* "mulberry *(morado),* or a dark color." The professors in 1666, also said that the gold had been added to the rays surrounding the Image and was already deteriorating. The rays and their background show considerable damage and discoloration where cherubim had been earlier added and later removed. It is probable that the original rays and aureole were very bright. Fifteen rays at the bottom of the Virgin's right side (our left) seem in perfect condition.

The bottom of the Image is problematical. The lowest part of the mantle and the entire "Aztec fold" of the tunic are not of the same colors as the rest of the mantle and tunic, and the angel has been criticized as not being of the extraordinary artistry that Our Lady shows. It has been suggested that these were all "add-ons" at some unknown time. However, if this were the case, one would expect the quality of the gold flowers on that part of the tunic to be different, but

they seem not to be. I assume with others, that because of all the friction endured by the bottom part of the Image until 1647, touch-ups (not add-ons) were eventually done. The gold flowers of that part of the tunic may not have needed any "restoration," because, according to artists whose competence and integrity cannot be doubted, the gold gives the appearance of having been put on the maguey threads before the tilma was woven! This is all the more remarkable, when we consider that the maguey threads are composed of twisted fibers (more on this in article on page 68).

Jody Brant Smith's infrared photos show that, while none of the rest of the Virgin's figure evidences brush strokes, the angel and the bottom of the mantle do. He doesn't mention brush strokes on the "Aztec fold." It has been suggested that an examination of the reverse side of the tilma might supply some answers to these riddles. Careful near-ultraviolet and near-infrared photographs have been made of the back of the tilma; but the results of their analysis seem not to have been made public yet.

In 1666, the university professors and the chairman of the ecclesiastical commission, Dr. Francisco de Siles, did examine the back of the Image, and to their surprise, found very subtle, fine greens, "soaked up by the material and incorporated into it." These colors are nowhere to be found on the front of the tilma; which they thought was quite surprising in view of the porosity of the maguey fibers. Fr. Francisco de Florencia, Dr. Siles, and others, examined the back of the Image on another occasion. Father Florencia reported that they found "large color stains" resembling the juice squeezed from various flowers and their leaves: green, white, dark purple, pink, blue, yellow; but all the colors were discreet, not blended one with another. In trying to imagine how such an effect could have occurred, they agreed that it was as if the picture had been stamped on the fabric by putting Juan Diego's flowers in a press, and what was left over from the Image soaked through to the other side, resulting in the "clear confusion" of colors that they saw.

Until her Papal Coronation in 1895, there seem to have been very few reproductions of the Image that do not show Our Lady wearing a crown. However, the newly publicized Codex 1548, possibly the oldest reproduction we have, shows her without a crown. It seems inconceivable that a copyist would presume to paint in a crown if the Image did not originally have one. Before the image was removed from the Basilica for the renovation there was a crown. When it was returned in 1895 the crown had disappeared. Opinions varied in regarding what might have happened. Don Alfonso Marcué, for many years the official photographer of the Basilica, says that the crown still exists, but is painted over. He is confident that the crown will eventually reappear. Regardless of add on or not, it is the face that attracts admiration and wonder.

There is a wonderful softness about the Guadalupan Image, especially the face, which even the finest copyists could not capture, in part because of the Divine Artist's economy of means, to such an extent that lack of pigmentation and flaws in the weave are used to lovely effect. Dr. Philip Callahan, who had the opportunity to study the color of the face from different distances was surprised to find, that viewed close-up, her complexion is whitish gray, that at a little more than three feet, it is a gray-green, and farther than that, it takes on an Indian or mestiza hue. Others report that about ten feet, the colors of the Image are strong and well delineated; but as one draws nearer, they fade, to be almost lost when seen through a strong magnifying glass. This phenomenon helps explain the extraordinary softness of Our Lady's face.

The Guadalupan face is soft not only in technique. It has been said, "She scarcely begins a smile, which gives her face a pleasant expression of kindness, as if inspiring confidence in those who come closer. She gazes softly, sure of herself, peaceful and serene as the message of protection and presence which she came to give us." Her eyes are cast down. "Peaceful, pleasant, perfectly formed and the color of bees' honey, they gaze with a mother's attention, with an expression of infinite tenderness and limitless mercy."

Materials Used in the Image

Miguel Cabrera, the great eighteenth-century Zapotec artist who painted more copies of the Image than any of his colleagues, was asked to examine the Image very carefully in 1751 and submit a report to an ecclesiastical commission. He and his fellow artists agreed that the Image seems to have been executed using four different types of media, a thing to their knowledge never before attempted, and especially difficult because of the total lack of sizing or other preparation of the tilma for receiving paint.

However, Dr. Philip S. Callahan, a biophysicist who is very familiar with the composition and properties of artists' paints, has been unable to identify the nature of the colorings used in the Image. In 1936, Dr. Richard Kuhn, a German chemist who later won the Nobel Prize in his field, found on analyzing a red and a yellow fiber from the tilma, that the colorings were neither animal, vegetable, nor mineral. Synthetic dyes were first derived after 1850, so that their presence on the tilma would be completely anomalous, to say the least. Dr. Charles J. Wahlig has reported that in 1963, the management of Kodak of Mexico found the constitution of the Image to resemble a photographic film on the surface of the tilma. This could explain both its lack of apparent brush strokes, and the fact that the front surface of the tilma is as smooth as silk, while the back is as rough as anything woven of cactus fiber would be. The heavenly process may have anticipated that of the Polaroid Land camera, which develops its image upon exposure to light!

Marvels and More Marvels

In 1778, a considerable amount of nitric acid was spilled on the Image while its new frame was being polished. The workman fled in terror, expecting to have seriously damaged his country's most treasured possession; but to everyone's astonishment, only slight stains appeared, which can still be seen in the upper right corner. In 1921, the explosion of a powerful bomb hidden in a bouquet of flowers on the high altar under the Image, bent a large bronze crucifix like a bow, but Our Lady's glass was not even cracked. The Image even rejects insects and dust. Fr. Mario Rojas has told me that according to LaValle, no matter what the surrounding temperature is, the Image itself remains at an even 36.5 degrees C, or 98.6 degrees F., the normal human body temperature.

Indian Princess or Mary of Nazareth?

We regularly come upon the belief that Mary of Guadalupe appeared as an Indian maiden and that she is dressed like an Indian princess. Pictures in the codices have failed to support this idea, and no documentation seems to be offered by those who hold the belief. Over their upper bodies, Indian women both noble and of the ordinary people, wore various styles of the *quechquemitl,* a triangular or rounded blouse-like garment. On their lower bodies, without exception, they wore the *cueitl,* a wrap-around skirt, sometimes sewn together at the end of the wrap-around. There are ample and beautiful pictures in the codices of women wearing these garments, and glowing descriptions of them in account after account of pre-Cortesian culture (Anawalt, passim). It is clear that Mary of Guadalupe is not wearing such garments.

On the other hand, Fray Jose Francisco de Guadalupe Mojica, O.F.M., has noticed that even today in the Holy Land, many women wear their mantle over their tunics just as Mary does in her Guadalupan Image. Their hair is parted in the middle and shows under the mantle. In winter, like Mary of Guadalupe, they wear two tunics, an inner one of white linen and an outer one of heavy cloth lined with fur. This tunic is so long that they have to lift it in front as they walk. They use a belt to hold the tunics in, and babouches, or slippers, on their feet, just like Mary of Guadalupe's. Father Jose notes that these garments were worn two thousand years ago, when Mary of Nazareth walked in Palestine. He believes that the Guadalupan Image is an actual portrait of Holy Mary, the Mother of God. I believe that the face of Mary of Guadalupe is the one that Jesus himself saw as he lay in Mary's arms and as he grew from childhood to adolescence in Nazareth.

The Iconography of Guadalupe

Dom. Columban Hawkins, O.C.S.O.

"*T*he Virgin is one of us - the Indians! Our Pure Mother! Our Sovereign Lady! She is one of us!" Thus cried the Aztec Indians who were first privileged to behold the miraculous painting of Our Lady of Guadalupe. Yet, strangely enough, when a Russian Orthodox priest, Fr. A. Ostrapovim, Dean of the Chair of Church Archeology in Moscow, and unacquainted with the history of Our Lady of Guadalupe, was presented with a copy of this picture for appraisal, he replied that it is an icon, definitely of the Byzantine type and presumably of Eastern-Asiatic origin. It was his opinion that the painter of this Icon deviated from the very severe canons of icon painting and introduced much of himself into it. How accurate his analysis was! For Our Lady, the Mother of Jesus and author of the unique picture of Guadalupe, did live in the East - in Palestine; and when she effected this, her own portrait, she did put herself wholly into it.

Unquestionably, the Sacred Image preserved in the Basilica of Guadalupe is symbolic, employing the symbols of Christian iconography in the traditional style. It is, of course, a matter of conjecture what these meant to Juan Diego and his people. In any case, what they saw was a most beautiful Lady, nobly clad, enveloped by the rays of the sun and standing on the moon, with stars adorning her mantle and clouds dispersing at her approach. Yet she, with folded hands, acknowledges One greater than herself. Hence, these elements need no longer be feared, nor worshipped as gods. This sweet, gentle, maiden is one of themselves, yet greater than all, except God; but even over Him she has an influence, that of a Mother. Perhaps this is what the Indians, enlightened by Our Lady's words to Juan Diego, saw in the picture.

Christian iconography is the science pertaining to representative ecclesiastical art and its visual symbols as established by the traditions of the Catholic Church. It describes the spiritual sentiments which our ancestors expressed in the language of symbols in whatever medium. *Icon* has reference traditionally to religious painting, especially that of the East; though originally it meant any image. Before printing came of age, Christian iconography was considered the "Bible of the Poor." Symbols represented truths of religious belief, and served to instruct the illiterate in the Faith and to lift up their hearts in worship. Of itself, a symbol cannot produce grace; but it can be a channel of grace inducing us to respond to the saving truths represented. For example: A lamb was always a lamb, but in Christian iconography it is the symbol of Jesus Christ, the Lamb of God Who takes away the sins of the world. The Eastern Church has been most faithful to the symbolic language of Christian iconography. In fact, an icon is frequently given an imprimatur to show that it's symbolism is free from doctrinal error.

To the extent that an icon expresses in color and form a mystic meaning, to that extent is it a great icon. An icon artist is qualified not only because he follows exactly the ancient norms of icon painting, but especially because of his own personal spiritual depth and vision. If he is to express a mystery, an artist must be graced with contemplative insight.

Now, the artist of the Image of Our Lady of Guadalupe is none other than the Mother of God, and in it she shows herself to be the "icon painter" par excellence. The main purpose of an icon is to express a mystery of the liturgy, and to draw one towards a practical and worshipful understanding of that truth in the form of a festal celebration. What is the mystery in the case of the painting of Our Lady of Guadalupe? Christian iconography has traditional styles or types to express certain mysteries. Clearly, in the miraculous painting of Guadalupe, it is the type taken from the Apocalypse of St. John: "a great sign appeared in the heavens, a woman clothed with the sun. . . ." In iconography, this type of the woman clothed with the sun represents either the Immaculate Conception or the Assumption. Since she first appeared on December 9th, the day on which the whole Church, East and West, at that time celebrated the feast of the "Holy Conception of Mary," it is evident that the picture is of the Immaculate Conception and not of the Assumption. In the West, the feast of the Immaculate Conception has been transferred to December 8th, while the eastern Church continues to celebrate it on December 9th.

In this Image then, effected on Juan Diego's coarse tilma, Our Lady—the masterpiece of God, the unspotted mirror of His majesty and image of His goodness—wishes to reveal herself in the traditional religious symbols of iconography. At Lourdes she told Bernadette that she was the Immaculate Conception. This, we may affirm, she expressed at Tepeyac using the language of symbols.

Meaning of the Symbols

Whatever serves to designate the character and position of the person in a painting is called an "attribute." Among the most important of these is the "aureole" or luminous area surrounding the figure. It is simply an extension of the nimbus, which is the radiance usually encircling only the head. Sometimes the aureole surrounds the entire body as a fringe of light. But it may also be composed of many simple or flame-like rays. Or again, as in the Image of Our Lady of Guadalupe, the rays may be alternately simple and flame-like. In Russian iconography there are many icons using this and other symbols similar to those in the Guadalupe painting.

The aureole is the symbolic mark of supreme power exalted to the highest degree. It is, therefore, an attribute especially characteristic of God, Who is in Himself properly and intrinsically the Center of Omnipotence. The aureole is bestowed upon the Persons of the Godhead and upon the Virgin Mary; though the latter application is rare, unless she is accompanied by her Divine Son, or when alone, in the imagery of the Immaculate Conception or the Assumption. Quite often, the aureole is surrounded by clouds which are but an extended form of the aureole, and they are symbolic of the unseen God. Under Our Lady's feet is the crescent moon, the symbol of her perpetual virginity. This symbol, though it is sometimes used in the imagery of the Assumption, is most often and principally found in representations of the Immaculate Conception. Christian iconography does not use the moon to symbolize the powers of darkness.

All of the garments of Our Lady are symbolic. In medieval art, blue was the symbol of eternity and of human immortality. It signified divine contemplation and godliness of conversation. For this reason, blue was mainly used in the garments of the High Priest in the Jewish dispensation. Because of the mystic signification of this color, how fitting it is that blue has been traditionally the color of Our Lady's mantle!

Stars, emblematic of heaven, are studded on the mantle of Our Lady of Guadalupe. They are frequently found painted on the domes of Russian Churches to typify the canopy of heaven over the faithful. The ceilings of churches too, were generally powdered with stars for the same reason. On Our Lady's mantle, stars have the added significance of her being the Queen of Heaven. Different pointed stars have different meanings. An eight pointed star, which is found in the painting of Guadalupe, means Holy Baptism and the regeneration-gifts God gave the Indians in such profusion through Our Lady. The limbus, or gold border on her mantle and on the edge of her robe and embroidered cuffs, signifies her royal dignity.

The rose-colored robe is symbolic of martyrdom for the Faith, and of divine love. It is lined with white ermine, which is the symbol of her purity and honor without stain - purity which regulates all her conduct. The stylized leaf and rosette design on her robe symbolizes paradise, which she enjoys and wishes to share with us. At her waist, her garment is fastened by a "zone" or "cingulum." This was worn by young unmarried women, and removed only upon their marriage. It is a symbol of perfect chastity. The golden encircled-cross brooch which fastens the neck of her robe, though the smallest of the symbols, is very rich in meaning. It signifies that she is sacred, like a holy temple, and protected against all profanation.

The angels too, have their meaning. In the Middle Ages, which was the golden age of symbolism, angels were usually clothed in tunics or ecclesiastical vestments. They were painted with human forms, but as young men to show their strength, and with wings to indicate their speed and unweariedness. In this painting of Our Lady of Guadalupe, the angel's red, white, and blue feathered wings are emblematic of loyalty, faith and fidelity. His red tunic is a symbol of his love for her whose garments he holds so serenely. His position proclaims that the Ever Virgin Mary has been raised above the angels by her prerogative of Mother of God.

From this study of the symbols used in the painting of Our Lady of Guadalupe, we are obviously led to the same conclusion as the Russian Orthodox priest quoted above, that this is definitely an Icon of the Byzantine type, using the recognized symbols of Christian iconography. These symbols reveal to us the traditional spiritual image of Our Lady. They manifest her as the ever-loving, ever-immaculate, sweet Mother of God and Queen of Heaven and Earth, adorned with all the virtues and exalted above the angels, clothed with the might and goodness of God, making intercession for us, her children.

It is true that Our Blessed Mother deviated from the very severe canons of Byzantine rules of icon painting, but necessarily so. She wanted to portray herself as she actually is, in her own natural, lovely form and features. Who is not moved to love and trust by this simple beauty of the Mother of God which her miraculous portrait reveals? In the words of Leo XIII: "Never before has it been granted us on this earth to see so lovely an image; and its loving-kindness moves us to reflect: 'How beautiful must Mary herself be, in heaven!' "

Pope John XXIII has said that, "the best assurance of reconciliation between Orthodox and Catholics is their common devotion to the Mother of God." Let us hope that this Icon, so rich in Christian symbolism, is destined to be the heaven-sent means of effecting unity and peace in the whole world according to Our Lady's promise at Fatima: "When my Immaculate Heart triumphs, then the world will have peace." Thus would be realized in fullest measure what is implored in the Eastern Rite Ritual for the blessing of an icon: "O Lord, Our God, send down the grace of the Holy Spirit upon this icon ... bless it and make it holy; grant it the power and strength of miraculous deeds. Make it a spring of recovery and health."

Our Lady has done her part. She has given us a portrait of herself, rich in the symbolism of the Mother of God. She has told us that she is our Mother and invited us to come to her with trust and love in all our troubles. Today she earnestly calls us to prayer and sacrifice to save souls. Is not her picture a loving summons to all her children to do their part?

This article [here condensed], which originally appeared in the 1962 special issue of IMMACULATA, is as relevant today as when it was written, showing the timelessness of the subject.

The Sacred Image is a ...
Divine Codex

Janet Barber, I.H.M.

A Codex is a pre-Conquest or early Colonial document, a record composed of pictures, an *amoxtli,* painted by Indian *tlacuilos,* painter-scribes, on a long strip of fanfolded paper made from maguey fibers or the bark of a wild fig tree. Some codices were done on specially treated deerskin coated with a white pigment. Bright vegetable and mineral inks were used. The art was continued until about 1560, with at least one document containing entries into the early 1600's. All of the material recorded in the codices was of interest to the people as a whole, rather than to an individual. Because of their importance to all the people, the Apparations of Mary of Guadalupe were recorded in Indian codices (See article on Historicity of Guadalupe pg. 184).

Over the last several decades, Father Mario Rojas Sanchez, of Hidalgo, Mexico, has discovered in Mary's Image precious and profound meanings which have gone unrecognized by Guadalupan scholars for centuries. In short, what can seem to be a fairly static and puzzling picture of the Blessed Virgin is really a codex itself, an *amoxtli,* printed on maguey cloth, filled with Christian teachings rooted in the Indians' own culture. There seems to be no end to the riches contained in the divine Codex. Father continues to find "new" elements in it.

The Stars on Mary's Mantle

Infrared examinations of the Image have led some persons to suppose that the stars on the Guadalupan mantle are add-ons. Father Mario doubted this, and wondered if the stars might not be imaging the constellations of the winter sky of 1531. He shared his hunch with his friend, Dr. Juan Homero Hernández Illescas, an amateur astronomer who has an observatory on his roof, a Spitz Planetarium, various computer programs which show the positions of the heavenly bodies (including Halley's Comet, overhead at dawn on December 12, 1531) at any time for centuries into the past, and astronomical journals and books and charts published by universities and researchers. The findings and methods of Hernandez and Rojas were published in 1983, to the effect that the stars on Mary's mantle are indeed the ones present over Mexico City just before sunrise on December 12, 1531, the morning of the Winter Solstice, which occurred that morning at 10:40, probably just when Juan Diego was opening his tilma before Bishop Zumárraga.[1] We must remember that the Julian calendar was still in use and had accumulated an error of some ten days in regard to actual sun time. The constellations are represented on her mantle as seen from outside the dome of the heavens, that is, in reverse.

After I had pored over sky charts for weeks in Los Angeles, verifying the two men's identifications of each star, my traveling companion, Eilene Berg, I.H.M., and I were privileged to meet Dr. Hernandez at his home in Mexico City, where he and his wife Doña Gloria showed us his original work on the project. We gasped when he held to the light a sky map corrected for "reverse" anamorphosis and Doña Gloria suddenly placed a photostatic copy of the Image behind it. The correspondences were overwhelming.

As we study the identifications, we must remember that the Nahuatl artists always represented the east at the top of their pictures, the south at the right, the west at the bottom, and the north to the left. We must also remember that the Divine Tlacuilo showed the stars "backwards," thus reversing north and south. The constellations wheel from east to west, from the top of her Image to the bottom. Those at the top are rising. Leo is directly overhead and if it were shown on the tunic, it would be over her womb. (We recall that Revelation 5:5 gives the Lion of Judah as a type of Christ, and that Regulus, the most prominent star in the constellation of Leo, means "Little King"!). The stars at the bottom are about to disappear over the western horizon. As a further confirmation of the accuracy of the two men's work, and to me, of the miraculous origin of the Image, the Great Northern Crown, the Corona Borealis, lies invisibly on her temples; Virgo, the Virgin, on her virginal heart; the Twins,

Castor and Pollux, on her knees, and Orion on the angel. The Nahuatl *tlacuilos* always dated the events recorded on their codices. *The Great Tlacuilo dated his Amoxtli also.* We now know the day was that of the Winter Solstice. And the year? Father Mario has found the year, placed exactly where Luis Becerra Tanco told us in 1675 that the tlacuilos dated their documents: "at the foot and the border." The part of Mary's mantle held at its border by the angel is a different color from the rest of the mantle, possibly because it had to be touched up from damage received during the 116 years that the Image was not protected by glass. Although it might have been the same blue-green of the mantle originally, it is now what we could call olive green. The Nahuatl word for both colors is *matlalli*. Their word for "ten" is *matlactli*. The Indians saw *"Yei citlalli ipan matlalli,"* "three stars on olive green (or blue)," and because of their associative way of thought, they could easily jump to *"Yei xictlali ipan matlaclli,"* "three placed on ten," which in their system of showing numbers equaled thirteen. According to the Aztec calendar, 1531 was 13 Acatl, "Thirteen Reed." Where is the reed? Next to the thirteen, touching Our Lady's foot! Reeds and arrows could be represented similarly, and this reed has a pronounced arrow tip[2]!

The Gold Work on Mary's Tunic

The exquisitely formed floral design on the tunic of Mary of Guadalupe has been misunderstood for centuries, and continues so in our own day. Beautiful copies of the Image reveal that the copyists either couldn't see the gold work on the tunic or didn't realize its importance. Their own flower designs honor Our Lady by their beauty, but they lose much of what the Great Artist is telling us through His own design, utterly divine in its execution and in the precise play of the multiple meanings.

Miguel Cabrera's examination of the Image in 1751 had revealed that the technique used in putting the gold design on the tunic was inexplicable. He hesitated to touch the gold, because it looked so much like the gold dust on butterfly wings that he was afraid it would come off on his finger. The gold looked as if it had been applied to the fibers before they were even twisted together and woven. On touching the lines, he realized that they were concave, as if they had been stamped onto the tunic, although there were no signs of the size or sizing which gold workers used when they stamped

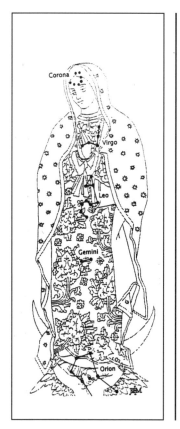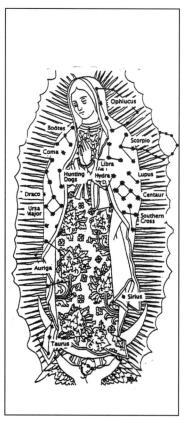

Left: The constellations on the morning of the Winter Solstice, December 12, 1531, as they would appear if there were stars on the tunic as well as on the mantle.

gold onto a fabric. To his further astonishment, he found that on both edges of the gold lines there was another line, as perfect and thin as a human hair. He declared that so far as he knew, no human artist could accomplish such lines or would even attempt them on such a surface. Infrared negatives of 1946 confirm the existence of these lines (Escalada, 1989, 63, 65).

Cabrera noted that although the flowers, "of strange design," do not follow the folds of the tunic, the gold seems darker over the sunken parts of the fabric. Some who have studied the Image state that no competent artist would have laid a flat floral design over the folds, and base on this their conjecture that the flowers were a later addition. Others suggest that the flowers are really on an invisible—and perforce narrow!—gauze sheath that the Virgin is wearing, over a tunic so full that it falls in folds.

The solution to the enigma turns out to be very simple: Father Mario was the first to perceive that the flowers are clever adaptations of Nahuatl glyphs. These adaptations easily conveyed Christian truths to the Indians without alarming those Spaniards who did not respect the Indians as rational human beings capable of being evangelized, Indians whom the Mother of God was addressing as her own children. The glyphs of this divine Codex, this Amoxtli, written on maguey cloth rather than maguey paper, could not fall into the folds if they were to be fully understood.

Thanks to Holy Mary herself, Father Mario realized that the four-petaled flower over her womb, the only one of its design, was beyond any shadow of doubt the *Nahui Ollin,* "Four Movement," the quincunx, the Flower of the Sun, a symbol of plenitude, representing as it did the four compass directions of the world, with heaven and the underworld vertically encountering earth in the center, in the "navel" of the world, or, to use the Nahuatl metaphor, in the navel of the moon, as they called the Valley of Mexico. The quincunx was the central organizing concept of their society. Placed over Mary's womb, the four-petaled flower announced that even though their Fifth Sun had died, the Sixth Sun was to be born of Mary of Guadalupe and *had* been born of her; Jesus Christ, the great Sun of Justice announced in Malachi, would be born to them liturgically at Christmas and could be born in them with Baptism.

The *nahui ollin,* the cross-shaped flower, was derived from their crossed sticks, the *mamalhuaztli,* with which they made fire. Because the life of fire is born of the friction, the *mamalhuaztli* are essentially a symbol of new life. New life for those who were on the edge of total despair as a result of the Conquest and the loss of their gods, their culture, family and friends, their sense of self-worth, their freedom, their sustenance; new life and hope in Jesus Christ. As if to emphasize this promise of new life, the *mamalhuaztli* are shown a second time, in the constellation of the same name, that is, in the three stars on the part of her mantle held by the angel, Al Debaran of our Taurus and his two companions (see article on Prolife Patron page 135).

Father Mario identifies the flower as the Mexican four-petaled jasmine. Its name in Nahuatl is *Huilacapitzxochitl,* "Flute-Player

Flower." Here it is important for us to know that "*in xochitl in cuicatl,*" "flower and song," was the Nahuatl metaphor for access to and experience of the divine, for truth, poetry, philosophy. For Nahuatl philosophers, flowers and song represented the only truth on earth. They were the loveliest things that the Nahuas knew. The flute-player flower on Mary's womb announced instantly to the Indians the truth of the apparitions, the truth of what she said to Juan Diego, the truth of the rest of the information on her Miraculous Image.

Seeds of the Gospel and Our Destiny in Christ

Then there are ten "eight-petaled" flowers which are sometimes confused with the Flower of the Sun. Actually, in some, the narrower "petals" are sepals, the modified leaves which protect the bud and form the calyx. First and foremost, these flowers can be identified with a Nahuatl glyph or symbol for Venus, the Morning and Evening Star. Venus as Morning Star was associated with their god and culture-hero Quetzalcoatl, who after his self-immolation was taken up into heaven as the Morning Star. Quetzalcoatl's teachings were so beneficent and his mythic role so life-giving, that he can be understood as one of the "seeds" of the Gospel which God has planted in all cultures. The Blessed Mother was giving the missionaries a tool which they could appreciate only much later.

Footnotes

1. Dr. Hernández gives complete documentation of his procedures, with many charts, in the expanded publication of their findings, *La Virgen de Guadalupe y las estrellas*, Mexico, 1995. The optical problem of representing on a plane, stars that are really spread over a sphere (anamorphosis) was taken into account by Dr. Hernández.

2. Indians had no problem seeing this reed or arrow representing a magnolia, hill, a bishop's mitre, a jaguar, a maraca, or rattle, a heart, etc.

Glossary for this and following article

amoxtli A Nahuatl codex, record composed of picture-writing

Anamorphosis An image produced by a distorting optical system or by some other method that renders the image unrecognizable unless viewed by the proper restoring device. Transferring the constellations from their positions on the "dome" of the sky to the flat plane of Mary's tunic was a problem involving anamorphosis.

Codex An Indian record composed of pictures.

glyph A hieroglyph, an Indian symbol used in picture-writing.

maguey The "century plant," the fibers from which Juan Diego's tilma was made.

mamalhuaztli Indian fire sticks, also a constellation, either the belt and sword of Orion or the Hyades group in Tarsus. Father Mario tends towards the latter, and identifies the three lowest stars on Our Lady's mantle as the mamalhuaztli, a symbol of new life.

nahui ollin Flower of the sun, used to symbolize the sun; four-petaled flower over Mary's womb. Another interpretation, "four movement or earthquake." It shows the four directions of the universe and the center, where heaven intersects earth.

Quetzalcóatl The "Feathered Serpent." An age-old god who rescued the human race from the underworld by personal sacrifice. A culture hero-king who was opposed to human sacrifice and taught civilizing and cultural skills to his people. A Christ figure, a "seed of the Gospel."

quincunx An arrangement of five things, with one of each corner and one in the middle of an expressed or imaginary square. A symbol of Quetzalcoatl.

solstice Simply one of the two points in the year at which the day is at its longest and the night is the shortest, or vice versa. After the winter solstice, around December 22, the days begin to get longer.

Tepetl A hill. The nine heart-shaped "flowers" on Mary's tunic are also hills or mountains.

tlacuilo A painter-scribe

The Codex that Breathes Life

Janet Barber, I.H.M.

N umbers were extremely important to the Mesoamerican peoples' world view and understanding of their lives. A period of sixty-five Venusian years corresponded to 104 of their solar years, at which point these two cycles also coincided with the beginning of their 260-day divinatory calendar, their *tonalpohualli*. This complex divinatory calendar provided the minute mesh of augury by which they lived their days. Imagine their joy on learning from the educated elite and/or Juan Diego that the eight-petaled flower imitates a configuration of their *tonalpohualli!* Although they had lost the public apparatus of their calendars and the ritual celebrations connected with them, Mary of Guadalupe was not leaving them bereft. From now on, their destiny was to be based not on good or ill omens, but on the rich and sufficient grace of her Son Jesus Christ, the loving and merciful Lord of all time and space (which the Nahuas conceived of as only one entity), the Lord in Whom all would be brought to unity in the end (Eph 1:9-10).

It is interesting to note that the eight-petaled flowers on the light half of Mary's tunic are imitating with their larger petals the precise position of the petals of the Flower of the Sun. Father Mario identifies them as jasmines with their sepals. We see that the eight-petaled flowers, which are in the shadow, have their principal petals exactly opposite the position of the corresponding petals of the Flower of the Sun. Those which are in the half-light have started to turn so as to imitate the Flower of the Sun! "The people that walked in darkness have seen a great light." (Is 9:2) "By your light, we see light." (Ps 36:9)

A New and Availing Sacrifice

There are nine of the large, triangular, heart-shaped flowers, six below her sash, one on each sleeve, and one on her bosom, below the little brooch. Father Mario points out that these can represent the nine levels of the Nahuatl underworld and has identified them as the *yolloxochitl,* the Mexican magnolia, (*Yollotl,* is heart in Nahuatl, and *xochitl,* "flower"). The design can represent either the magnolia's bud or ovary, which becomes its seed pod. *Yolloxochitl* was an Aztec metaphor for the palpitating heart torn from the body of the sacrificial victims. No longer, then, were the Indians to rely on endless human sacrifices to enable the life-giving sun to come up each day. No, they were to rely instead on the new and divine life offered them through the once-for-all sacrifice of Mary of Guadalupe's Son, the Son of God. The seeds of several varieties of magnolia are bright red, recalling the infinite value of her Son's drops of blood shed on the Way of the Cross.

But the *yolloxochitl* is read as another glyph, too: *tepetl,* hill, and precisely, Tepeyac Hill, which means "Nose of the Hill," for it was the last and smallest of the range of hills which end there, at what used to be Lake Texcoco. We see the nose inside each flower—and other flowers bursting forth on all the Tepeyacs! The large, graceful, virile stems with their leaves are an adaptation of the Nahuatl glyph for water, the water of life which flows through Tepeyac and emerges as the water of the Holy Spirit which will well up in Christians to eternal life (Jn 4:14). But the leaves are not just water; they are also Nahuatl flames. A Christian equivalent easily found in these is the fire of the Holy Spirit which Jesus came to kindle upon earth and yearns to see spread (Lk 12:49).

Mary, Mother of the Church

The glyphs for hill and water combine to make the new meaning of "city." Because the *tepetl* also resembles a Bishop's mitre, the Indians could read that the Mother of God had come down from heaven with a message for the bishop in the great city. Mary of Guadalupe is Mother of the Church. It is inconceivable that she would have circumvented the Bishop-elect, the one chosen by Charles V and by heaven, just as surely as Juan Diego was the one chosen to be her intermediary, her ambassador. Mary was pointing her Indians toward Christ and toward His Church.

Father Mario understands that the three flowers sprouting from the stems of the yolloxochitl are buds. But in addition to this, three was the number of Quetzalcoatl, the mythic intermediary who not only rescued from the underworld the bones of the humans who had lived in the previous era, but brought them to life by bleeding his member on them. Three, then, is the number of mediation, of intercession. The three buds or flowers can be taken to express the role of Mary's Son and the Holy Spirit in our redemption, and to set forth one of our most important ministries as other Christs: to intercede before the Father that all hearts may turn to His Son and accept His offered redemption (Hb 7:24-25; 2 Cor 5:18-20). I have been given to understand that the little ball at the tip of each flower is its fruit, the lasting fruit we are to give as branches grafted into the Vine (Jn 15:5, 16). We are represented on Mary's divine Codex not only as recipients, but as channels of the grace of God.

How Beautiful Upon the Mountains

Father Mario suspected that the nine tepetl glyphs might furthermore represent specific volcanoes of Mexico, and his idea turned out to be correct! If we take the Flower of the Sun as our point of reference and observation, and let it represent Tepeyac, then the *tepetl* on her right sleeve is Ixtaccíhuatl and the one on her left sleeve, Popocatépetl, with the white cotton on her cuffs representing their snow! The mountain on her bosom is La Malinche, in the state of Tlaxcala, brooding over the neighboring Valley of Puebla. The star on her left shoulder is Citlaltépetl, "Star Mountain," known to us as the Pico de Orizaba. The small cross at her neck marks Nauhcampatépetl, the "Hill of the Four Directions," El Cofre de Perote! The highest star on her right shoulder represents the volcano Chicnautla, the spur of the Sierra Madre Oriental range. When a slide of the Image is projected onto a map of Mexico done on a scale of one centimeter to 1,000,000 centimeters, the distances correspond exactly from the foot of Malinche (where the middle of the Virgin's index finger touches the flower) to the Pico de Orizaba to El Cofre de Perote. The other *tepetl* glyphs represent, but not to scale, the great horizontal volcanic axis of Mexico.

In a dazzling yet simple display of His power and tenderness, Almighty God represented the Nahuas' very earth on His Amoxtli, their majestic volcanoes, the horizons and reaches within which they lived their lives. He echoed their unique ideas of time and space, found in the stars and the compass directions, through their own picture language with which they recorded their history and myths, their keys to the meaning of their own views of reality. It was as if their *Huel Nelli Téotl Dios*, their One True God, were returning their culture to them, purified and fulfilled in Jesus Christ. They were being affirmed by heaven. *They too were God's beloved sons and daughters in whom He was well pleased* (cf. Mt. 3:17).

Father Mario points out that the Indians saw in the Image that heaven, the mantle with its stars, is touching, covering, and protecting earth, the rose-colored tunic with its vegetation. Gone are the profound celestial causes for their vital anxiety, their constant terror of falling into nothingness. Heaven is now benign, a source of the love and nurturing that none of their former gods could offer them, not even Quetzalcoatl. The Image goes on to tell the Indians that heaven is our true home. The stems of the nine great flowers emerge from the mantle. They are clearly rooted in heaven! Heaven, our source, our sustenance, and our destiny! Has not God made us such that our hearts are restless until, trusting in His unconditional love, they find rest in Him?

In fact, the Indians easily saw in the Image that Mary of Guadalupe was kissing them. For the Mesoamericans, the angel with his outspread wings represented Juan Diego, whose Indian name had been Cuauhtlatohuac, "Eagle Who Speaks." *"Quitennamiqui!"* they would exclaim, which meant both "She is kissing him!" and "She is touching him with the edge." She is kissing Juan Diego with the borders of her mantle and her tunic! And, because Juan Diego represents not only all of Mexico, but all humanity also, she is kissing us too!

Although Mary of Guadalupe looks static to some, she nevertheless portrays forward motion, and dancing. The Indians see by her bent left knee that she is walking, as we all must, on the inner pilgrimage and in response to Our Lord's call to take the Gospel to others. She is also dancing, with her hands clapping to the rhythm of the maracas! The Indians see many signs in the large heart-shaped flower, and one of them is *ayacachtli,* which means "rattle" or "maraca." She will change their mourning into dancing, she will clothe them in joy! (Ps. 30:11) *(See editor's note on page 80.)*

The Nahuatl word *xihuitl* expresses "grass," "leaf," "year," "comet," and "turquoise." Her turquoise-colored mantle and the vegetation of her tunic are signs of Mary's virginity, while the mantle in itself is enough to bespeak her sovereignty as Mother of God and Queen of Heaven, since only the emperor could wear that color. Her mantle and the Flower of the Sun told the Indians that she was Virgin-Mother. The lone leaf over the left thumb of the angel is that of the *cuetlaxochitl,* "flower of [our] flesh," the poinsettia! When the Indian saw the leaf and the Image on the tilma, they would exclaim, "The angel is carrying the Flower of Our Flesh!" This taught them that she is not a goddess, but rather the loveliest Flower of our human race, come to give us the Fruit of her womb, Jesus.

The 70 flowers and buds on her tunic told them that she was singing, because they associated their word for an abundance of flowers, *xochihuica,* with *xochicuicatl,* "blossoming song." Father Mario has found — and played for us — musical rhythms in the details of the Image, using a deer antler and a turtle carapace, typical pre-Colombian instruments. From the heavenly bird song, as Juan Diego began his great adventure, to the fresh, dew-covered flowers on the barren hill and all through the centuries right to our own day, the Guadalupan Event is lush with Flower and Song. All that the Great Tlacuilo had put in his Amoxtli for them — and for us — is trustworthy. He had spoken to them in their own terms, using their own pictures and their own language, even using their own maguey cloth to write it on. Since for the Nahuas the tilma stood for the man who wore it, they realized with absolute certainty that the Heavenly Tlacuilo was profoundly honoring Juan Diego and all of them too; and they were of one piece with their culture. He was affirming it and honoring it and giving it back to them in the hands of His and their Mother.

Just one more precious detail, of the many left in our maguey-fiber bag. Mary of Guadalupe is radiant, she is shining. Because the Nahuatl verb "to shine," *mihiyotia,* also

The mountains near Mexico City on the Image.

means "to breathe," the Indians said "She is breathing!" Indeed, everything about Mary of Guadalupe speaks of life, the life breath of Jesus Christ. John Paul II said in the Basilica on May 6, 1990, that Mary's maternal heart is beating there. Yes, Almighty God maintains a continuous Miracle in Blessed Juan Diego's tilma and the Portrait it holds, the loveliest Icon and Codex ever given to His sons and daughters, the Image of the Perfect Virgin, Holy Mary, Mother of God. In her advocation as Guadalupe, she has come

Image (Heb 4:12), and in her loving response to the cries of her sons and daughters.

*Editor's note: *In another part of this book Our Lady's hands are described as in prayer. To both Western Christians and pre-conquest Indians she is seen as human in prayer, and not as a goddess. This did not prevent the Indians from seeing other meanings in the position of her hands. In Psalms 149 and 150, God asks us to praise Him in dance, and even today, with the blessing of the Church, Indians perform their centuries-old dances on Our Lady's feasts. One has to see their religious dance to understand that this is in no way profane or worldly. It is part of their culture and their way of expressing a deep religious experience.*

Our Lady of Guadalupe — Model of Prayer and Holiness

Ten million Indians embraced the Catholic Faith in less than a decade following the Guadalupe apparitions in 1531, while the Franciscan missionaries had only produced scarcely one million converts in the previous decade. Bro. Peter of Ghent, O.F.M. alone baptized over a million Indians in the wake of the heavenly visitation, and one location 3,000 were baptized and married during Christmas day in 1538. What was the secret of the holy Virgin's success? What lesson does this loving Mother teach the faithful, especially missionaries, regarding efficacious evangelization? Simply put, the salvation of souls depends upon grace and she is the Mediatrix of all grace that comes to man. We could all be effective evangelizers simply by allowing Mary to use us as instruments in her hands for the salvation of souls. In her life and in all her apparitions she points the way by word and example — keeping the commandments, living in union with Christ through prayer and sacrifice.

We see the perfect, ever Virgin Mary of Guadalupe preeminently manifested in the sacred Image as the *"woman"* absorbed in deep prayer. What is more, from the sash about her waist the Native Americans immediately knew she was with Child, and that Jesus the God-Savior was abiding in her. *"Abide in Me, and I in you."* (Jn. 15:4). Because of her perfect union with the Most Holy Trinity and her unparalleled sanctity, it comes as no surprise that her maternal presence in Mexico begot the life of grace in millions of wandering souls. *—Fr. Maximilian, F.F.I.*

PART V

Scientific Studies of the Tilma

Is it the imagination of the devout, or a scientific fact that a reflection of a man is found in the eyes of Mary of Guadalupe? Today, there is incontestable evidence, verified by men of science that, indeed on the Tilma, the image of Juan Diego is reflected in Mary's eyes.

A young Mexican couple contemplates the first apparition of Our Lady to Juan Diego, before one of the murals of the chapel on the "little hill." Our Lady appeared to Juan Diego in the pre-dawn darkness of December 9, 1531, on the site of this chapel.

An Analysis of Dr. Callahan's Infrared Study

Bro. Thomas Mary Sennott

In 1756, Miguel Cabrera, the most famous colonial artist of the day, examined the tilma and reported:

> I believe that the most talented and careful painter, if he sets himself to copy this Sacred Image on a canvas of this poor quality, without using sizing, and attempting to imitate the four media employed, would at last after great and wearisome travail, admit that he had not succeeded. And this can be clearly verified in the numerous copies that have been made with the benefit of varnish, on the most carefully prepared canvases, and using only one medium, oil, which offers the greatest facility; and of these, I am clearly persuaded, that until now there has not been one which is a perfect reproduction as the best, placed beside the original, evidently shows.

Cabrera knows whereof he speaks, for his own copy of Our Lady of Guadalupe is considered the most faithful to the original. It was at the dramatic unrolling of this canvas that Pope Benedict XIV exclaimed, *Non fecit taliter omni nationi.* "Not with every nation has He dealt thus."

In 1979, in the tradition of Miguel Cabrera, Dr. Philip Serna Callahan, a biophysicist at the University of Florida, an expert in infrared photography, and himself a painter, was allowed to examine and photograph the Image. Callahan, a devout Catholic, after setting up his infrared equipment on a platform, asked for and obtained permission to receive Holy Communion before he began photographing. Concerning the utility of infrared photography in the study of the holy Image, Callahan writes:

> Infrared photography is recommended before any restoration or cleaning is attempted on old paintings. It is most important because one can often detect undersketching accomplished before the artist applied paint to the canvas. Infrared photography also enables one to determine the nature of the sizing under the paint, provided the layers are not too thick. No study of art work can be considered complete until the techniques of infrared photography have been utilized, and certainly no valid scientific study is complete without such an analysis.

Callahan, who also has a background in entomology, makes the interesting comment that some of the effects of the painting are impossible to accomplish by human hands, but are found in nature in bird feathers and insects. He pointed out:

> It is a simple fact that if one stands close to the painting, the face is very disappointing as far as depth and coloring are concerned. At a distance of six or seven feet, however, the skin tone becomes what might best be termed Indian-olive (gray-green) in tone. It appears that somehow the gray and "caked" looking white pigment of the face and hands combines with the rough surface of the unsized hue. Such a technique would be an impossible accomplishment in human hands. It often occurs in nature, however, in the coloring of bird feathers and butterfly scales, and on the elytra of brightly colored beetles . . . By slowly backing away from the painting, to a distance where the pigment and surface sculpturing blend together, the overwhelming beauty of the olive-colored Madonna emerges as if by magic. The expression suddenly appears reverent yet joyous, Indian yet European, olive-skinned yet white of hue. The feeling is that of a face as rugged as the deserts of Mexico, yet gentle as a maiden on her wedding night. It is a face that intermingles the Christianity of Byzantine Europe with the overpowering naturalism of New World-Indian, a fitting symbol for all the peoples of a great continent!

It has been known for some time that there have been some additions to the Image and that these are beginning to flake off, much to the delight of the anti-apparitionists. But Callahan concludes that the original Image cannot be explained in natural terms

> The original figure, including the rose robe, blue mantle, hands and face . . . is inexplicable. In terms of this infrared study, there is no way to explain either the kind of color luminosity and brightness of pigments over the centuries. Furthermore, when consideration is given to the fact that there is no underdrawing, sizing, or over-varnish, and the weave of the fabric is itself utilized to give portrait depth, no explanation of the portrait is possible by infrared techniques. It is remarkable that after more than four centuries there is no fading or cracking of the original figure on any portion of the agave tilma, which - being unsized - should have deteriorated centuries ago. Some time after the original image was formed, the moon and the tassel were added by human hands, perhaps for some symbolic reason since the moon was important to both Moorish-Spanish and Aztec mythologies. Some time after the tassel and the moon were added, the gold and black line decorations, angel, Aztec fold of the robe, sunburst, stars and background were painted, probably during the 17th century. The additions were by human hands and impart a Spanish Gothic motif to the painting. In all probability, at the same time the tilma was mounted on a solid support, the orange coloring of the sunburst and white fresco were added to the background. The entire tilma for the first time was completely covered with paint . . .

Callahan's conclusions regarding extensive human additions to the tilma might well be true, but I suspect he is overdoing it. This suggestion of a 17th century date for most of them can't possibly be true. In 1570, just 39 years after the apparition, Archbishop Montúfar sent King Philip II of Spain a copy of the miraculous Image which was placed in the flag ship of Admiral Andrea Doria in anticipation of the Battle of Lepanto. (See article on page 101). This copy is now enshrined in the Church of San Stephano in Aveto, Italy. The Lepanto Image is identical to the original Miraculous Guadalupe Image, which means that any additions had to have been made well before 1570.

The *Codex Seville*, called the "oldest book in America," is an Indian calendar in picture writing that was begun around 1407 and ends around 1540. It is reproduced to size in an overleaf of the Historical Records and Studies, Volume XIX, September, 1929, of the United States Catholic Historical Society. It is about three and a half feet long, with small paintings illustrating important events. Reading from the bottom up, just above the symbol for 1532, is a tiny figure of Our Lady of Guadalupe about an inch high. The codex was probably kept up to date year after year by Indian scribes and the tiny figure of Our Lady was entered in 1531, the year of the apparition. Demarest and Taylor describe it in *The Dark Virgin*:

Under magnification, the tiny figure of the Virgin is startlingly similar to that of the Holy Portrait. The position in which she stands, her manner of dress, the way she holds her hands in prayer are the same; the colors are the same in tone, and figure is surrounded by clouds bordering the rays of the sun, indicated by thin streaks of yellow. When one considers that this miniature is painted on a very rough, thin, fibrous paper, it is astonishing that the likeness is so closely achieved. . . . It is obviously intended as a figure of the Virgin . . . as above her head there is a great crown, and there are the clouds and sun rays.

We can see from the *Seville Codex* that the Image was not just a simple figure originally, as Doctor Callahan suggests, but from the first there were clouds and the rays of the sun, and evidently the tilma was completely covered with color from the very beginning. It is possible that on top of the miraculous colors, additions could have been made without sizing, but being unvarnished, they are now beginning to flake off. I suspect that all the additions were made almost immediately by Indian artists, to enhance the pictogram nature of the Image. Doctor Callahan concludes his study:

"The additions to the Image of the Virgin, although by no means technically elegant compared with the original Image, nevertheless add a human element that is both charming and edifying. Any single addition - whether moon, Aztec fold, gold and black border, angel or whatever - does not alone enhance the portrait. Taken together, however, the effect is overwhelming. As if by magic, the decorations accentuate the beauty of the original and elegantly-rendered Virgin Mary. It is as if God and man had worked jointly to create a masterpiece."

The above article is an excerpt from the unpublished manuscript for a book, "Acheiropoeta: Not Made by Hands" (The Miraculous Image of Our Lady of Guadalupe and the Holy Shroud of Turin) by Bro. Thomas Mary Sennott, used with the permission of the author.

The Man in the Eyes of Our Lady

Fr. James Meehan, S.J.

*I*s it imagination inflamed by devotion or scientific observation that sees in the eyes of Our Lady of Guadalupe the reflection of a man? Fifty years ago, it would have been considered pious imagination. Not today. A greatly enlarged photograph of the face of the ancient image reveals a person who has been tentatively identified as Juan Diego, the Indian whom Our Lady chose to speak for her to the Bishop of Mexico in 1531.

In 1962, Dr. and Mrs. Charles Wahlig, O.D., of Woodside, New York, while looking at a photo of the eye enlarged 25 times thought they discovered what looked like three persons reflected in Our Lady's eyes. A colleague of Dr. Wahlig, Dr. Frank T. Avinone, professor of optics at Columbia University, suggested to Dr. Wahlig to set up an experiment to show how three persons could be reflected in the eye of Our Lady's Image. This he did with the help of family members. He was able to catch the reflections in the eyes of his daughter Mary of Mrs. Wahlig, their daughter Carol and himself. [His experiment was immensely successful in drawing attention of the public to the scientific dimensions of the Image. Even more revealing and up-to-date is the article immediately following].

Today there is little doubt of the image reflected in the eyes of Our Lady's miraculous portrait. Juan Diego is identified from various paintings, traced back to the 17th century, that depict him with full beard and head of hair. This reflected image brings to a skeptical modern mind a disposition to accept the evidence for the truth of the Miracle. The hard fact is, we have proof as incontestably strong as photography and modern scientifically verifiable evidence can be. These images were reflected in the eyes of Our Lady of Guadalupe over 465 years ago, when Our Lady was present, invisibly to all, looking down on Juan Diego and Bishop Zumárraga and others as Juan Diego gave the Bishop the "sign" he had requested. At that moment Our Lord produced an exact picture of Mary on the tilma of Juan Diego, faithful even to minute details of reflections in Our Lady's eyes.

This is the face of Mary of Nazareth, whom Jesus beheld as a little Baby, the face His tiny hands caressed, the face He looked on during His life on earth, the face He admires in heaven today.

A condensation and updating of an article by the late Fr. James Meehan, S.J., which originally appeared in the "Jesuit Bulletin," April, 1970.

The Indescribable Face

On Epiphany night, January 6, 1960, I had the rare and altogether wonderful experience of examining the Portrait of Our Lady of Guadalupe at eye level from a scaffold positioned with its floor at the bottom of the frame. It was an experience very hard to write about since it was so overwhelming, so ineffably beautiful.

We had about an hour altogether, and could study the Image carefully. The more we looked, the more miraculous it appeared. In some places there is scarcely any paint (if it is paint) at all. And all of it is like a wash...a thick wash of some sort on a very coarse canvas almost as open as burlap. When you see the broken seam, you wonder how it hangs together. The expression of Our Lady's face is altogether indescribable. It is so tender, so loving, so human, and in her enigmatic smile, far more challenging than that of the famed "Mona Lisa" of Leonardo da Vinci. Reproductions do not convey the gentleness and softness of the molding of the eyes and lips. In some reproductions, the eyes seem to bulge, and lips almost to pout; but there is none of that in the original; the contours are all lovely. And the great feature is, of course, the eyes, which do not look like the painted eyes in a portrait, but like really living, human eyes, with the proper eye contours.

To me, the strangest thing is this: ordinarily, when one is close to a painting, the detail is sharper than from a distance. But with the Holy Portrait, this isn't so. Close up, you can scarcely see the stars in her robe; yet they are dazzling from a distance. And from the nearness of the scaffold, her robe is not the greenish blue (robin's egg) one sees from a distance, but a much darker, bluer blue up close. The pink of her gown is very pale, yet very rosy at some distance. This reversal of nature intrigued me to no end, and baffled all of us. And it is, or must be, part of the phenomenon of "change in size" one encounters when the Image looms so large mid-way up the Basilica aisle, and shrinks to "normal" when you get close. That, too, is a reversal.

And always, there is the tremendous sense of Presence, of magnetic graciousness, which has never been my experience with any other painting, religious or secular, that I have ever admired and loved. And I have seen, studied, and admired many masterpieces in my twenty-five years in New York City: those of El Greco, Goya, Leonardo, Michaelangelo, Rafael, Verneer, Holbein, Rembrandt, Raeburn, Titian; be it in the permanent collections of museums, private collections, or in the great loan exhibition for the World's Fair. There is nothing comparable to Our Lady's Portrait. She left something of her presence with it, that is all I can say.

−Coley Taylor

Latest Scientific Findings on the Images in the Eyes

Janet Barber, I.H.M.

*M*iguel Cabrera wrote of Our Lady's eyes in 1751, "Her eyes are downcast, and like a dove's, so peaceful and pleasant that just to see them causes joy and reverence." When I contemplate the Guadalupan eyes at length, I have an overwhelming sense of Holy Mary's purity, her serene commitment to God's will, her complete absence of self-seeking, her tender love of all creation. In Mary of Guadalupe, Almighty God has given us the truest of all icons, the sustained contemplation of which can lead us from the sight of our eyes, to the sight of our spirit and a sharing in the transforming grace of her Son.

Scientific interest in the eyes of Mary of Guadalupe has commanded center stage since the early 1950's, and with good reason. It all got off to a "false start" in 1929, when the official photographer of the Basilica, Don Alfonso Marcué González, discovered the reflection of a man's bust in the right eye of the Image. Church authorities asked him not to reveal this to the public, possibly because of the complexities and strain of Church-State relations. Proper investigation of his discovery would have been next to impossible, and publicizing it at that time would have been most imprudent. In 1951, however, Carlos Salinas Chavez "rediscovered" the figure. An intensive examination by reputable ophthalmologists revealed that both eyes contain the reflection of a bearded man. These are also accompanied by the corresponding "Purkinje-Sanson" reflections.

In 1832 and 1838 respectively, Purkinje and Sanson had discovered independently of each other that whatever is reflected in a normal human eye is reflected three times: first, on the front surface of the cornea, right side up; second, on the back surface of the lens, right side up; and third, on the front surface of the lens, upside down and smaller. Around 1980, Father Mario Rojas Sanchez found two relatively large gaps in the tilma's weave in the iris of each eye, at the level of the pupils. In view of the fact that in order to perform an examination of the Purkinje-Sanson images the pupils must be dilated as much as possible, we might speculate that the gaps compensate in some way for the fact that her eyes are lowered. At a certain distance, color is seen in the gaps even though there is nothing to which it could adhere.

Ophthalmologists have testified that even though they are opaque, both eyes in the Image show depth and become filled with light when the ophthalmoscope's light is trained into them. They have asserted that it would be impossible to produce with paint such perfectly placed reflections in eyes offering so little space with the Virgin looking down and on such rough material as the tilma.

The figure has been generally taken to be that of Juan Diego. The features correspond well to those of the portrait of him seen in the large painting, "The First Miracle," on exhibit in the Basilica Museum. In it, Juan Diego is the figure at the end of the altar, who, with his hands in the same position as the Virgin's, is looking up at the Image, one of the very few persons in the large assemblage who *are* looking at her!

In 1981, Dr. Jose Aste Tonsmann, a systems engineer, electrified lovers of Mary of Guadalupe by announcing that his computerized blowups of photos of her eyes have revealed microscopically small figures which, he suggests, could be Bishop-elect Zumárraga, Juan Diego with his open tilma before the Image appeared on it; the interpreter Juan González, a black woman, an Indian family consisting of a young woman with a baby in her rebozo, a small child, and a man; a seated Indian, and a bearded Spaniard. It is quite possible that the latter could be Don Sebastián Ramírez de Fuenleal, Bishop of Santo Domingo, who had recently arrived as president of the Second Audiencia and may have been staying at Zumárraga's residence until he could find his own lodgings.

Dr. Jorge A. Escalante Padilla, a surgical ophthalmologist, considers these reflections to belong to the type which have been described by Tscherning (on the back surface of the cornea) and by Vogt and Hess (at the center of the lens). Such reflections are very difficult to detect, and are not modified by changes in the direction of the ophthalmoscope's light. Dr. Escalante has also reported the discovery of small veins on both of the eyelids of the Image. In the 1970s, a Japanese optician who was examining the eyes fainted. When he recovered, he said that the eyes were alive and looking at him!*

*From Tepeyac, Organ of the Center for Guadalupan Studies, October 1988, pg. 7

The facts known to date about the Guadalupan eyes should be enough in themselves to change the minds of persons of good will who have assumed the story of the Apparitions to be mere "legend" and the Image a Franciscan concoction. The reflections in the three-dimensional eyes solemnly and permanently attest to the divine origin of the Image.

Editor's note: Aste used photographs of the Miraculous Image in his computer digitalization. Anyone somewhat familiar with photography, knows that the light-sensitive silver halloids that capture the image in front of the film can be quite grainy. When prints are blown up many times, graininess becomes more visible, thus affording many interpretations. The figures outlined in the photographs in the book by Aste, according to Fr. López Beltrán, seem to be extremely distorted, and at times unrecognizable. The late Dr. Rafael Torija Lavoignet, a well-reputed oculist who gave strong support to the original Purkinje-Sanson study, felt that Aste's scenes were unrealistic and optically impossible. Aste's high-tech study came shortly after Dr. Serna Callahan's infra-red study of the tilma, in which he conducted his research directly on the actual tilma (see page 83).

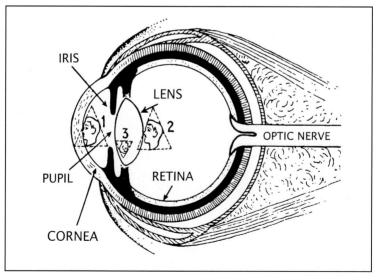

The triple reflection of Juan Diego in the eye of the miraculous Image, according the Purkinje and Samson effect, is shown in the above diagram.

Above: The first public miracle before the Image of Our Lady of Guadalupe, a dead Indian is restored to life. Juan Diego is probably the person to the right of the Image with hands folded and looking up. Bishop Zumárraga is to the left of the sacred Image. See page 94 for the complete story on painting of the first miracle.

PART VI

Where Miracles Abound

"Somehow or other an extraordinary idea has risen that disbelievers in miracles consider them coldly and fairly, while believers in miracles accept them only in connection with some dogma. The fact is that it is the other way around. Believers accept them because they have evidence for them, while disbelievers deny them because they have a doctrine against them."

—G.K. Chesterton

The Portrait of the First Miracle

Hanging on the wall of the Basilica museum is the ancient and large painting (9 x 20 ft.) of the first miracle which occurred before the Image of Our Lady of Guadalupe on Dec. 26, 1531. Bishop Zumárraga had arranged a grand procession for that day to transfer the Sacred Image from his church in Mexico City to a new chapel which had been constructed in an amazingly short two weeks. People from all walks of life had participated in making it a most notable event.

Present were Bishop Zumárraga, Bishop Garcés of Tlaxcala, members of the Second Audiencia, whose President was Bishop Ramírez de Fuenleal. Hernando Cortés was accompanied by his captains. Besides these notables, there were many Mexican nobles and a large number of Indians from nearby towns. When they arrived at the chapel, the precious Image was placed above the altar. The chapel was blessed and the first Mass was celebrated. At that sacred event, as the conquerors and conquered embraced each other before the Real Presence of Jesus and the Sacred Image, a new race and nation was born.

The first miracle portrait is a painting-within-a-painting. The insert in the upper right shows the procession making its way toward the chapel. We can see that at that time Mexico City was surrounded by a lake and connected to Tepeyac by a causeway. As the native entertainers were processing, playing their musical instruments and dancing, during one of their mock battles on the lake, a native was accidentally shot in the neck by an arrow. Filled with grief they brought the dead man before the Sacred Image. There, they removed the arrow and all implored Our Lady to restore him to life, which she did.

This painting is actually a copy of the original, painted by three artists in the middle of the sixteenth century. As these artists were probably acquainted with the principals portrayed, we have here faithful likenesses of all the important characters present at that event. It is quite likely that Juan Diego is the second person to the right of the Sacred Image, with hands together, directing his gaze upon Our Lady's Image. It may be assumed that the figure at the extreme left is Bishop Zumárraga. When it was decided to restore this old Basilica in 1965, the painting which had been forgotten, was found. Discovering the painting at this particular time when there is much interest and devotion to Juan Diego, is providential as it helps to establish his identity. Its disclosure complements the other related discoveries of a scientific nature which confirms that the Sacred Image is indeed a heavenly portrait of Our Lady.

—Dr. Charles Wahlig

Guadalupe Miracles
for Her Beloved Children

Martin Herbert

For centuries, Mexicans have experienced many times, as an essential part of their history, Our Lady of Guadalupe's intervention through miracles. The foremost among these is the actual Image of Our Lady on the tilma of Juan Diego. Its miraculous and instantaneous appearance on the tilma at the Bishop's residence in 1531 was an unprecedented miracle in the history of the Church. The Image is an on-going, unexplainable miracle preserved over centuries, yet it has lost none of its original beauty and freshness on the flimsy tilma which should have disintegrated within the space of thirty years. Besides this, no matter what the temperature of the surrounding area, the temperature of the tilma is always the same 98.6 degrees, normal human body temperature. It is as if Mary is reminding us of her living presence at the shrine of Guadalupe. The late Coley Taylor experienced this vibrant presence (page 88) while examining the miraculous image at close range. Artists and men in different fields of science have examined the tilma carefully and are at a complete loss to explain how it happened and how it remains perfectly intact and unchanged over 465 years.

The miraculous cure of Juan Bernardino, the uncle of Juan Diego, was the first and only time, to our knowledge, that Our Lady appeared to one person (Juan Diego) and at the same moment appeared to and cured someone else (Juan Bernardino) miles away. The next miracle had an even greater impact because thousands witnessed it. While solemnly transferring the Sacred Image from Bishop Zumárrraga's church to its new home at Tepeyac, an Indian involved in the celebration was accidentally killed when an arrow pierced his neck. The dead man was taken to the foot of Our

Above: A Mexican dancer pays honor to his Queen.

The rich traditions and culture of the Aztecs was not lost when they accepted Christianity. It was "baptized" when they were received into the Church.

The statuary group of native Americans paying homage to Mary of Guadalupe is situated in the beautiful gardens of the shrine.

Lady's Image, while the whole congregation of low and noble birth, Aztecs and Spaniards alike, besieged Our Lady for a cure. As the arrow was removed, the dead man was instantly restored to life. A fresh scar on either side of his neck where the arrow had passed was the only evidence of his brush with death. (This miracle is immortalized in a painting of this incident reproduced on page 92).

Beyond a doubt, the greatest miracle story of all is the conversion of the Aztecs and the neighboring tribes - eight million souls in less than seven years. Prior to this mass conversion the Franciscan missionaries had been getting very few conversions, understandably, in light of the exploitation and suppression of the native population by a few unprincipled Spanish leaders. Even to this day, the Mexican nation remains 94 % Catholic. On visiting the shrine of Our Lady of Guadalupe one sees whole families on pilgrimage to the shrine, school children in large number, individually and collectively, visiting their Patroness.

In 1545, the terrible *cocolixti* plague struck the area around Mexico City, carrying away over 12,000 people in a matter of months. The Franciscans organized a procession of six and seven year olds to Mary's shrine. These innocents caught Our Lady's ear and the plague soon abated.

Another manifestation of Mary's power to stay natural disasters came during the period of the great flood in 1629, during which an estimated 30,000 Indians died in five years, and an additional 50,000 Indians and Spaniards fled the city. So bad was the flooding of Mexico City (remember it was built on an island in a lake) that there was serious consideration of abandoning the city to rebuild on higher ground. It was only after a lay sister had a vision of the "Lady of the Tilma" propping up the walls of the city (reminiscent of the dream of Pope Innocence III of St. Francis of Assisi holding up the walls of the Lateran Basilica) that the city officials decided not to abandon the city. Was not their city dedicated to Mary Immaculate, whose Sacred Image was a short distance away? The extent and the seriousness of the disaster prompted both civil and religious authorities to give permission to have the Image transferred to Mexico City from Tepeyac. It was brought to the cathedral where the inhabitants renewed their supplications to their great Patroness. Though the waters did not recede in one dramatic instant, the city was saved and rebuilt. All classes of citizens recognized her intervention. From the Royal Audience down, they publicly attrib-

The plague is arrested through the prayers of the faithful to Our Lady of Guadalupe.

uted their preservation to divine intervention, and as such entered it in various official records. After the waters had receded, the Sacred Image was brought back to the shrine with great solemnity in May of 1634.

In 1737, another miraculous deliverance of Mexico through prayers to Our Lady of Guadalupe occurred. This time all of Mexico was struck with a plague that killed 700,000 people in eight months. It was characterized by a fearful fever, accompanied by violent spasms, abundant bleeding from the nose and finally ending in death. When all natural means had failed, the Mexicans turned again to Our Lady. After much prayer and frequent reception of the Sacraments, they vowed to consecrate Mexico to Our Lady of Guadalupe. The vow was ratified with great solemnity and enthusiasm. Historians agree that the plague was lifted at the exact time her Patronage was decreed, since during the height of the plague, an average of a hundred bodies were received in the morgue each day, but on the actual day of consecration there were only three. That generation and succeeding ones have had no difficulty in attributing this great miracle to Our Lady's love for the Mexican people.

During the period in Mexican history from the middle of the sixteenth century to the middle of the eighteenth, there were also countless individual miracles attributed to Our Lady of Guadalupe. One particular example recalls the miraculous cures at Lourdes which are thoroughly investigated and validated by a Medical Bureau of doctors. Sister Jacinta of St. Catherine's Convent in the city of Puebla suffered from a perforation of the stomach which caused daily hemorrhages. At the age of twenty-eight she was totally prostrated by acute peritonitis. She was unable to talk, her eyes were insensible to light and she was breathing in gasps. The doctors who examined her, declared her to be a terminal case, with no hope of recovery. A copy of the picture of Our Lady of Guadalupe was placed in the hands of the dying Religious, and this she held close to her breast. As the sisters in the convent later learned, she silently prayed that her recovery would be for the honor of the Virgin of the Apparitions and the fame of her Holy Image. On the date that she was expected to die, December 12, 1755, the feast day of Our Lady of Guadalupe, she suddenly sat up in perfect health and radiant with life. This case, as at Lourdes, was documented after extensive medical and ecclesiastical investigation.

If one tends to discredit the miracles that happened years ago in spite of historic validation, the twisted, heavy iron crucifix that is on display in the Basilica is a permanent reminder, not only of a miracle but of the extremes to which evil men will resort to destroy the Faith and Mary in her images. On November 14, 1921, a stick of dynamite was hidden in a bouquet of flowers placed directly below the Sacred Image. The explosion tore out marble blocks from the altar, broke windows and threw the twisted crucifix to the floor. The Sacred Image, in direct line of the explosion, was untouched, even including its protective glass.

In the museum adjacent to the old Basilica, there is a gallery with hundreds of paintings in which people who have received a favor from the Madonna, illustrate, albeit in a rather simple way, how the Virgin of Guadalupe came to their aid in every imaginable circumstance of life.

Regarding *all* miraculous interventions of heaven, what better way to conclude than from G. K. Chesterton's, "Orthodoxy," written years before he became a Catholic:

"My belief that miracles have happened in human history is not a mystical belief at all; I believe in them upon human evidence as I do in the discovery of America. Somehow or other an extraordinary idea has risen that disbelievers in miracles consider them coldly and fairly, while believers in miracles accept them only in connection with some dogma. The fact is quite the other way. The believers in miracles accept them (rightly or wrongly) only because they have some evidence for them. The disbelievers in miracles deny them (rightly or wrongly) because they have a doctrine against them."

Our Lady of Guadalupe at the Decisive Moment in
the Battle of Lepanto

Dr. Charles Wahlig

*W*hen Pius V ascended the throne of St. Peter in 1566, he found himself faced on all sides with turmoil and crises. In northern Europe the Church was being destroyed by the Reformation. In the south the Albigensians were ravaging the Latin countries. To the east the frightful threat of the conquering Ottoman, or Turkish Empire, was threatening Christian Europe.

The situation St. Pius V faced is very analogous to our present day predicament. We too experience terrible threats from the east. The recent resurgence of Communism in Russia and some of the Eastern Bloc countries, the stepping up of the persecution of Christians in Red China, leads one to believe that we have not heard the last of the Communist threat. The very tenuous peace in the Near East makes one wonder if we are not on the verge of Armageddon. We can take hope, in placing our trust in she who is the Hope of the hopeless. The Church has faced many similar crises in the past and ever triumphed. One of the most serious was that of a Moslem threat.

After more than 700 years of struggle, Spain had finally driven its Moslem rulers out, and in 1453 had again become an independent kingdom. In the east, however, a resurgence of Mohammedan power and a thirst for conquest in the rapidly expanding Turkish (Ottoman) Empire had taken place. The capture of Constantinople by the Turks in 1453 had encouraged their desire to conquer and enslave all of Christendom. Their armies invaded the Balkan peninsula and subjugated all of the eastern Mediterranean countries. By the middle of the 16th century their navy had captured Cyprus and was menacing Venice.

The Turkish plan was to build up the greatest navy the world had seen to that time, and then use it to conquer all the European countries bordering on the Mediterranean Sea. From there they would push upward until they had all Europe in their power. Faced with this monstrous threat, Pope Pius realized that he had to take drastic action. By skillful diplomacy he persuaded the Spanish and Italian powers to set aside their own rivalries and unite to form the Holy League to oppose the advance of the infidels.

While all this was taking place, something else was happening that turned out to be of world-shaking importance. Don Fray Alonso de Montúfar, Second Archbishop of Mexico, became an enthusiastic champion of Our Lady of Guadalupe as he witnessed the continual flow of miracles wrought through her intercession. Being very alert to the impending crisis in Europe he had a small reproduction of the Sacred Image made and touched to the original. He sent it as a present to King Philip of Spain in 1570. Montúfar expressed the hope that when the battle was imminent, the King would place this copy of the Sacred Image in a suitable location in the Christian navy, being confident that she would work a miracle for the Holy League as she had done so many times for the Mexicans. King Philip complied and had it mounted in the cabin of Admiral Giovanni Andrea Doria in anticipation of the battle of Lepanto.

The Forces of the Holy League

The naval forces of the Holy League assembled in the straits of Messina. There were two large squadrons, one from Spain under the command of the Marquis of Santa Cruz, the other from Venice which had Veniero and Barbarigo as their principal admirals. The smaller squadrons from the Papal States, Parma and Savoy, were joined to the Genoese forces under Prince Giovanni Andrea Doria. The supreme command was given to Don Juan of Austria, halfbrother of King Philip of Spain.

The Christian forces comprised 300 galleys which carried the naval crews, 3,000 soldiers and 8 ships loaded with artillery. The Turkish fleet consisted of about an equal number of ships. The supreme commander was Ali Pasha. Their ships were lined up just inside the entrance to the Gulf of Lepanto (now the Gulf of Corinth in Greece), and stretched almost from shore to shore in the form of a crescent. Ali Pasha was in the center. To his north

*Under the command of
Don Juan of Austria, the
Christian forces won a
resounding victory over
the Moslems at Lepanto
in 1571, lifting the threat
of Moslem domination of
Christian Europe.*

Mahomet Sirocco, and to his south Uluch Ali were in command.

The Christian allies had to deploy around the headland on the northern side of the Gulf and then come abreast of the Turkish ships. The allies had formed into three squadrons: in the center the Spanish ships, to the left the Venetians, and to the right the squadron commanded by Andrea Doria. The left and center flanks came under the full fire of the Turks, and the Christians suffered what appeared to be a disastrous blow.

Uluch Ali maneuvered Andrea Doria, separating him from the center force and then he broke through the gap so created, and was in a position to cut Doria's fleet to pieces. It is reasonable to assume that when Andrea Doria realized his fleet, and possibly all the Christian armada was facing destruction, he would have rushed to his cabin and prostrated himself before Our Lady of Guadalupe's Image, begging her to save them. The fact that his crew attributed the subsequent victory to Our Lady of Guadalupe strongly inclines us to that belief. In any case, a tremendous wind came up at that critical moment which threw the whole Moslem navy into complete disarray. Panic spread through their squadrons, and most of their fleet was either captured or destroyed.

The Battle of Lepanto was remarkable in two ways: it was the last sea battle fought with oar-propelled vessels, its casualties were enormous. The Christians numbered about 8,000 killed and about 16,000 wounded. The Turks counted almost 25,000 killed and an unknown number wounded. Some 15,000 Christians who had been chained to the oars in the Turkish galleys were freed.

Lepanto Marks the End of Moslem Threat

The victory at Lepanto brought to an end the Moslem sea power, never more to be a threat to the Christian world. Some historians have mentioned that after the victory, the crew attributed the triumph to Our Lady of Guadalupe but did not go into their reasons. Moreover, the Guadalupe element was obscured by the general belief, sponsored by the Holy Father, that the victory was given to the Christians by the Blessed Virgin in answer to a Rosary crusade he had promoted in anticipation of the conflict. The obvious thing for him to do was to ascribe the victory to the Queen of the Rosary, evidently not having known anything about the presence of the miraculous Image of Our Lady of Guadalupe. The part the Rosary played in the victory at Lepanto, of course, is universally recognized, but this does not exclude a more proximate instrumentality of the Icon of Guadalupe as the means of Our Lady's intervention.

To express his and all the faithfuls' gratitude for this deliverance, the next year St. Pius V established the feast of Our Lady of Victory, to be celebrated on Oct 7th. He died that year and was succeeded by Gregory XIII, who changed the title of the feast to Our Lady of the Most Holy Rosary, and decreed that the month of October should be devoted to reciting the Rosary.

The disclosure that the Blessed Virgin probably performed as Our Lady of Guadalupe the vital act which brought victory out of what appeared to be utter defeat at Lepanto, would seem to nullify the widely held notion that the Guadalupe miracle exists just for Mexico, or that it is an "Indian cult." Beginning in 1531, the mass conversions of the Indians in the New World, through the apparitions of Mary of Guadalupe and her miraculous Image more than compensated for the number of Catholics that were lost to the Faith during the Protestant Reformation in Europe. Then just 40 years later (1571) the same likeness of Mary was apparently the instrument through which she rescued Christianity from the infidels in the Old World.

In other words, Our Lady of Guadalupe intervened to rescue the Catholic religion from one of the greatest threats to its survival, and paved the way to the enormous expansion it enjoyed in subsequent centuries in South and Central America. How fortunate all of us Americans are to have such a treasure! What a comfort to know that she is still here with us ready to bring deliverance from similar crises!

The small size reproduction of the Sacred Image remained in the possession of the Doria family until 1811, when a descendant, Cardinal Doria, made a present of it to the people of the town of Aveto in Ligouria north of Genoa. It has remained there to this very day, enshrined in the church of San Stefano d'Aveto. Miracles and favors followed in such profusion as a result of the fervent devotion to Our Lady of Guadalupe by the inhabitants of Aveto and surrounding areas, that Pius VII was impelled in 1815 to grant the shrine the faculty of an Office and Mass of Our Lady of Guadalupe, as well as several indulgences. Leo XII granted perpetual privilege to the altar of Our Lady of Guadalupe in San Stefano d'Aveto.

Adapted and updated from the original article by Dr. Charles Wahlig in <u>A Handbook on Guadalupe</u>.

Our Lady as Healer

Patricia Treece

*H*is face dark with worry, the young doctor suddenly loomed over my hospital bed. "It's going to take a lot of TLC to pull you through," he sighed. Then, as if running from the doubtful outcome, he abruptly turned and left. His father, whose practice he had just joined, would not have been so insensitive. More experienced in dealing with patients, the older man understood I was dying from terror as well as from disease.

I was twenty-seven years old, pregnant, and my body was being overwhelmed by a massive kidney infection that had me vomiting constantly and in severe pain. Blood transfusions were necessary because my hemoglobin was so low. But where lay the root of all this? Was it TB in the kidney, was it . . . urologists, gynecologists, internists huddled together in the hall, murmuring names of strange diseases. I was so petrified because my mother had died at age twenty-seven and pregnant. The doctors had found the bowel obstruction that caused peritonitis only during an autopsy.

"Are you sure I don't have a bowel obstruction?" I kept insisting.

"No, that's not it," my doctors kept answering.

When the young doctor turned me to emotional jelly with his unthinking remark, I had been supposedly stabilizing a bit - enough to be sent home later that week to lie in bed all day with my pain pills, nausea pills, antibiotics, and yes, tranquilizers! The doctors would do a blood transfusion every two weeks, keep me in bed the remaining six months of the pregnancy, and hope I could make it. If I worsened, they intended to turn to abortion to save my life. Abortion had not saved my Presbyterian mother's life. I had always said I would never have an abortion. Now, I shrank from the fearsome thought of having to choose whether to have my baby and myself both die or to let someone kill my child so that *perhaps* I might live.

I knew the right thing to do and had only to think of my father to know the horrors of remorse; still I feared what I might do, in my terror, if put to the test.

A Catholic convert of several years standing, I made a novena to Our Lady of Guadalupe, attracted by her promise to Juan Diego, "I am a merciful mother to all who call on me," and her assurance that his uncle was cured. I asked for life for myself and for my baby and that my child would not be damaged by all the medications, tests and x-rays. The ninth day of my novena came. And with it a knock on my door. I opened to a stranger who introduced herself as a practical nurse living just two doors away. She had heard about me from my landlady and wanted to loan me a book.

I was reading two or three books of fiction a day to keep away the terrors but this was non-fiction. It was titled, *"Let's Have Healthy Children,"* by nutritionist Adelle Davis, and dealt with dietary ways to ensure a healthy baby and a healthy pregnancy for the mother. Because it came on the final day of the novena and from the hand of a total stranger, I felt this had to be God's answer to my prayers. I devoured the book that day. I even called my husband at work asking that on the way home he pick up the various foods and vitamins it recommended.

I began to eat these foods, some of which, like liver, I would have never touched at one time. I also took the vitamins, and in two weeks, surprised doctors found I did not need my next blood transfusion. They stopped talking death and abortion. I wrote Adelle Davis and asked her to plan a diet just for me and my condition, for by now the medical men had come up with a diagnosis. I had polycystic kidneys, an hereditary disease, and my life span would be short. But thanks to the novena, I had new hope in nutrition and a new impetus to develop my spiritual life. After six months as an invalid, I had an uneventful labor and a healthy son.

For almost two years I fought drug-induced allergies and then found myself pregnant with my second child. Relying on the diet "Our Lady sent," I had only a mild kidney infection *after* my second little miracle was born. As each child reached the age of four, they were subjected to a kidney pyelogram because I *had* to know if they had the same kidney problem. I prayed fervently to Our Lady each time. Both children were cyst free. As for my "short" life, that remains to be seen. I only know that my kidneys, like the rest of me, have been given to me by Him Who when addressed plaintively, "Lord, if You will, You can make me whole," answered immediately, "I will. Be thou healed."

Our Lady of Guadalupe
As Our Protector

Sister Sally Castro, M. C-M.

*T*he Virgin Mary became "God's dwelling place among people" (cf. Rev. 21:3). Just as Mary had set off in haste to the hill country of Galilee to help Elizabeth, she also hurried to the mountain of Tepeyac in 1531, to liberate a whole nation. Out of the blood and ashes of an old society which did not want to live because its gods had been defeated, its temples destroyed, its men enslaved, and its women violated, a new generation with hope was born.

"Why do you worry, Juanito? Am I not your Mother? I love you and have come to stay near you so I can help and protect you in all your afflictions." From the beginning Our Lady of Guadalupe is seen as Our Protectress. *"La Morenita"* conquered the heart and the imagination of her people. It was truly an apparition with a divine meaning, a constellation of signs coming from heaven to transcend the divisiveness caused by sin and the alienation from God.

No longer will the Mexicans be considered illegitimate orphans cut off from their cultural roots, but the children of the Mother of God. From a people of a violated "mother culture," the Mexicans would become a nation under an Immaculate Mother. Indeed, Our Lady of Guadalupe is, in particular, the Mother and Protectress of the Mexicans and the Mexican-Americans of the United States, as well as all who love her and invoke her.

The Mexican-Americans have been fighting for justice against all possible odds for well over a hundred and fifty years. History shows a remarkable tenacity in persevering in *"la lucha,"* even when humanly speaking, there appeared to be no possibility of victory — or even survival of their culture. Their hope for a better day was strengthened by their faith and devotion to Our Lady of

Guadalupe.

In World War II, the Hispanics in the Armed Forces were the most decorated ethnic group. In the service, many of them experienced a new fraternity which they had never experienced in their local communities. They found a new spirit of community. In times of armed conflict on the other side of the ocean, the Mexican-Americans felt the protection of *Nuestra Madre, la Virgen de Guadalupe.*

In the year 1965, Cesar Chavez, the charismatic leader of the United Farm Workers' movement in California, rallied his followers under the Mexican Flag, the Banner of *"La Huelga"* and the Banner of Our Lady of Guadalupe. Chavez and the *campesinos* praised, honored and thanked *"La Morenita"* for all victories. They were reassured, marching under the Guadalupano Banner, that they were walking beneath her protective love.

In 1991, some women were sent to a San Joaquin Valley prison for defying an injunction against migrant-worker protests. The prisoners had no money. However, someone had a New Testament, and another found a picture of Our Lady of Guadalupe in her pocket. A farm-worker woman took the silver paper from a chewing gum wrapper, braided it and made a frame for the picture and hung it on the jailhouse wall. All through the night a vigil of prayer was kept. Mary was their only power and protection. They were confident she would obtain their release. The Mother of God did not abandon her children; their prayers were answered and they were set free.

Mary's role as Protectress is illustrated again in the following example. A woman coming home from work late at night noticed that there were only two other passengers on the bus. The woman felt that these two men were up to no good. She began to feel very frightened because in a few minutes she would reach her stop and would have to walk home alone in the dark. Silently, the woman began to pray. She held in her hand the medal of our Lady of Guadalupe which hung from her neck. Frantically, the lady invoked La Virgen de Guadalupe. *"Acompaname y no me dejes al deseo de los enemigos."* (Come with me and don't let harm overcome me). The bus stopped, and sure enough the men also got off.

But on the corner there was a large white dog who seemed to be waiting for the woman. The dog began walking beside her. The men upon seeing the dog, went off in a different direction. When the woman reached home safely, the big white dog disappeared.

Young and old, singly and in families, they come to pay homage and seek help from the Mother of God, the ever Virgin Mary.

Never, before nor after, had a white dog been seen in the neighborhood. Naturally, the woman thanked Our Lady of Guadalupe for having made her guardian angel visible as a dog. She felt the protection of a loving Mother and praised God.

Our Lady of Guadalupe did not just tell Juan Diego to build a Temple. She sent him to the Bishop — the symbol of authority in the Church. It is the Church, especially its leaders, with the heavenly aid and protection of *La Virgen de Guadalupe,* who are to build the new Temple of compassion which will right the wrongs and alleviate the affliction of the poor and oppressed.

The Virgin of Guadalupe brought forth a cultural symbiosis which is very apparent at her shrine today. She likewise appears throughout Mexico in the huge murals on buildings, in movies and literature, in tattoos, in homes and on medals. She rushes to places where there is indifference to suffering, offering protection and giving hope to the oppressed. Our Lady of Guadalupe is our Protectress against the evil one. She helps us to turn away from sin and return to Jesus, her Son and our God.

PART VII

Guadalupe in Society

"Every serious student of Mexican history and culture, whatever their religious or political leanings, has to acknowledge that the only factor uniting a country separated from earliest times by extraordinary barriers of geography, language, culture, revolutions and persecutions, is Our Lady of Guadalupe." —Donald Demarest

Guadalupe Cult ...
in the Lives of the Mexicans

Donald Demarest

*I*n 1951, when my little family first went to Mexico City to go to school on the G.I. Bill, we were typical Sunday-go-to-Mass Catholics. We knew little about Mexico and nothing about its Dark Virgin. But you can't avoid her for long in that city. On the dashboards of any bus or taxi, in ads for mouthwash, on billboards, on bullfighter's capes, there is that ever present Image of the dark-skinned Maiden of Nazareth standing on a half moon. You learn why she is the center of Mexican life. She appeared to a middle aged Indian in 1531 and left to the world a Miraculous Portrait of herself, which is miraculously preserved to this day. She appeared dressed as an Aztec Princess, and in much the same way that young women in the middle east dress even in our day.

What happened on the rocky hillside of Tepeyac on three days of December 1531—an event only recently known and publicized in North America—dramatically determined the history of the Americas, in particular, South and Central America. Twelve years after Cortés had landed at Vera Cruz and claimed Mexico for the Spanish Crown, sixty-nine years before the pilgrims landed on Plymouth Rock, Our Lady appeared to a humble Indian convert, Juan Diego, and told him to go tell the Bishop that she wanted a church built on the barren slope of a hill where she appeared. Here she would: "Show my love and compassion for you and all your people, and all who would call upon me."

"And so it happened," Pope Pius XII proclaimed in a radio message beamed to Mexico in 1945, "the sounding of the Hour of God . . . when on the shores of Lake Texcoco there flowered the Miracle . . . brushes which were not of this earth painted an Image most tender, which the corrosive work of the centuries has marvelously respected."

At that time, Mexico, the seat of the most advanced civilization in the New World, was facing a crisis of an imminent revolt. The successors of Cortés' valiant 600, unscrupulous adventurers motivated by greed, were plundering the wealth of the country and working the native inhabitants to death in the mines. In spite of the efforts of a handful of Franciscan and Dominican friars efforts to carry out the mandate of Christ: *"Go out into the whole world and preach the gospel to every creature..."* (St. Mark 16, 15-16), conversions had practically ceased. It seemed that the Mexican Indians would face the same fate, perhaps even more swiftly than their brothers north of the Rio Grande.

And then, at that sounding hour, when Juan Diego unrolled his cactus fiber cape at the feet of Bishop Zumárraga to display the Miraculous Portrait, word spread instantly from one end of that vast country to the other. Almost immediately, crowds of Indians were camping on the grounds of the Bishop's residence, just as they do today around the huge Basilica on Tepeyac. Mass conversions took place on a scale such as the world has scarcely ever seen. According to the heroic Fray Toribia de Motolinía, nine million were baptized in his time alone.

From such a devotion, miracles were bound to follow: from the cure of Juan Diego's uncle of typhus, to the rescue of Mexico City from successive plagues and floods that struck not only Mexico City but the whole country, to our century when a bomb was planted underneath the portrait of Our Lady during a Pontifical High Mass (See article on page 95).

That miracles continue can be attested to by the thousands of silver ex-votos and painted scenes depicting the circumstances surrounding many miracles, which can be found in all of Mexico's churches today. My wife and I believe that our son was miraculously cured of polio when he was just thirty days old, through her intervention.

Since Our Lady promised her protection to the people of Mexico—and to come to their aid when called upon—the Miraculous Portrait has been in the forefront of all of the momentous events in that country's history. The wars that led to independence from Spain began in a small country church in central Mexico on September 16, 1810, when Padre Hidalgo proclaimed from the pulpit: "Long live Our Lady of Guadalupe! Long live independence! Down with bad government!" She was the rallying banner he carried into battle. During the terrible years of oppression, when the dictator Calles and his Redshirts tried to stamp out religion, closing churches, exiling and executing priests, devotion to *La Morena* kept the flame of Faith burning in Mexico.

Every serious student of Mexican history and culture—whatever their religious or political leanings—has to acknowledge that the only unifying factor which holds together a country separated from the earliest times by extraordinary barriers of geography, language, culture, revolutions and persecutions, is Our Lady of Guadalupe. *In the Meeting of East and West,* F.S.C. Northrup wrote: "Nothing to be seen in Canada or Europe equals the volume or vitality of its moving quality or in the depth of its spirit of religious devotion." Even the agnostic, I.M. Altamirano, declared in a newspaper editorial in 1945: "The day when the Virgin of Tepeyac is no longer venerated in this land, not only will Mexican nationality have melted away, but even the very memory of the inhabitants of present-day Mexico will have vanished." Just recently in an interview with this author, the celebrated novelist, Carlos Fuentes, declared: "One may no longer identify himself as a Christian, but you can not truly be considered a Mexican, unless you believe in the Virgin of Guadalupe."

Because of the distances involved, and the loss of documentation, it was not until 1754 that Benedict XIV officially allowed an Office and Mass to Our Lady of Guadalupe. The Vatican again recognized and gave its enthusiastic support of Guadalupe when Pope Leo XIII in 1884, repeating the famous saying attributed to Pope Benedict XIV, declared: *"Not with every nation has He dealt thus."* He not only promoted devotion to La Morena but also saw to it that her Guadalupe Image was crowned. Benedict XV proclaimed her his own Patroness. St. Pius X declared her Patroness of all Latin America. Pius XII named her Queen of Mexico and Empress of all the Americas. Pope John Paul II made the first of his many worldwide pilgrimages to the shrine of Our Lady of Guadalupe. In 1990, on his second visit there, he beatified Juan Diego.

Unfortunately, it has taken too long for Catholics north of the border to appreciate the enormous favor accorded our continent. It wasn't until 1938 that a convention of the Holy Name Society in California invoked her protection. And in 1939, they sent a delegation to add the Stars and Stripes to the flags of all the Latin American countries which have long graced the Basilica. In 1948, a Trappist Abbey in Oregon was named after her. The Queen of the Americas Guild was founded in 1979 to spread her devotion in the United States and Canada. Pilgrimages from the States have in-

creased continually from year to year over the past twenty years. Incredibly, North Americans have been more aware of the European apparitions of Our Lady of La Salette (1846), Lourdes (1858), and Fatima (1917), than of Our Lady of Guadalupe, which is on their front door step. Yet the number of pilgrims to Tepeyac now far outnumber the other shrines to Our Lady in the world. However, the Mexicans accept the miraculous cures and divine interventions at the shrine casually, as it is such an everyday occurrence in their lives. One can hardly meet a family which does not claim such a blessing for one of its members.

In her masterpiece, *Death Comes for the Archbishop,* Willa Cather, from the state of New Mexico, describes her prelate's visit to Tepeyac and his conclusion:

> "Where there is great love there are always miracles...one might almost say that an apparition is human vision corrected by divine love. . . . The miracles of the Church seem to me to rest not so much upon faces or voices or healing powers coming suddenly near to us from afar, but upon our perceptions being made finer, so that for a moment our eyes can see and our ears can hear what is there about us always."

Parts of the above article appeared in the Introduction to "The Dark Virgin," a documentary anthology on Guadalupe, edited by the author and Coley Taylor, Copyright 1953.

Our Lady of Guadalupe and La Conquistadora in the Southwest

by Pedro Ribera-Ortega*

This chapter is a tribute to the long-standing traditional Marian devotion of the Hispanic population in Southwestern United States. In 1998 the city of Santa Fe, New Mexico commemorated the 500th anniversary of the city. The establishment of the Pueblo of Santa Fe was the beginning of the Catholic-Hispanic culture in the South West, with its great devotion to the Mother of God. This chapter is a combination from two articles by Pedro Ribers-Ortega, one of which originally appeared in Sept/Oct '96 IMMACULATA. —The Editor

"Our Lady of Conquering Love of All peoples," La Conquistadora, of the South-western United States is unique, but Mary's place in Spanish history is not. Catholic Spain's great love for and veneration of the Blessed Mother goes back much further than what was written in the chapter on "Catholic Spain" (page 19). The history of the Church in Spain goes back to apostolic times. According to tradition it was St. James, the older brother of the beloved Apostle St. John, who was sent to evangelize Spain when it was still a province of the Roman Empire.

But "Santiago" (the Galician name for Saint James) was winning few converts. He did consecrate six bishops, and in their company headed back to Jerusalem to report to St. Peter. On their way they camped on the bank of the river Rio Ebro at Zaragosa (named after the Roman Emperor Caesar Augustus). It was here, according to Spanish tradition, that Our Lady appeared to him. It is said that after Pentecost, before the apostles set out to the four corners of the world, Our Blessed Mother promised them: "If you ever need my help, at any time, dearest sons and Apostles, pray to Our Divine Lord and ask Him to send me to help you."

*He is the director of the Confraternity of La Conquistadora.

Remembering Our Lady's promise, Santiago along with his companions prayed fervently to Maria Santisima la Real de Jerusalem to come to their aid. They saw a vision of angels in the sky, escorting la Virgin Santisima Maria. The angels were carrying a pillar. She greeted the surprised Santiago and explained to him that the pillar was a symbol of the faith in Christ that would never die in Spain. This promise was not without the accompaniment of the Cross of her Son. Since Roman times the Church in Spain has had a history of bloody persecutions, the latest being the Spanish Civil War, 1931 -1939, when 8,000 priests and religious, including a number of bishops, along with 4,000 lay persons died for the Faith. To this day Our Lady of the Pillar of Zaragoza is the greatest Marian shrine in Spain. The present Holy Father, Pope John Paul II, visited it in 1989.

Another popular Marian shrine that figures greatly in the history of Spain and New Spain, which brings us closer to that of Conquistadora, is the famous shrine of la Virgin de Guadalupe de Extremadura. The interesting story of this shrine is covered in the chapter which begins on page 24 of this book. What has not been mentioned thus far is the origin of the name Santa Fe. After the battle and victory in Granada in 1492, which finally drove the Mohammedans from Spain, the army of Queen Isabelle wanted to name the rebuilt city on the sight of the destroyed one after the popular queen. She reminded them that 774 years of bloody struggle to liberate Spain succeeded through the cross. Thus the rebuilt city was called Santa Fe de la Vega de Granada (Holy Faith of the Valley of Granada). After eight long centuries the Mohammedan Crescent was finally replaced with the Christian Cross.

The connection of the Guadalupe Shrine in Spain with the Guadalupe in Mexico is explained earlier in this book. As conquistadors and Spanish colonists moved north into what is now the southwestern United States, they brought with them the devotion to La Virgin Santisima de Guadalupe del Tepeyac. But the early settlers had their own unique Madonna. (What follows is the account from the IMMACULATA magazine.)

More than 370 years ago, long before Martha Washington became our nation's first lady, a small, wood-carved statue of the Blessed Mother had already earned historical and spiritual rights to the title, "First Lady of Our Land." The formal name for this regal lady is "La Conquistadora," short for "Our Lady of the Rosary, the Conquering Lady of Hearts of All People."

Shortly before Christmas in the year 1625, Father Alonso Benavides, Spanish Franciscan, superior of the New Mexico missions, brought a thirty-one inch tall wooden image of Mary to the parish church of the Assumption in Santa Fe. (At the time, southwestern United States was part of the Spanish colonial empire, with Santa Fe the capital of the "Kingdom of New Mexico" since 1610). She had been carved in Seville, Spain, years earlier by an unknown artist. La Conquistadora first journeyed to Mexico, the "Viceroyalty of New Spain," as the nation was then called, before Benavides lovingly carried her to Santa Fe along the El Camino Real, the historic trail that stretched two thousand leagues between Mexico City and Santa Fe.

The Spanish settlers who first colonized the area in 1598 were thrilled with the statue of bright arabesque patterns over gold leaf, representing the Assumption. Later generations clothed her as a Spanish queen, and she thus became the "Queen of New Mexico" for the settlers and admiring local Indians. Her "subjects" then began calling her La Conquistadora because she had come to this new land in the days of their founding parents and grandparents, the Conquistadores.

In 1680, the local Pueblo Indians staged an uprising after long-standing tensions with several bad Santa Fe governors. During this "Pueblo Revolt," twenty-one missionary Franciscan friars were martyred. The people of Santa Fe had to fight their way out of the pueblo, leaving behind many of their personal possessions, but not their Conquistadora. She was saved, although the parish and her shrine were destroyed. The colonists fled to the Guadalupe Mission at El Paso del Norte (now Juarez, Mexico). On the outskirts of this city they built a temporary capital in exile, naturally dedicating its chapel to La Conquistadora.

Late in 1693, under the famed Governor Diego de Vargas, the Spaniards set out to reclaim Santa Fe under the protection of their patroness. De Vargas vowed to "rebuild her temple and throne." The Spaniards fought hard to reclaim the city, and eventually triumphed.

The following year, 1694, the colonists began an annual thanksgiving observance of their victory by taking La Conquistadora from the parish shrine to the encampment site outside of Santa Fe's walls where they had prayed for victory. A temporary shrine of boughs was erected every year for the event. There a novena of Masses was sung, and then the statue was brought back to the shrine in another solemn procession. This surely is the oldest Marian festival in the United States. It is continued to this day by the Confraternity of the Conquistadora of St. Francis Cathedral and the archdiocese of Santa Fe.

Holy Mary of Guadalupe, Mother of the Poor

The original shrine, attached to the Assumption parish of 1626, was destroyed during the Pueblo Revolt. De Vargas built a temporary shrine and church in 1695, which was replaced by a permanent church in 1717, in honor of St. Francis of Assisi. When Santa Fe was named a diocese in 1850, the adobe Church of St. Francis was raised to cathedral status. The French archbishop, Jean Baptiste Lamy, whose story is told by Willa Cather in her well-known novel Death Comes to the Archbishop, built the present stone cathedral in 1884, and the adobe structure was pulled down. But the Conquistadora chapel was partially spared, its outer half continuing as her chapel today.

There is also a secondary shrine, "The Rosario," built in 1807 at the old encampment site of 1693. It is still used as the gathering site for the annual thanksgiving processions in the beginning of summer.

The diminutive but festively adorned La Conquistadora has been venerated and feted continuously to this day. It is not a miraculous statue or image as is that of Our Lady of Guadalupe in Mexico City, though we are told she was blessed at Tepeyac before leaving for the far away New Mexico missions. Nor does she represent the triumphalist conquering of a weaker people.

Instead, La Conquistadora is a historical treasure and a long-enduring symbol of a people's unfailing love for the Mother of God — whether they be Indian, Hispanic or Anglo. The Holy Catholic Church has acknowledged this devotion with an Episcopal coronation in the Marian Year of 1954, when La Conquistadora visited every parish in the archdiocese; and in 1960, when the Holy Father Pope John XXIII granted a unique papal coronation.

When you come to Old Santa Fe, one of America's favorite pilgrimage and tourist sites, please come and visit La Conquistadora — America's oldest Madonna. We pray to her daily as "Our Lady of Conquering Love of All Peoples."

Symbolism in the Dialogue
between Mary and Juan Diego

Sr. Rosa Maria Incasa, C.C.V.I.

*T*he dialogue between Our Lady of Guadalupe and Juan Diego took place on December 9, 10 and 12, 1531. These words were recorded in Nahuatl, Juan Diego's native language, in a document known as the *Nican Mopohua* (meaning, "Here it is narrated"), published by Luis Lasso de la Vega in 1649. The *Nican Mopohua* is a little known masterpiece of Christian literature, rich in symbolism, which provides penetrating insights not only into Mary's mentality but also into the mestizo (Nahuatl and Spanish) culture which produced the Mexican people.

The indigenous people worshipped a God of duality—masculine and feminine—the principle of all things. For this reason they saw an inherent duality in all nature. Thus, expressing the same idea with two words is their predominant literary characteristic. This trait is frequent in the *Nican Mopohua*. Human beings are recognized by their "face and heart," the deepest truth is expressed through "flower and song," a city is referred to as "water and hill," the world as "heaven and earth", creation begins at "night and in silence," war is expressed as "dart and shield."

Juan Diego, in Nahuatl symbolism, is the historical man but he is also the universal and oppressed man of the past, present and future—us. The story tells how Juan Diego arrived at the hill (symbol of strength), the hill of Tepeyac, a religious place (where the house of an Aztec deity had been built). It was dawn (the end of night, beginning of a new day) and he heard the sweet music of the birdsong coming from the direction of the rising sun (God). Then there was silence (the time of death and oppression was ending) and he heard his name being called "Juantzin, Juan Diegotzin," the ending "tzin" meaning "worthy of reverence," signifying the indigenous people were being restored to their dignity as human beings. The Lady was standing as Juan Diego came to meet her. This is important because both the Aztec and Spanish leaders gave their orders sitting down. To greet him standing showed respect for him, an equality among all beings, including Herself. In the words of the narrative the rocks and cacti seemed to shine like emeralds and turquoise. In Nahuatl culture turquoise was a sign of new life. At Tepeyac a new life coming from God through Mary was being born for the indigenous people in the same desolate landscape from which they had been expelled by the Spaniards as a conquered race. And she begins the dialogue by asking him where he is going, allowing him to speak first and to explain his moment in history. Juan Diego responds with words of respect and intimacy: "My Lady and child, I am going to Tlatelolco to learn about the things of God."

Meaning in Numbers

Numbers have a symbolic meaning in Nahautl thought. Ideas expressed in twos mean, in addition to inherent duality, that something is beginning. Three expresses intercession. Four represents wholeness/perfection. Five means center, where God is found. In the *Nican Mopohua* the story begins with the words "Here it is narrated and set down (beginning)." In her dialogue with Juan Diego, Mary uses numerical groupings to signify the proper symbolic context for her messages. Thus, she tells Juan Diego that she will show four things: love, compassion, help, defense (all that is needed). Those who love, invoke and trust her (three) will become her intermediaries. Then she goes on to say that she herself, as intermediary, will cure our troubles, miseries and sufferings.

She sends Juan Diego to the Bishop to tell him all he has seen, heard and admired (three). Upon being admitted to the Bishop's presence, he entered, bowed down and knelt. And the Bishop, in due time, telegraphing his own intermediary role, tells how he will hear, examine and think about the message. Three's lace the dialogue between Mary, Juan Diego and the Bishop in order to emphasize their respective intercessory roles. When Juan Diego reports the disbelief of the Bishop to Mary, he displays a crisis of self-confidence. He urges her to replace him as messenger from among the powerful, well-known, respected and esteemed (four). Yet, once again, God chooses the weak and insignificant (in their own eyes) to carry out the work of salvation. The stone rejected becomes the cornerstone.

Mary's Total Concern

Later in the story Mary illustrates the totality of her concern for Juan Diego (us) by a double couplet of fours. She tells him to "listen and understand." that what "frightens and causes him (us) pain is nothing." "Don't let your heart be troubled, don't fear this sickness, nor any other sickness or sorrow." Finally, in a wonderfully climactic sequence of concepts expressed in the form of five questions to Juan Diego, she illustrates the completeness of her solicitude for him (us). Even more, each concept includes a beautiful symbol. "Am I not here, I who am your Mother?" "Are you not under my shadow?" (Like God's shadow in the desert or the Holy Spirit's at the Annunciation). "Am I not the source of your joy?" "Are you not in the hollow of my mantle?" "What else do you need"?

The entire story is enclosed in a parenthetical couplet of symbols. The story is initiated with the singing of birds, as if the music were opening a parenthesis in which the communication of truth is to be shared. And when the flowers appear at the end the parenthesis is closed, indicating that the story that was narrated is true. The story begins: "He heard singing at the top of the hill; it sounded like the song of several precious birds; once in a while the singers became silent; and it seemed as if the mountain responded. Their song was sweet and pleasant, it was more beautiful than that of the 'coyoltotol' and of the 'tzinizcan' and of other pretty birds that sing."

Toward the end, the Lady asks Juan Diego to go to the top of the hill and to cut the flowers he finds there. Now Juan Diego must climb the hill and cut, gather and bring the flowers as an intermediary (three). He is astonished by all the blooming, open flowers of every kind, lovely and beautiful, when it was not their season, like precious pearls (of great price?), full of dew. Our Lady sees, touches and places the roses on Juan Diego's lap. Along the way to the Bishop he marvels at the fragrance of the different kinds of flowers. And the Bishop and those with him were astonished by how fresh they were, how open their corollas, how good they smelled.

At that point, Juan Diego reminded the Bishop that the hill was not a place for growing flowers, but a place for meeting God:

there were many "rocks, thistles, thorns, cacti and mesquites" (five-the center, the place of God). In the midst of this dry, pain-filled land, new life flowered again, just as through the message of Guadalupe, the indigenous people were renewed in their hope and celebration of life.

In her last words to Juan Diego, Our Lady showered a flurry of active verbs on him as if to charge him with an active outlook in facing the work and suffering necessary to bring the Good News of love and compassion to all nations. "You will narrate everything to him (the Bishop); you will tell him I asked you to climb the hill, so you would cut the flowers there, and tell him all that you saw and admired, so that you may convince the Bishop to grant his help in order that the temple which I have requested be erected and built."

We must not forget that, as Juan Diego was charged, so we are charged to become his collaborators in loving her, invoking her and trusting her by living as her true children and as brothers and sisters of her Son, carrying out her project of justice and love, particularly towards the poor, weak and suffering.

The Coronation
of Our Lady of Guadalupe

*T*he Coronation of Our Lady of Guadalupe's Image in 1895 was an epochal event in Mexican history and an outstanding witness of a whole nation's devotion to the Mother of God. When Pope Leo XIII received the petition for the coronation in March of 1887, not only did he allow it, he ordered it. The Guadalupans decided that nothing short of a complete renovation of the Basilica would do for such a solemn event. Since Mexico at that time was economically under-developed and poor, fund raising for the renovations took much time - time which was well spent in the spiritual preparation of the people. The reason and basis for the crowning were thoroughly explained, her special sovereignty over Mexico and all the Americas was recognized and preached, and prayer services were introduced. Due to this added attention to Our Lady of Guadalupe, there was a general effort to amend one's life and conduct among both rich and poor, educated and illiterate, as a proper preparation for the great event.

Special consideration was given to the design of the crown which would be rich in symbolism and ornamentation. A dozen of the leading ladies of society sought the privilege of having their gold and diamond jewelry wrought into a precious diadem for Mary of Guadalupe. The design was Mexican, the execution Parisian. In addition, a beautiful silver facsimile of the crown was wrought by Mexican artists for everyday use. This crown was presented by twelve young girls who had no mothers, thus expressing their desire that Mary be their Mother.

While renovating the Basilica it was necessary to transfer the Miraculous Image to the nearby Capuchin Sisters' church. Seeing their Sacred Image taken away from its usual setting, caused an outburst of vocal concern. The emotions of the people were intensified when they saw the old Abbot kneeling in a corner, with streams of tears rolling down his face. On September 30, 1895, exactly seven years, seven months, seven days from the date that the Image was removed, February 23, 1888, it was returned to the renovated Basilica, where it remained until October 11, 1976, when it was moved to the newly completed Basilica of Guadalupe (see article on page 207).

After the transferring of the Sacred Image to the Basilica, the festivities began. Every day in October was celebrated, although the solemn day of crowning was October 12th. From the early hours of the morning, it seemed as if the whole city was moving out to Tepeyac and the shrine. Many were going on foot, even the well-to-do. As the pilgrims approached the shrine, many would travel the final distance on their knees, which is a practice still seen at the shrine.

By noon, forty bishops, some from the United States, and hundreds of priests were in their places. Only a small fraction of the vast multitude of the faithful were able to find a place in the Basilica. As the *Regina Coeli* was intoned by the celebrant, a personal delegate of Pope Leo XIII in whose name the coronation was being made, four Bishops brought the crown to a platform where two Archbishops raised the Crown to its place. The thunderous and sustained cry of: *Viva la Virgen de Guadalupe!* resounded throughout the Basilica. The crowd outside the Basilica picked up the acclaim and shouted it out repeatedly as church bells sounded their joyful peal throughout the city and the whole of Mexico. Even the secular paper, *El Tiempo,* waxed eloquent in reporting this epochal moment:

"In all present there was a veritable explosion of gladness of exultation, of enthusiasm. Men and women wept for joy, and the scene became sublime. All felt themselves possessed by the Faith of the early Christians, while their souls were filled with an undefinable sweetness." One of the two Archbishops who crowned the Image kissed it before putting the crown in its place. The other Archbishop who was deeply moved, descended the platform in tears. (See illustration on page 175.)Twenty-eight Indians from the neighboring village of Juan Diego, one to represent each diocese in the Republic, had a conspicuous place in the ceremony expressing in their native dress and dance, their loyalty and submission to their Sovereign Queen."

The celebration was not only confined to the shrine of Our Lady of Guadalupe. Devotions were held throughout Mexico in parishes and shrines. The more distant the places, where many could not make the long journey, the more elaborate their celebration.

There seemed to be a competitive spirit in each sanctuary in giving local expression of the people's devotion to Mary of Guadalupe. In some cities, nine churches had Exposition of the Blessed Sacrament on succeeding days, the last day being on the day of the Coronation. It was reported that the number of Communions was greater, this, at a time when frequent Communion wasn't common.

The Mexicans, so fond of fireworks and bands to liven up their fiestas, found that neither were available just prior to the celebration. The fireworks were sold out and bands were no longer available. Accompanying the religious fervor were signs of devout love of country. The Mexican national colors were seen everywhere, despite the lack of support from the political party governing the country at that time.

The Constitution of 1873 clearly applied the doctrine of Separation of Church and State in a literal sense which ended up in supporting a secularisitic society which excluded religion from everyday life. By applying literal interpretation of certain clauses, petty officials who wished to win favor with the anti-religious party in power at that time, tried unsuccessfully to dampen the Guadalupan fervor of ordinary Catholics. Municipal regulations were issued, but were ignored and supplied a comic relief as policemen stood guard over belfries and even took away bell ropes so that the bells could not be rung. Though there was no bloody confrontation, it did point to the persecution that was to come in the twenties under the brutal Calles regime, when many priests, religious and lay people gave up their lives for the Faith, Blessed Padre Miguel Pro among them.

When Pope John Paul II visited Mexico in 1979, upon arrival at the airport President Jose Lopez Portillo gave him a stiff and formal welcome. But, throughout his five day visit record crowds welcomed him with enthusiasm wherever he went. He actually could have been liable to a prison term for wearing his pontifical and clerical dress in public, according to the Mexican Constitution of 1917, not favoring one religion over another (read anti-Catholic from a long standing Masonic influence). By the time of his second visit, the government had abolished that restriction on religion and since then has been much more open and friendly to the Church in Mexico. The Mexican people, as was demonstrated so many times in their history, turned to Our Lady of Guadalupe rather than to civil authority in their every necessity.

The fidelity of Catholics to the Faith in Mexico (and the Pope singled out Mexico as *semper fidelis*) is not in *spite* of persecution in the past, but *because* of persecution as is the case in the long history of the Church. There is no doubt their fidelity is due to their complete trust in Our Lady which is outstanding. Could not those memorable words she addressed to Juan Diego be applied also to the Mexican nation: *"...in you I place my absolute trust."* Mary of Guadalupe is now extending her trust to all of the Americas. Will other nations respond as Mexico has?

The above article is based largely on Chapter 15 of the book Our Lady of Guadalupe, *by Fr. George Lee, C.S.Sp. It is, to our knowledge, the first book published in English on Our Lady of Guadaluple.*

PART VIII

Guadalupe and the Mission of the Church

Juan Diego was commissioned to the lay apostolate by no less than the Mother of God. Providentially, he who was instrumental in the conversion of millions of natives of the New World, was beatified at a time when great emphasis is being placed on the vital role of the laity in the mission of the Church.

A Model and Patron
for Lay Apostles

Fr. Christopher Rengers, O.F.M. Cap.

"*Thy Kingdom come,*" the daily petition of the Our Father, has always needed for its fulfillment the work and cooperation of the laity. Not only to the clergy, but to all those baptized and confirmed, the commission has been given to make Christ and His teaching known and loved. The "*Spirit breathes where He will*" (Jn. 3,8) and the People of God have always had charisms (gifts) to help spread God's kingdom on earth.

But our era needs laymen more than ever. Because of advances in communication, in industry, in the physical and social sciences, there are many new fields of human endeavor where laymen have control and are expert. The Church can do little to bring the spirit of the Gospel to these areas except through laymen.

Recognizing the ancient truth and the new need, the Second Vatican Council issued the Decree on the Apostolate of the Laity. For the first time in the history of the Church a conciliar document set forth the concept of the layman as necessary in the mission of the Church, and spelled out the goals to be attained. The conclusion is inescapable that to be a real Christian is to be an apostle, that the perfect example of spiritual and apostolic life, is the most Blessed Virgin Mary, Queen of the Apostles. While leading on earth a life common to all men, one filled with family concerns and labors, she was always intimately united with her Son and cooperated in the work of the Savior in a manner altogether special. Now that she has been taken up into heaven, 'with her maternal charity she cares for these brothers of her Son . . .' All should devoutly venerate her and commend their lives and apostolates to her motherly concern.

Accordingly, it seems appropriate to suggest that the Patron for all Lay Apostles should be one who will lead men to Mary, the per-

fect example of the apostolic life, who ever directs men to her Divine Son. There have been many great sainted Marian apostles. But there is one obscure layman, as yet to be canonized, whose life story exemplifies very well the life and virtues of the Lay Apostolate. Juan Diego, the seer of Guadalupe, leads men with singular and irresistible charm to Our Lady. To choose him would serve to emphasize the "motherly concern" of Mary, and to highlight a relatively modern chapter in the loving care of the Queen of the Apostles for her children.

His story, wonderful in its beginning, still continues today as something living and enduring. It lives in the long lines of pilgrims, most numerous of any Marian shrine; it lives in the Faith of a new nation. It endures in the continuing Miracle of the only Portrait in the world that was not painted by human hand, but rather as Pius XII has said, "by brushes not of this world." The actual result of Mary's Guadalupan message in which Juan Diego played the key role, was to bring to belief in Christ and the original grace of baptism eight million persons within a decade. There is no greater Pentecostal example in the history of the Church.

During that period Juan Diego lived constantly near the marvelous Picture, quietly caring for it as Joseph had cared for Mary herself. He was part of the story of the wonderful Lady, her representative, her salesman, a living proof that heaven had smiled on the humble and lowly. As with St. Joseph we don't know all the details. But we do know the quality of this man's charity and it was magnetic. *"By this shall all men know that you are my disciples, if you have love one for another."* (Jn. 13:35)

The Decree on the Apostolate of the Laity has a special chapter entitled, "The Preservation of Order." It begins: "Whether the Lay Apostolate is exercised by the faithful as individuals or as members of organizations, it should be incorporated into the apostolate of the whole Church according to a right system of relationships. Indeed, union with those whom the Holy Spirit has assigned to rule God's Church is an essential element of the Christian apostolate." In the case of Juan Diego, he received the call by Mary herself. The message was given to him by Mary but she sent him to the Bishop. "Go to the Bishop of Mexico and tell him that I sent you."

The Spirit breathed on Juan, but judgment and authorization were reserved to the Bishop. It is true that usually the Spirit breathes in a less dramatic way. But the case of Juan Diego shows both that the inspirational grace for a great work in the Church may first come to a layman, and that the favored person then cooperates with the proper authorities. Juan Diego's humble fulfillment of an unwelcome and embarrassing task paved the way for the marvelous bestowal of heaven's favors. At the same time, as a sidelight, we also have illustrated here the fact that the layman may push his point, and that in pushing his point he is not necessarily disrespectful. The Bishop needed convincing, and Mary herself told Juan to go back and try again.

Juan Diego was told that he was necessary for the fulfillment of the plans of heaven. When he protested his inability and urged Mary to send a person better known and respected, her answer was: "Listen, the least of my sons, you must try to understand that I have many messengers and servants whom I could charge with the delivery of my message and cause to do my will. But it is altogether necessary that you yourself should undertake this entreaty and that through your own mediation and assistance my purpose should be accomplished..." The importance of the most humble person in fulfilling the divine plans can hardly be more pointedly exemplified. Mary did not go directly to the Bishop-elect Juan de Zumárraga and inspire him. Nor did she choose the messenger most suited by ordinary human judgment. She chose one particular, unknown, middle-aged widower who would have preferred to quietly practice his Faith in an ordinary way. She told him that he was her man. He was the necessary instrument of Divine Providence chosen to evangelize his people. One unlikely, obscure layman was to be the key to the unlocking of graces for the conversion of a whole nation.

Juan Diego is like Nathaniel, *"an Israelite without guile."* He was a simple and sincere man. Children are fascinated in the retelling of the story and his conversations with Mary on Tepeyac. Their dialogue has a quality of tenderness, of immediacy, genuineness and uniqueness that make rare literature. In the Indian idiom Mary called him her *xocoyote*, her favorite son, the least of her sons. He addressed her as *xocoyota*, his littlest daughter, his lady and his child. To listen to this conversation you must love both Juan and his Lady.

Today and in the decades and centuries to come, people of the emerging nations will be able to identify with Juan Diego. He is humble and chose to be identified with the poor, not entangled in the meshes of western political or cultural history, readily understandable in any era. How appropriate to have a layman like Juan Diego who has universal appeal as an inspiration and example for other lay apostles.

In recent years a number of examinations of enlargements of the eye of Our Lady of Guadalupe, shows the image of a bearded man, identify as Juan Diego, reflected in the eye of the Sacred Image. If Juan Diego is in her eyes, possibly she wants him to be before ours. It would seem that his being recognized as the special patron of the Lay Apostolate is tied in with his official recognition as a saintly person who can be imitated in his heroic practice of virtue. After a four-and-a-half-century wait, Pope John Paul II in his second pastoral pilgrimage to Mexico beatified Juan Diego on May 6, 1990, the day he arrived in Mexico City. In his homily at the Mass the Holy Father placed particular emphasis on Juan Diego's association with Our Lady in bringing the Gospel message to the New World.

"At the dawn of the evangelization of Mexico there is a prominent and unique place for Blessed Juan Diego . . . His kindly figure cannot be separated from the Guadalupe event . . . Like the ancient biblical personalities who represented all the people, we could say that Juan Diego represents all the indigenous people who received the Gospel of Jesus, thanks to the maternal assistance of Mary, who is always inseparable from the revelation of her Son and the establishment of the Church, as was her presence among the apostles on Pentecost.

"The recognition of the veneration that has been given for centuries to the layman, Juan Diego, assumes a particular importance. It is a strong call to all the lay faithful of the nation to assume all their responsibilities in the transmission of the Gospel message and in the witness of a living and operative Faith in Mexican society. From this privileged place of Guadalupe, the heart of ever faithful Mexico, I want to call all the Mexican laity to commit themselves more actively to the re-evangelization of society . . . may Juan Diego also shine before you, raised by the Church to the honor of the altars, and whom we can invoke as protector and advocate of the indigenous peoples."

The feast day of Blessed Juan Diego is December 9, just three days before the feast of Our Lady of Guadalupe and the day after the feast of the Immaculate Conception. In regard to his canonization, Monsignor Enrique Salazar, vice-postulator for the Cause of Juan Diego, went to Rome in May, 1994, to present final documents. He reported on his return that he expects Juan Diego to be canonized in the near future. Letters asking for the further honoring of Blessed Juan Diego as a Saint and as Patron of Lay Apostles may be sent to the Bishop of any diocese.

The same request and reports of favors received - or perhaps of a miracle - may be sent to one's Bishop or to *Franciscans for the Cause of Juan Diego*, Box 15314, Philadelphia, PA, 19111; or to *Queen of the Americas Guild*, 345 Kautz Road, Box 851, St. Charles, IL 60174.

Holy Mary of Guadalupe, Prolife Patron

Janet Barber, I.H.M.

*T*he Blessed Virgin Mary best reveals herself as Patroness of the Unborn in her advocation of Guadalupe. In her Image, which she left us in Advent of 1531, miraculously stamped and conserved on Juan Diego's cloak, she is represented "*with child.*" Her pregnancy is recognized by the high position of her sash, from the slight swelling of her abdomen most visible to the right of the sash, and with the four petaled flower over her womb. Until recently, she was judged to be in her first trimester. However, an analysis by a leading gynecologist/obstetrician of Mexico City, Dr. Carlos Fernández Del Castillo, now suggests that she is very close to giving birth. Dr. Fernández believes that the Infant is resting vertically, head down, and that the four-petaled flower over her womb, symbolizing life, lies directly over the left shoulder of the Infant, in the best place for listening to his heartbeat.

The four-petaled flower over her womb is the only one of such design among the 57 flowers and 13 buds on her tunic. This unique flower is the Flower of the Sun, the Nahuatl symbol *Nahui Ollin*, which announced to the conquered Indians that the Sun of the New Era was about to be born liturgically and in their lives, that is, the great *Sun of Justice* announced in Malachi, the last book of the Old Testament.

The Indians of the Mesoamerican cultures were accustomed to finding several meanings in their symbols, just as we do in our own. They easily saw in the four-petaled flower the additional meaning of their *mamalhuaztli*, the crossed sticks they used for making fire. Every 52 years, on the night of their New Fire, the Lake peoples waited in dread for the three stars of the constellation which they called "Mamalhuaztli" to cross the zenith, thus showing that their world would not end as the previous ones had. As soon as the danger was over, they would kindle new fire with their *mamalhuaztli* in the empty heart cavity of a fresh sacrificial victim, and with that fire, light a huge bonfire that told the fasting, frightened people that the universe would not end. The new fire was carried by runners to the city and towns, to light the extinguished family hearths. As the three stars sank below the western horizon, the life-giving sun would rise in the east, and their new "year bundle" would begin. The primary meaning of the sign *mamalhuaztli*, then, is *new life,* and this they read over the Virgin's womb.

While every type of symbol on the tunic of Holy Mary of Guadalupe has several specific meanings relating to our new life in Jesus Christ and His life in us, the overarching meaning of her Image to the Mesoamerican Indians was simply *xihuitl,* life. Life in the vegetation of her tunic, life in the five great streams of living water represented as the stems of the heart-shaped flowers, stems which were adaptations of the Nahuatl sign for *atl,* water. The water of Baptism and the water which they would draw from the wells of salvation, water that would bubble up in them to eternal life.

Needless, then, were their vain attempts to prolong life on earth by feeding the Aztec sun god Huitzilopochtli with human blood, the divine liquid which he needed if he was to be strong enough to battle his way through the underworld and rise anew each day to cross the sky. Needless were their liturgies involving infant sacrifice; sacrifices which were continued at night for years behind the backs of the Friars. From now on, the only Sacrifice that could indeed give them life was that of Jesus Christ on the Cross, represented on Holy Mary's tunic by the nine large magnolia blossoms, their symbols for the *yolloxochitl,* the Heart Flower, which had formerly been a metaphor to them of the hearts of their countless sacrificial victims.

Just as Holy Mary of Guadalupe has extinguished human sacrifice in the Aztec world of the sixteenth century, standing for life and offering the abundant new life won by the self-sacrifice of her Son, so too can she be importuned to end the sacrifice of millions of babies in our own world today. It is altogether appropriate that she become the focus of our prayers on behalf of these innocents.

Through the earliest known account of her apparitions, the *Nican Mopohua,* we know that Mary of Guadalupe came to Mexico

The Pyramid Teotihuacan: Human sacrifices took place by the thousands atop these pyramids. After their hearts were torn from the victims their bodies were rolled down the sides of the pyramids and cannibalized.

in 1531 asking for a Little House of God in which she would reveal the love of God to her sons and daughters through her own love. She would cleanse their wounds of suffering and anguish, as any loving mother tenderly cleanses her child's bleeding, dust and grit-filled wounds. She promised that if we seek her and love her (which includes seeking and loving the Christ she came to give us) we would be protected in her shadow, carried in her cloak, nestled against her breast or on her back, as Indian women still carry their babies and young children today.

Whatever our burden, Mary and her Son yearn to carry it for us, now, as in 1531. While Juan Diego trotted miles through the darkness to find a priest for his dying uncle on that longest night of the year, the night of the Winter Solstice, his heart was heavy with fear and anxiety. He thought he had to solve his problem alone, avoiding the Woman who is a "compassionate Mother of all who would seek her."

Interestingly, his detour led him to the eastern side of Tepeyac, the side of the hill on which the sun would rise several hours later, and where he came into her healing presence. She told him to have no fear, and then uttered the tenderest series of words of any of her recorded apparitions on earth, beginning with, "Am I not here, who am your Mother?" Then she sent him higher. His tired legs had to carry him in pitch darkness to the top of the rocky hill, but what a reward he found there!

Holy Mary of Guadalupe, Patroness of the Unborn, offers us no easy solutions. But if we face the sun, continue to climb and "do whatever she tells us," she can then keep her promises and exercise her gentle motherly care in ways we cannot foresee.

Of Aztec Human Sacrifice

*A*t the time of the 500th anniversary of the discovery of America there was a proliferation of articles in secular publications, as well as history books which gave a new interpretation of the circumstances and personalities surrounding the discovery and conquest in the New World. It reflected pretty much the mind set of the secular-humanist world in which we live. These writers who had little love for religion in general and the Catholic Church in particular, would have us believe that Catholic Spain and the conquistadors had anything but high motives in the conquest of Mexico.

Besides generalizing that all the conquistadors were unprincipled and cruel they questioned the imposition of a foreign culture, and even of Christianity, on the native people in the New World, the Aztecs in particular, who had a very advanced civilization. The revisionists held that the native Americans would have been better off left alone to pursue their way of life, rather than have their art, institutions, religion, etc. be almost completely obliterated by the conquistadors. The modern historians considered it a grave mistake and injustice on the part of the Spaniards.

Apart from the facts that there were abuses, such as Pizarro in Peru, the first audiencia in Mexico, (see page 48), from the standpoint of the many suppressed Indian tribes, the conquest of the Aztec Empire was a liberation from one of the cruelest tyrannies the world has ever known. This sort of advocacy reporting doesn't take into account that the Indian nations and tribes under Aztec rule were severely taxed and suppressed. Whenever they could not pay the tribute levied on them, their people would end up on the sacrificial altars of the Aztec demonic gods, such as Huitzilopochtli, god of war or Tezcatlipoca, god of phantoms, *"He Who Is at the Shoulder"* as the tempter. Enemy warriors captured in the "Flower Wars" provoked by the Aztecs were offered as sacrificial victims to their literally blood-thirsty gods. The Aztecs argued that the gods would perish without human blood, that mysterious fluid of life

gushing from the torn-out heart of the victims. Is it any wonder that Cortés was able to conquer the Aztecs when he was able to win allies among the neighboring tribes, who supplied porters and warriors to fight the hated Aztecs?

The historian, Warren Carroll, author of, "Our Lady of Guadalupe and The Conquest of Darkness,"[1] from which most of this material is drawn, writes:

"Many primitive peoples have practiced occasional human sacrifice and some have practiced cannibalism. None has ever done so on a scale remotely approaching that of the Aztecs. No one will ever know how many they sacrificed; but the law of the empire required a thousand sacrifices. . . . in every town with a temple, every year and there were 371 subject towns in the Aztec Empire. . . .The total number was at least 50,000 a year, and probably more. The early Mexican historian, Ixtlilxochitl, estimated that one out of every five children in Mexico was sacrificed. It is known that entire tribes, numbering in the tens of thousands, were on several occasions exterminated by sacrifice. . . .

"An almost universal symbol in Mexican religion was the serpent. Sacrifices were heralded by the prolonged beating of an immense drum made of the skins of huge snakes, which could be heard two miles away. Nowhere else in human history has Satan so formalized and institutionalized his worship with so many of his own actual titles and symbols."

The most feared and evil leader in the later days of the empire was Tllacaellel, who on the occasion of dedicating a new pyramid-temple in 1487, accordings to Chroniclers at that time, sacrificed between 20,000 and 80,000 men in a period of four days. An Aztec annalist summarized his evil career thus, "It was he who established the worship of the devil Huitzilopochtle, the god of the Mexicans." One of Cortés' captains estimated that there were 100,000 skulls of victims on one skull-rack. The Satanic nature of the latter-day Aztec worship is well attested to by the three earliest experts and writers on the Aztec culture: Fr. Bernardino de Sahagún, a Franciscan; Fr. Diego Durán, a Dominican Friar, and Fr. José de Acosta, a Jesuit. All three were familar with Nahuatl, the language of the Aztecs, and had studied extensively their culture for the purpose of formulating more effective ways of evangelizing them. All three agreed that the native people were subject to satanic power through their religion.[2] However, one does not have to be an expert in Aztec culture at the height of its dominance in central America, to appreciate the fact that human sacrifice and cannibalism is contrary to the natural law, written in the hearts of all men, at all times and in all lands.

It would seem that today in our nation in which the "culture of death" is so pervasive and is supported by the highest political leaders in the land and especially the mass media, we are attempting to outdo the Aztecs. They killed, as mentioned above, one out every five children. Each year, in our national capital abortionists kill more babies than are delivered alive. Nationally, over a million and a half babies are killed each year, not counting the early abortions by abortifacient birth control pills. Now the time is near when the lives of the elderly, handicapped, unproductive members of society will be terminated (murdered) as having little or no value. Where will it end?

If history repeats itself, we are on the very same slippery slope as the Aztecs and another "superior race" took four hundred years *after* the Aztecs, which led to the gas ovens of Auschwitz, and ultimately to divine retribution. But where is the media reporting on the slaughter of so many innocent lives in our times? There is a news black-out here, as well as with the modern-day secular historians who rewrote the history of the times when the great pagan Aztec Empire fell and Our Lady of Guadalupe was there to pick up the pieces.

—The Editor

1. See summary of the book in Bibliography, page 224.
2. Nuestra Señora de Guadalupe, Mother of God, Mother of the Americas, a catalogue for an exhibition conducted by Bridwell Library at the Southern Methodist University in Dallas Texas.

The Missionary Image
of Our Lady of Guadalupe

Daniel J. Lynch

*T*he Missionary Images are two actual size (4' x 6') photo-graphic replicas of the original Miraculous Image of Our Lady which she left on Blessed Juan Diego's tilma. They are gifts from the Catholics of Mexico to the Catholic people of the United States through the Basilica of Our Lady of Guadalupe. In 1991, each was named a "Missionary Image" and blessed as such by the late Cardinal Posadas of Mexico on behalf of all the Mexican bishops and by representatives of the Basilica, who supported the mission with their prayers. They defined Our Lady's Mission: to end abortion and convert millions. Cardinal Posadas prayed, "Lady, help us support your Mission with our prayers in order that your Missionary Image may be well received in America for the glory of God and the honor of His holy Mother!"

The guardian of the Missionary Images, Daniel J. Lynch of St. Albans, Vermont, a judge, retired lawyer, author and public speaker coordinates the journeys of the Images. He also accompanies the International Missionary Image and speaks at Missions and Con-ferences throughout the world. The National Missionary Image is sent to local guardian teams who have requested visitations, and in-cludes churches, abortuaries, monasteries, convents, prisons, hospi-tals, nursing homes and schools. They prepare the reception and co-ordinate all liturgical events with the local pastors and bishops.

The Journey Visitations

The Missionary Image began her journeys in June of 1991. From the International Rosary Congress at the National Shrine of the Immaculate Conception, throughout America and the world, the Image has visited over 1,000 parishes in every state of the U.S.A., the Caribbean Islands, Canada, Mexico, Ireland, England, Europe, Russia, China, the Philippine Islands, Japan and Israel. The Image has been venerated by hundreds of thousands. There have been thousands of Masses, Confessions, hours of adoration before the Blessed Sacrament and Rosaries said in the presence of the Image. Our Lady's Image has led the largest pro-life Rosary processions ever seen in various cities including Dublin, Ireland; Port of Spain, Trinidad; Melbourne, Australia and Pittsburgh, Pennsylvania. Many abortions have been averted and at least twenty abortuaries have been closed through Our Lady of Guadalupe's intercession. The Irish clergy credit the voting down of a proposed Constitutional amendment to "legalize" abortion in Ireland to her intercession. Many conversions, healings, reconciliations and graces have also been reported.

One priest, who had sponsored the visitation of the Image, reported, "Our Lady melted hearts everywhere she went! In her travels near Dayton, Ohio, Our Lady visited five abortuaries, and two grade schools totaling over 1,000 students, 13 parishes, a university chapel, a renewal center, and a women's prison. Almost everyone who venerates the Image is touched in one way or another. Some are given an inner strength to deal with their problems and adversities; others receive confirmation of their prayer petitions; many are led to Confession and Communion or to Eucharistic adoration; and some are miraculously healed."

A visitation to the Rio Grande Valley in Texas attracted an estimated 34,000 Valley residents with their prayers, their hopes, their fears and their dreams before the Missionary Image during a nine-day pilgrimage for life with Fr. Frank Pavone, National Director of Priests for Life. "What a marvelous pilgrimage it was!", said Fr. Pavone. "It was like a powerful retreat for me, and I was inspired by the faith of the people and the jubilation and beauty that marked the celebrations." The Image visited 25 churches and an abortion center where the precious life of an unborn baby was saved. Local guardian, Sr. Nancy Boushey, O.S.B., acknowledged that the child's life was saved through "the intercession of Mary and the prayerful presence of those who accompanied the Image and counseled the mother not to destroy the human life she was carrying."

The residents responded with love and some with tears of joy,

Father Frank Pavone, National Director of Priests for Life, with Helena and her daughter, Guadalupe. Helena, intending to have an abortion, caught sight of this priest outside the abortion "clinic," and changed her mind.

as they gazed upon and touched or kissed the Image. People came from across the Valley to participate at Mass, to adore Jesus in the Blessed Sacrament, sing hymns to our Blessed Mother, pray the Rosary and pray for their families and for life. More than 100 people attended classes in preparation for making the total consecration to Our Lady according to St. Louis de Montfort, which Pope John Paul II had made as a young man and has had such a profound influence in his spiritual life.

The Image also visited a juvenile center where television cameras focused on the conversion stories of 20 young prisoners who said they would henceforth totally consecrate their lives to Jesus through Mary. As the visitation ended at St. Anthony's Church in Harlingen, men, women, youth and small children followed the Image to the parking lot for an emotional farewell. They reached out to touch the Image one last time, sang Marian hymns and waved good-bye when the Image was lifted into a pick-up truck for its departure.

In Wichita, Kansas, the Missionary Image visited an abortuary where late-term babies are being killed and cremated in an incinerator on the premises. As the Image was processed around the killing center, people smelled a strong fragrance of roses. Then, they saw rose petals miraculously flaking from the Image in all directions. An eyewitness to this extraordinary event, experienced an overwhelming peace and said that it seemed as if heaven had come down to earth and Our Lady was saying, "It is good for you to be here; as I too stood at the foot of the Cross silently watching and praying as my innocent Son was crucified."

Through her Missionary Image, Our Lady has melted the hearts of many women who had planned to have their babies killed. Cathy, a professional journalist, interviewed Dan Lynch at a Marian Conference. She asked him, "How will Mary end abortion?" He replied, "She will melt hearts and the melted heart of a mother would never consider killing her innocent, helpless child; she will reverence the life within her and bring it to birth!" At this point, Cathy broke down, crying and told him, "I had an abortion ten years ago. You are the first person in the world that I have told. I named my son Joshua and have asked him to forgive me." Mr. Lynch quickly arranged for her to receive the sacraments of Reconciliation and Eucharist that day, for the first time since her abortion. They both felt great joy at her response to Our Lady's call to come back to the Sacred Heart of her Son and His holy Church. She now evangelizes youth in chastity and the reverence for life.

Her Knees Began to Shake

One day, while the Missionary Image was placed in a public park for veneration, a pregnant mother named Vicki walked by. She had already decided to abort her baby, but when she looked at the Missionary Image, her knees began to shake and she spontaneously began to cry. "When I saw the Missionary Image, it was like the Holy Spirit was coming into me and waking me up after many years." Although Vicki was unaware of the significance of the image of Our Lady of Guadalupe, she heard an interior voice say to her, "You are called to motherhood!" She instantly decided against killing her baby, chose life and put her trust in God. God rewarded her trust and she gave birth to a healthy boy in a Catholic hospital. She has returned to the sacraments after years of involvement in the New Age movement, and has decided to spend the rest of her life helping mothers and their unborn children. "It's made all the difference in the world," Vicki said, "to know that there are people who are ready to help, people who care."

On another day, a pregnant mother named Helena, who was waiting inside a "clinic" to have an abortion saw Fr. Pavone and a group of pro-lifers outside, praying beside the Missionary Image.

Above: Vicki and her son. Left: The Director of the Missionary Image, Dan Lynch, and other noted pro-life activists, Joan Andrews Bell and Joe Scheidler.

When Helena looked out, and saw the Roman collar she thought, "There's a priest out there! What am I doing in here?" Helena changed her mind, came outside and received help from the pro-lifers. She later gave birth to her child, who was baptized by Father Frank and appropriately named *Guadalupe*.

One repentant mother-victim, a victim of abortion was ashamed to confess it, "I did not confess this horrid sin until after learning about Our Lady of Guadalupe. The Image drew me to herself, she who is beautiful, loving and who guided me towards self-knowledge. I finally found the love and peace that is only possible through the sacrament of Reconciliation." Our Lady of Guadalupe also saved a mother who had had four abortions! She said, "I now consecrate myself daily to the holy Virgin Mother of Guadalupe and I ask her to make me an instrument to end abortion by melting hearts. I believe that Our Lady of Guadalupe will heal all those who have been wounded by the grave sin of abortion and that she is the shield that will protect unborn children and their mothers."

In November, 1992, a four-year-old girl named Alex Schuhmann lay dying in a Kentucky hospital of a rare lung disease, *bronchiolitis obliterans*. Local Missionary Image Guardian, Debbie Womack, brought the Image into Alex's hospital room on the day doctors had predicted she would die. Alex was lifted up to the Image and she tenderly touched and kissed Our Lady. The next day, the doctors went to Alex's room, they were shocked to find the little girl playing and eating a hamburger! Alex's mother credits this healing to Our Lady of Guadalupe through her Missionary Image. The saving of so many lives by the Visitation of the Missionary Image should give us the courage to march on with confident hope towards the Great Jubilee Year 2000!

Apostolate's Mission of Evangelization

Pope John Paul II in *Mission of the Redeemer* said, "People today put more trust in witnesses than in teachers, in experience than in teaching, and in life and action than in theories. The witness of a Christian life is the first and irreplaceable form of mission." This is the mission of the apostolate of the Missionary Image - to be witnesses for life and for Jesus, to bring conversions and end abortion through the intercession of Our Lady of Guadalupe.

The Holy Father asked for a "new evangelization" to usher in the Great Jubilee Year 2000. Our bishops entrusted this new "evangelization" to Our Lady of Guadalupe. They said, "We entrust our commitment to giving birth with new fervor to the life of the Gospel in our hemisphere, to Our Lady of Guadalupe, Patroness of the Americas. She truly was the first Christ-bearer; by her maternal intercession, may her faithful sons and daughters be renewed and discover afresh the joy and splendor and promise of being bearers of the good news."

Pope John Paul II prophesied, "The light of the Gospel of Christ will shine out over the whole world by means of the Miraculous Image of His Mother." May she end abortion and convert millions in the "new evangelization" of the Americas just as she ended human sacrifice and converted millions in the First Evangelization. May we help her by our act of total consecration and by living that consecration through reparative prayer and fasting. May we walk in step with the Holy Father behind Our Lady of Guadalupe toward the Great Jubilee Year 2000!

To schedule a visitation of the Missionary Image, please send a written request and more information will be provided. For a comprehensive account of Our Lady of Guadalupe's historical role and further explanation of her mission and journey today, please refer to the book *Our Lady of Guadalupe and Her Missionary Image* by Daniel J. Lynch. Missionary Image of Our Lady of Guadalupe, 144 Sheldon Rd., St. Albans, Vermont 05478 phone: 888-834-6261; fax 802-524-5673.

Our Lady of Guadalupe:
Protectress of the Unborn

Father Paul Marx, O.S.B., Ph.D.*

*W*ho would have thought that a small one room office in Washington, D.C. would, in just 15 years, develop into the world's largest pro-life, pro-family organization? Or who could have imagined that in the same amount of time a people once steeped in superstition, pagan ritual, and bloody human sacrifice, experienced such an outpouring of grace that over nine million of them were baptized? The answer? "What is impossible for man, is possible for God." He alone imagined it, and He alone accomplished it, through the miraculous intervention of Our Lady of Guadalupe.

The appropriateness of hailing Our Lady of Guadalupe as patroness of our apostolate is remarkable. Of all the many manifestations of Mary's loving presence among us throughout the centuries, in this apparition alone does she appear to us as a pregnant mother. She holds within her the unborn Christ, proclaiming the sanctity and blessedness of life within the womb. Her reverence and tenderness communicate to us the joy and awe with which we must approach each nascent life. In contemplating her simplicity we find the strength to emulate her faith, and proceed with confidence in the knowledge that God will overcome the seemingly insurmountable barriers looming all around us in the world today.

When Mary first appeared to Blessed Juan Diego in 1531, Mexico had been in the hands of Christian leaders for only a short time. Human sacrifice, in which the blood of infants was often spilled to appease the thirsty demons of the old rite, was still prac-

---

*Founder of Human Life International

ticed surreptitiously, a gruesome continuation of the country's long enslavement to pagan fears. Into this cavern of darkness and ignorance, Our Lady of Guadalupe brought a message of maternal compassion. "I am the merciful Mother, the Mother of all of you who live united in this land, and of all mankind, of all those who love me, of those who cry to me, of those who seek me, of those who have confidence in me. Here I will hear their weeping, their sorrow, and will remedy and alleviate their suffering, necessities, and misfortunes." No more did the people need to cower in abject terror before the bloodthirsty gods who demanded the death of their children. They found refuge beneath the gracious protection of a gentle Mother.

As our world is poised at the dawn of the third millennium, how much we need her! In ever greater numbers society sacrifices our young and aged at demonic altars, hurrying them to destruction through abortion, sex education, prostitution, pornography, infanticide and euthanasia, foolishly believing that just a little more contraception, just one additional population control program, and we will be blessed with the happiness and peace that we so desire.

Against the darkness of this era, we must cry out for the assistance and protection of Our Lady of Guadalupe. Her face radiates the very light of God, while her example reveals authentic feminism. Only by imitating Our Lady's respect for life from the moment of conception can we hope to inherit Life itself. Under her gentle direction we find not only shelter and rest, but confidence and strength to go forth to battle the evil. Through her intercession we can expect tremendous miracles. Though they were few in number, the first Franciscan missionaries in Mexico reaped an unprecedented harvest of souls for God in just a few short years, all under the patronage of Mary. Likewise, the pro-life forces, like David versus Goliath, stand firm against a vast array of anti-life organizations, imperialistic governments, and literally billions of dollars, yet continue to flourish. Countless children have been rescued from the slaughter, an entire generation that will live to praise God. Thousands of souls have been turned away from fear and death, to embrace life and joy. Families the world over have learned to look to pro-life forces in the Untied States for support and encouragement against what the Holy Father has termed "a culture of death."

And the pro-life movement, in turn, looks to Our Lady of Guadalupe, who is held in great reverence. She is indeed the

"Mother of all mankind," and we in the pro-life movement cherish a special allegiance and devotion to her banner. Though she is known as the "Queen of the Americas," she has extended her influence to every continent through her servants in the pro-life cause, bearing the message of love and life to all nations.

The miraculous image of Mary carrying within her womb the unborn Jesus, shows us more poignantly than words that the child is the heart of the family and the family is the foundation upon which a peaceful society will be built. This is the soul of our mission. Daily we feel her blessings. Didn't Mary tell us that this would be the case when we busied ourselves with her work and left our cares in her hands? "Listen and be sure, my dear son, that I will protect you; do not be frightened or grieve, or let your heart be dismayed, however great may be the illness that you speak of. Am I not here? I, who am your Mother? And is not my help a refuge? Am I not of your kind? Do not be concerned . . . Is there anything else that you need?"

Only through the Heart of a Mother so benevolent and powerful can we hope to achieve our ends. If my many years of world travels have taught me anything, it is that we are always the underdog. The opposition is always bigger, better funded, and has the support of the government and the media. We are like a ragged little dog against a bully with a stick. But Mary assures us that we need not worry or be frightened. We need only to ask her intercession and she will see to the victory, despite the most overwhelming odds.

It is a combination that cannot lose. Our Lady of Guadalupe appears to us as the Mother of Christ, who is Head of his Church. She directs us to look to her Son, to "do whatever He tells you," to uphold the teachings of His Body, the Catholic Church. Therefore, we promote and defend the teachings the Church without exception, without compromise. Indeed, it would be the greatest foolishness to do otherwise. Time and again I have seen that once a society has accepted contraception, abortion follows. The 'slippery slope' goes down fast from there. Abortion ushers in the greatest disrespect for human life and human sexuality and heralds the inception of innumerable evils: pornography, child abuse, infanticide, and euthanasia. Catholics who were once faithful begin using contraception and suddenly lose all apostolic zeal. The family begins to disintegrate and society starts to self-destruct.

There can only be one solution: to turn in true faithfulness to the teachings of Christ and accept the peace and freedom that He offers us, especially through His emissary Our Lady of Guadalupe. She is the model of the obedient virgin, the faithful subject, the loving mother, the gentle spouse, and the charitable woman. Her virtues extol the grace of God, her obedience His wisdom, and her miracles His power. We are in this battle until God wins. We will not be deterred by opposition, government interference, political correctness, and the alliances of the devil. As Saint Paul said: "We will fight the good fight."

With the help of Our Lady of Guadalupe, we cannot falter. The first miracle of Jesus at Cana was on behalf of a family, and undertaken at Mary's request. That alone tells us that we are in the right business and have her blessing! Then 1500 years later in Mexico, in the midst of seemingly impregnable darkness, she shone forth radiantly as a champion of the family, a pregnant mother standing against the horror of human sacrifice. Beneath the mantle of Our Lady of Guadalupe, we shall not only survive, but prosper. Our Lady of Guadalupe, pray for us!

A Guild for
the Queen of the Americas

Frank Smoczynski

*W*hen Bishop Jerome Hastrich was made the Ordinary of the Diocese of Gallup, New Mexico, the poorest diocese in the United States, he was sad to find so few conversions among the native Americans. Since Juan Diego, to whom Our Lady had appeared at Guadalupe, was a native American, Bishop Hastrich reasoned that spreading the account of that wonderful intervention of the Mother of God to one of their own race might very well be the way of reaching the people of his diocese, most of whom were Indians. But, he was dismayed to find that in the United States at that time, 1970, there was little general interest and knowledge of the "Virgin Mary, Mother of the True God" as she had identified herself at Guadalupe.

He came in contact with other devotees of Guadalupe over the years who were also surprised at how few Catholics in the United States were aware of the apparitions of Our Lady and the on-going Miracle of the tilma of Juan Diego in the Basilica of Our Lady of Guadalupe in Mexico City. A meeting was organized under the leadership of Bishop Hastrich at a Catholic Retreat center in Emmitsburg, Maryland.

The Bishop shared his vision and dream with the group, and they all agreed that there was a need for more concerted, united action. The group, made up of lay people for the most part, were anxious to meet again the following year, and it was in 1980 that the Queen of the Americas Guild was founded, with Bishop Hastrich as its Spiritual Director. Bishop Hastrich asked me to take a leadership role in the Guild and I was pleased to assume the responsibility of President of the Guild for most of its sixteen years of existence.

The Guild is loosely structured, but nonetheless is very consistent and effective in its goal of spreading information about and devotion to Our Lady of Guadalupe. Each year, the Guild holds an annual conference in a different location. Highlights of the last ten years were: the 1987 meeting in Gallup, New Mexico, the "Indian Capital of the World;" in 1989 the Guild returned to Emmitsburg to celebrate its 10th anniversary; in 1991, for the 500th anniversary of the evangelization of the Americas their conference was in Mexico City under a big tent set up adjacent to the shrine itself. The conference in Birmingham, Alabama in 1993, was honored and inspired by the presence of Mother Angelica, founder and chairman of the board of the Eternal Word Television Network (EWTN).

There have been some outstanding Guadalupe apostles who have been a part of the Queen of the Americas Guild, such as Dr. Charles Wahlig, contributor of a number of articles in this issue of the *Handbook* and author of the first biography in English on Juan Diego. He has done much to propagate knowledge of and devotion to the Mother of the Americas in this country. Manuel Perez, whose center in Los Angeles has distributed many Guadalupe pictures and books, translated the first *Handbook* into Spanish. Although both Perez and Dr. Wahlig are deceased, we are confident, they are still working for the cause. The musical talent of Our Lady's Troubadour, Marty Rotella who writes and produces his own music, is one of the features of every Guild conference. One of his CDs, titled "I Wait on Tepeyac," has 13 original songs, each teaching the story of Our Lady of Guadalupe in a different way.

For many years the Guild had its own English-speaking representative at the Basilica in Mexico City. Fr. Jacob Joerger, O.P., was the first to fill this important post. When he left for another assignment in his Order, Bishop Hastrich asked Guild member, Susan Maloney, to fill the post. The few years that she served at the English information office at the shrine were very eventful for this zealous woman. "Every day has been filled with adventure," she reported with a smile, "and most important of all, with the love and support of many in the name of Our Lady." She talked with familiarity to dignitaries as well as to the ordinary, devout pilgrims who had walked many miles over mountainous roads, bringing their bedroll, food, and charcoal stoves. (See article "The Late Susan Maloney Reports" on p. 155.) She conveyed with enthusiasm the splendor and solemnity of the celebration of big feasts, such as Easter when people came to visit their Mother, Our Lady of Guadalupe; of how the ordinary people of Mexico celebrated these feasts in an extraordinary way with much music, mariachi bands, dramas, fireworks and native dances.

This humble woman was greatly respected by all who knew her. So much so, that her wish of being buried close to the Woman she had served so well was respected by the Mexicans; and so she is interred in the crypt of the old Basilica among the other notable people associated with the shrine.

Through the years, the Guild has distributed hundreds of thousands of images and much literature on Our Lady of Guadalupe to churches and religious groups, as well as to individuals. The most popular is the plastic holy card with her Image on one side and the motherly words which she addressed to Juan Diego on the other. During the Gulf War, I contacted the chaplains of the various branches of the military, asking them whether they would be interested in receiving these beautiful photo reproductions of the Holy Image for the men and women under their

Bishop Jerome Hastrich founder of the Queen of the Americas Guild with Fr. Christopher Rengers, OFM Cap on his left and Fr. Jacob Joeger, OP on his right.

command. Following their enthusiastic response, more that 60,000 of these durable cards were printed in record time and shipped to Saudi Arabia. One grateful chaplain wrote, "Many thanks for providing the Our Lady of Guadalupe holy cards for our service people with Operation Desert Shield/Storm. I am sure that, through her

Above: the founding members of the Guild who attended the original conference at Emmitsburg.

powerful intercession, we were spared a long conflict with massive casualties."

The most ambitious project of the Guild, without a doubt, is the plan for an English-speaking Retreat Center near the shrine in Mexico City. After 12 years of searching and negotiating, I finally found the perfect site which we had envisioned for a Center. On December 13, 1991, the day after the feast of Our Lady of Guadalupe, the contract for the property was signed in the sacristy of the shrine.

The property is at the base of Tepeyac Hill, where Our Lady appeared to Juan Diego. There is nothing to obstruct the view of the hill and the beautiful Basilica gardens. Glass walls will afford a panoramic view of the rose gardens at the base of the hill. Just 200 yards from the front entrance of the Basilica, the center will be a cloistered haven from the urban sights and noises that abound in the surrounding streets. The retreat center will have its own chapel, meeting rooms and dining facility. Acquiring the property was the first major step; now the immediate goal of the Guild is to put up a modern up-to-date building on this providential site.

In May of 1995 members of the Queen of the Americas Guild were saddened by the death of Bishop Hastrich, the Guild's Founder. When I visited the Bishop shortly before he died, we talked about the Queen of the Americas Guild, its past and its future. He was very pleased with what we had accomplished since 1980 and was honored to be a part of it. He had very clear hopes for the future. We also talked about the retreat center and he expressed the hope that our dreams for the center would not die with him. With another special friend in heaven, we of the Queen of the Americas Guild, still feel strongly confident of its continuation and growth.

The apostolate of making Our Lady of Guadalupe better known in the States is not only a national effort, but local Guild Chapters are being formed under the titles of the two places where she appeared. The first, Tepeyac, is named after the hill where she first appeared to Juan Diego and has as its purpose the same overall purpose as the national organization, with great emphasis on devotion to Our Lady. The second is named after Tulpetlac, the town eight miles north of Tepeyac, where Mary appeared to Juan Diego's uncle, Juan Bernardino, and cured him of a mortal illness. Their emphasis is on works of charity such as caring for the sick and elderly and helping poor and troubled people.

The Guild continues its mission of making Our Lady of

Guadalupe better known as the special Patroness of **all** the Americas. Through the propagation of her Holy Image, literature and conferences, the Guild is making its contribution in hastening the day when she will be recognized Queen of the Americas. When she appeared in 1531 in the center of the Americas, (North, Central and South America), before there were any national boundaries she assured all of us in the western hemisphere that she is indeed: "The merciful mother of all of you who live united in this land." It is up to us now to recognize that Queenship.

For further information: QUEEN OF THE AMERICAS GUILD, 345 Kautz Road, P.O. Box 851, St. Charles, IL 60174 Phone: (630) 584-1822.

The late Susan Maloney
Reports from the Shrine

Susan was the director of the English-speaking office at the shrine for only a few years, but in that short space of time she endeared herself to everyone. She wrote the following article, which highlights her enthusiasm and love for Our Lady of Guadalupe.

How do you sum up two years of being at the Basilica? I've come to the conclusion that there is only one way to express it - The Wonder of it All - as fresh today for me as it was two years ago. The stream of pilgrims never stops. They come in all types of weather, in a constant flow. Recently, we have had heavy rains, deluges and still they come -

The late Susan Maloney at her post in 1990.

individually, families, pilgrimages - a continuing source of amazement to me.

Some of the highlights of the two years are some of the very special groups. On Palm Sunday afternoon, the bird vendors of Mexico City came with all types of beautiful birds in cages decorated with flowers and ribbons and always with the Image of Our Lady. These cages fit on top of each other and, at times, reached six feet tall. These were placed on the main altar, and what a lovely sound as the birds sang to Our Lady!

One of my favorite stories concerns this pilgrimage. I was taking snapshots on the main altar when I saw a beautiful parrot in his decorated cage. I asked the vendor if the parrot talked. Before the vendor could reply, the parrot said in perfect Spanish, "I love my Mother, also." It is true of all creatures great and small. Another of my fa-

vorites, are the clowns of Mexico City. They come in full regalia with their families. What a wonderful sight as they come in procession up Guadalupe Avenue! Last year they not only came, but with them came a lion and a tiger in cages and three elephants - Mama, Daddy and Baby. The elephants came into the main plaza, and when the clowns entered the basilica for Mass, the elephants knelt at the entrance to be blessed.

The fireworks manufacturers came in November with their fireworks. The main plaza became a dazzling two-hour display of all types of fireworks - all in honor of Our Lady of Guadalupe. Fantastic! During December, taxis become difficult to find since every day a different association brings its decorated, beribboned taxis to be blessed. One of the most unusual sights for me was one day as I came home, there were the garbage trucks from all parts of the city, cleaned, shined and decorated with the employees in spotless white uniforms. Where else could it happen? I think for me the surprising

groups are the businesses, hotels, restaurants, airlines, banks, markets - all kinds, all types. And so they come - by foot, truck, bus, metro, car, taxi - to visit Our Lady, Our Mother.

PART IX

Guadalupan Theology and Spirituality

1. Guadalupe, Franciscans and . . .
the Immaculate Conception
Fr. Peter Fehlner, F.F.I.

2. Guadalupe in the . . .
Bible and Liturgy
Fr. Martinus Cawley, O.C.S.O.

From the very beginning, the Image of Mary of Guadalupe was identified by Spaniards and Indians alike, as the Immaculate Conception. But, few knew the intimate connection between Guadalupe and the Friars of the Immaculate Conception, as the Franciscans were known at that time.

Guadalupe, The Immaculate Conception and the Franciscans

Fr. Peter Fehlner, F.F.I.

*I*s there a link between Guadalupe and the Immaculate Conception? From the time of the apparition and first glimpse of the Miraculous Image on the tilma of Bl. Juan Diego, Catholics: Spaniards and Indian, American and European, have always believed there is a relation between Mary Immaculate and Guadalupe.

But toward the end of the "age of enlightenment," the 18th century, voices increasingly more strident have denied any such connection. Clearly, these "voices" are often identical with those who doubt or deny the historicity and/or supernatural nature of the apparitions. The arguments they use and the conclusions they reach exactly parallel those of modernists who claim one can deny the historicity of the infancy narratives, but still believe as a Catholic in the "symbolic" value of Marian dogmas such as the divine motherhood and perpetual virginity.

As so frequently happens, those attacking the truths of Faith unwittingly draw the attention of believers to the importance of facts easily discovered, yet commonly overlooked, which justify the traditional belief. In this case it is the role played by the Franciscans who assured that the link, intended by Our Lady, would be seen. That link has been explained over the centuries to rest upon the Franciscan influence in Spain and the New World.

During the first 200 years after the apparition, belief in a link between Guadalupe and the Immaculate Conception usually is evident in discussions of the "Woman clothed with the sun" (Apoc. 12,1 ff) plainly recalled by the Miraculous Figure of the Mother of God on the tilma. By 1531 it was commonplace among Catholics to identify the Woman of the Apocalypse the Woman who crushes the head of the serpent (Gen. 3,15), with the Mother of God, Coredemptrix and Queen, under the title of Immaculate Conception. The popular awareness of that identity and of its significance is the result of the role played by the Franciscan Order. It was the Franciscan theologian, Bl. John Duns Scotus (1266?-1308), who worked out the classic theology of the Immaculate Conception. Since then, Franciscan preachers and missionaries, guided by his profound insights, effectively contributed to the acceptance of his "thesis" throughout the Church. A good example of this kind of "borrowing Franciscan insights" without mentioning the Franciscans, is to be found in the writings of the Mexican Miguel Sánchez (1594-1674). As long as one is aware of and accepts the assumptions of the Franciscan "thesis" about the Immaculate, then the reference to the text of the Apocalypse mirrored on the tilma clearly says: She is the Immaculate Woman.

More recently, defenders of the tradition have brought forward arguments based on the words which our Lady used to identify herself to Juan Bernardino (see article page 179). Thus, Helen Behrens popularized the view that in identifying herself Our Lady used, not the Spanish name *Guadalupe*, but a word in Nahuatl: *Quetzalcoatl*, i.e., I am the one who has crushed the head of the serpent (who demands human sacrifice). To Spanish ears that word spoken by Juan Bernardino would have sounded like *Guadalupe*; whence the link with the Spanish shrine and the popular name of the Mexican shrine.

Now, the meaning assigned *Quetzalcóatl* in this thesis (crushing the head of the serpent) has come under considerable fire from students of Nahuatl and of Aztec culture. The sometimes heated exchanges, concentrating on what is a secondary point in regard to our theme, distract from the essential contribution of Helen Behrens. She called the attention of the English speaking public to some true facts.

First, Our Lady of Guadalupe in Mexico really is the Immaculate, the "Perfect Virgin" of the *Nican Mopohua*. In bringing about the conversion of nations to Jesus she does in some real sense crush the head of the enemy of the Savior and our salvation, whatever form this opposition takes. She, the Mother of mercy, because she is the Immaculate, intervenes in history to secure the conversion, sanctification and salvation of all peoples.

Second, *Quetzalcóatl*, the word used by Juan Bernardino, what-

The Statue of the Immaculate Conception in the Estremadura Shrine in Spain, placed in the shrine by the Franciscans toward the end of the 15th century.

ever it means in Nahuatl, when pronounced does sound like *Guadalupe* in Spanish! But to say that the link between Guadalupe and the Immaculate is based only on the misunderstanding of the word *Guadalupe* is a capital error. This fails to take into account the role played by the Franciscans at both Guadalupan shrines.

By the end of the 15th century the Franciscans had placed in the shrine of Our Lady of Guadalupe in Extremadura a statue of the Immaculate Conception, one which soon became a popular object of veneration. There is also good evidence that the same statue had already been made known by the Franciscan missionaries in Mexico to the Indians and that perhaps a reproduction was already venerated in the vicinity of Tepeyac.

Now, the similarity between the depiction of the Immaculate in the statue placed by the Friars Minor in the sanctuary of Extremadura and the Image on the tilma is extraordinarily close, so close that anyone from the region of Extramadura, like the Spanish translator in the Bishop's palace, hearing what sounded like *Guadalupe*, would have spontaneously associated this Image with the Immaculate Conception statue in Spain.

In the Franciscan tradition the Immaculate is Our Lady, Queen of the Angels, whose *Portiuncula* (Little Portion) was the chapel where Angels were often seen to descend and ascend, waiting on their Queen and her clients, "the rest of her offspring," i.e., the rest of the Savior's brethren (cf. Apoc. 12:17). This is the place where St. Francis came to understand his vocation, found his Order and where he died.

When, therefore, the good Bishop beheld the roses spilling on the floor, it was not only a sign that he could believe Juan Diego, but an answer to his own prayer for a sign assuring the success of the evangelization and the pacification of the two peoples. When he saw the image of Our Lady supported by an angel at her feet on the tilma, he could not help but recognize the Franciscan mode of conceiving the Immaculate as Queen of the Angels. The link between Guadalupe in Mexico, Guadalupe in Spain and the Immaculate Conception was fixed. The core of the *Perfect Virgin's* message at every authenticated appearance since, because she is the Immaculate, rests upon her maternal mediation as Dispenstrix of God's mercy and grace. It is she upon whom the Angels wait, the Angels venerated at both Guadalupe shrines.

The sacred Image of Guadalupe has a striking resemblance to the statue in Estremadura Shrine.

The association between Guadalupe in Mexico and the Immaculate Conception was perceived immediately, not only in Mexico, but in Europe as well. More and more as the Miracle came to be known representations of the Immaculate Conception reflected the likeness on Bl. Juan Diego's tilma. With the decisive victory of the Christian fleet over the the more powerful Moslems at Lepanto, lifting the threat of the infidels over the whole of Europe, through a copy of the Icon (described in the article on page 101), the Immaculate Conception came to occupy center stage in the Catholic counter-reformation. She is the *Auxiliatrix Christianorum* - Help of Christians.

This, therefore, is what the tradition uniformly assumed. To get around the obvious, skeptics interpreted references to the Woman of Apocalypse, such as those of Miguel Sánchez, the 17th century commentator, as inspired by *criollo* patriotism, rather than as they always have been understood: testimonials to the common belief in the Immaculate Conception reflected by the Image on the tilma. There is no indication that Sanchez or Bl. Juan Diego or our Lady anticipate a liberation theology interpretation of the *Magnificat.* The proof is all to the contrary.

The role of Franciscan piety in the origins of Guadalupe is understandable in the context of the Franciscan influence in Spain and Mexico, an influence explicitly and almost aggressively "Immaculatist." At the time of the apparitions the Franciscan Order was popularly known as the one which "preached the Immaculate Conception." Our Lady appearing at Tepeyac made use of Franciscans and their long tradition of devotion to the Immaculate, first of all in the person of Bishop Zumárraga, who openly supported the building of the first church at the site which she indicated.

The Franciscan spirituality, plus the urgency of the times, inspired and impelled Christopher Columbus, a Third Order Franciscan, in his expeditions (see article on page 19). He was quite familiar with the Apocalypse, in particular chapter 12, with its account of the opening of the Ark of the Covenant in heaven and the appearance of the Woman clothed with the sun, who literally is the Ark. This is the same biblical reference which played so central a role in the iconography of the tilma. There Our Lady blots out the sun, indicating she is greater than the sun god whom the Aztecs worshiped. She has the moon beneath her feet and stars on her robe which places her above and beyond mere terrestrial creation.

Guadalupe is not an explanation of the Immaculate Conception as such. Rather it is a heavenly confirmation of the basis for her universal maternal mediation as the Immaculate One, and so provides the key to the understanding of the successful evangelization of Mexico and of all people and nations. It is no accident that in every authentic appearance of our Lady since 1531, in some way these two themes: Immaculate Conception and Marian mediation are involved. In a word, the appearance of the *Perfect Virgin* declares the wonders of divine grace and glory over a world darkened by sin: the degradation of false worship involving human sacrifice, and the enslavement of neighbor through unjust amassment of riches.

Similarly, today vast numbers of souls are enslaved by the idolatry of sensual pleasure. Instead of worshiping the Child of the Virgin as Our Lady of Guadalupe asked, they sacrifice their offspring and their fecundity to the demands of lust and greed. How needed it is to look upon and listen to the Mother of Tepeyac, the Mother of Life and heed her requests to build a temple for the Holy Spirit in their souls in imitation of the Immaculate Virgin's purity, modesty and chastity.

Guadalupe, then, is no mere symbolic myth as one prestigious anti-apparitionist claims and this book refutes. Guadalupe is above all a person, the *Perfect Virgin*, our Mother of mercy, a model to be imitated, and a living Mother who anticipates our needs as when she intervenes in our history: for the sake of our salvation, for the sake of our welfare as pilgrims in this world. As a Mother to all she deliberately spoke in a way that both nations, Indian and Spanish, would understand the same mystery at Extremadura and at Tepeyac - the Immaculate Virgin in her unique role as Mother of all men.

Before airing questions of inculturation, politics, economics, etc., there is need for unity of Faith in her Son. This is possible only when she is humbly acknowledged to be the Mother of God as in Mexico by both nations through the erection of a temple in her honor. Where this is not recognized, there will be constant conflict and revolution. The genius of Catholicism, of Catholic political philosophy and culture, is the *Perfect Virgin*.

"Behold your Mother," Jesus says to St. John (Jn 19:26). To all his "beloved disciples" could He not also be saying before the tilma of Bl. Juan Diego: Behold the Woman of Revelation, the Immaculate? The more we grasp and live this mystery, the foundation of the Virgin's compassionate, motherly mediation, the greater our understanding of the person and work of her Son and Savior, and our sharing in His life. Blessed, indeed, those who behold their Immaculate Mother and, as the Son asks, take her into their homes by true devotion to Mary: by total consecration to the Immaculate.

The Franciscan Role in
Promoting the Immaculate Conception

From its founding by St. Francis of Assisi the Friars Minor have been recognized as a Marian Order, Marian because it strives to live the hidden life of Mary Immaculate and so identifies with the poor, crucified Christ. Their Marian piety has ever been characterized by total consecration to the Mother of God under the title of Immaculate Conception, Mediatrix of all graces. Throughout its 750 year existence we see this exemplified in the many great Marian saints of the Order, the latest being St. Maximilian Mary Kolbe.

Even centuries before Franciscan Bishop Juan Zumárraga beheld the miraculous image on the tilma of Bl. Juan Diego as the Immaculate Conception, there was a close association of the Immaculate Conception and the Franciscan Order. It was one of their theologians, Bl. Duns Scotus (1266? - 1308), whose theological argumentation, eventually accepted by the Church, which cleared the way for the definition of Mary's Immaculate Conception in 1854 by Pope Pius IX.

The Marian spirituality of the Seraphic Order played a predominant role in shaping the mind and heart of Catholic Spain during the late 15th and 16th centuries, making her a bulwark of Catholicism at the moment of the division and disintegration of Christendom. We need only recall the work of the Franciscan Cardinal Ximenes in the reform of Spanish Catholicism and the political system of Spain. The great Franciscan reform movements and the writings of the Franciscan mystics* prepared the way for great saints of other orders: Teresa of Avila, John of the Cross, and many others such as Louis of Granada and Ignatius of Loyola were indebted to the spirit and theory of this spirituality with its accent ever on the Immaculate Conception of Mary.

—Fr. Peter Damian M. Fehlner, F.F.I.

---

*Alonso of Madrid, *The Art of Serving God*; Francisco de Osuna, *The Spiritual Alphabet*; Bernardino of Laredo, *The Ascent of Mount Sion*; St. Peter of Alcantara, *Golden Book of Meditation*; Miguel de Medina, *Spiritual Childhood*; Bl. Nicholas Factor, *The Three Ways*; Diego de Estella, *Meditations on the Love of God*; Juan de los Angelos, *Marian Slavery*; Melchor de Cetina, *Devotion to the Virgin*.

Guadalupe in the Bible and Liturgy

Fr. Martinus Cawley, O.C.S.O.

*I*n the Acts of the Apostles, St. Paul tells the story of his conversion to two separate audiences: a throng of Jewish Zealots in
the Temple (Acts 2:.40-22:21) and the secularized King Agrippa
in cosmopolitan Caesarea (Acts 26:2-23). He charms both audiences
by speaking to each in its own language and echoing its own ways
of expression. It is the same with the Guadalupe story: when printed for Spanish readers, allusions to the Bible are accounted a precious ornament; but when solemnly recited to Aztec listeners,
adornment of another kind is needed.

The classical Nahuatl narrator catches his Indians' attention by
naming their suffering and the needs uppermost in their daily lives.
He uses his powerful eloquence to pile up striking phrases that give
the sufferings dignity. He insists that the needs are known to a
heavenly Lady, whose motherly concern he describes in images familiar from village life. He weaves into his discourse, not the far-
away world of the Bible but the nearby landmarks of parish life, the
divine titles from the catechesis, the prayers known by heart, the
sacraments: those realities that link the daily sufferings with the
lofty hopes entertained for the hour of death. He strives to set the
hearer at ease with Mother Church, ready to face suffering and
death with contented confidence.

Of the early Spanish narrators, just one stands out for his biblical allusions, Miguel Sánchez, and he stands out very sharply. He
published his Guadalupan narrative in 1648, bolstering it with letters to and from his friends. These friends form with him a "new
breed" of Mexican-born clergy, trained in the new style of the
Council of Trent and in the new Baroque approach to the Bible, the
Fathers, the Liturgy and to piety in general. Even recreational ban-

ter among such men can become a game of dominoes: mention any name and I'll match it with an echo from the Bible; match my echo, and I'll match another word of yours! Were it not for their mutual sensitivity, this could slip into one-upmanship; but such was Sánchez' courtesy, and such charm was there in his voice, that he was one of the city's favorite preachers. Far from affectation, they found his style a guide to their identity as a group.

Sánchez' main biblical allusion is ever to the heavenly Woman of Apocalypse 12. He guides us through this chapter three times over, spending some 50 pages to do so. His whole thrust could be paraphrased: "The heavenly Woman, who first appeared to John on Patmos, has now reappeared to another John, near another island, the lake-bound City of Mexico. She thus inserts Mexico into Sacred History and gives to the conquerors and clergy of this land a divine charter and a divine call." This was "heady stuff" for Sánchez himself and for the minor clergy among his friends. Little wonder they thronged to his sermons and urged him to get them into print. They wanted his biblical allusions in full force.

But Spanish layfolk, unfamiliar with the Latin of Sánchez' citations, found his whole text tiresomely long. These mainly wanted his basic story, but would also welcome a few sidelights, connecting it with familiar landmarks and with other devotions already dear to their prayer life, such as the feast of the Immaculate Conception and the shrine of Los Remedios west of the city, as well as the older Guadalupe back in Spain. Precisely these basics and these sidelights were supplied for them when, in 1660, the popular Mateo de la Cruz did an abridged edition of Sánchez' work. He does retain one Apocalyptic allusion, but drops its patriotic reference and makes it hint at the Immaculate Conception.*

"Blessed are the eyes that see what you are seeing!"

Very different was another biblical allusion, made almost 100 years earlier. It was the mid-1550s, and miracles were being reported

---

*Editor's Note: Nevertheless, Sánchez' reference to Guadalupe in terms of the Immaculate Conception is not without basis in the Apocalypse. For in Chapter 12, St. John identifies the Woman clothed with the sun, with the Woman of Gen. 3:15, the Woman whom the Church understands to be the Mother of the Savior, conceived without stain of original sin, and so worthy to be the Ark of the Covenant (cf. Revelations 11:19).

An imaginative portrayal of the Trinity collaborating in the painting of the image of Our Lady of Guadalupe. Since 1680, the words Non Fecit Taliter Omni Nationi (Thou has not done the like for any other nation) have been applied to the Mexican nation.

at Tepeyac in abundance. The newly arrived Dominican Archbishop, Alonso Montúfar, was familiar with the great miracle shrines of Spain and the moral uplift they brought to their cities. Thus he was most eager to have such a shrine bring refinement to his own frontier See. But before he could make canonical inquiries, leading Franciscans took alarm, for they feared that the Indians would expect automatic miracles and inevitably be disappointed to the verge of apostasy. Rumor of such nasty comments led Montúfar to announce from the pulpit that, while the individual miracles of healing were still under investigation, one thing was already clear,

Guadalupe's popularity had been bringing the town a moral transformation which all Christians should applaud.

He made this announcement in a sermon whose theme he epitomized by opening it with the text: "Blessed are the eyes that see what you are seeing!" (Lk 10.23; cf. Mt 13.16). If Sánchez tended to force biblical texts, Montúfar was forcing nothing: he was giving his text exactly the meaning it had in the Gospel, where it contrasts the "little ones," who recognize Jesus, with the "wise and clever," who miss his point.

In itself, Montúfar's insight was simple enough. Visitors to Tepeyac even today are moved to similar acclaim of the faith they behold in the faces of the ordinary pilgrims. But his choice of that text, using so correctly the very words of Christ, deserves to be immortalized in the Guadalupan liturgy.

She Has not Done the Like for Any Nation

Another text has long since become a leitmotif both of Guadalupe's liturgy and its iconography: the last verse of Psalm 147. This Psalm had always been sung at Vespers on feasts of Our Lady, aptly applying to her its crescendo of enthusiasm for Mother Jerusalem. The climax comes in this final verse with the words: "He (God) has not done the like for any nation, nor made so manifest to them His decisions."

It so happens that the Latin here leaves open the gender of the pronouns, "he/she," allowing the singer to think "she" for "he" and "her" for "his." In this way, with all the rich overtones of the Word of God, the choir sings out: "SHE (Mary) has not done the like for any nation!" Heady stuff for the Mexicans! And as early as the 1680's prominent Guadalupans were stamping these Latin words on medals and holy cards in Our Lady's honor: NON FECIT TALITER OMNI NATIONI.

By the 1750's the words had become so popular that they were proposed for use as a refrain in the Guadalupan liturgy. The Pope at the time was known to be somewhat of a stickler, and it was dreaded that he might not like that shift of gender in the verb. But the story arose that, during the interview about the new texts, he was suddenly shown a copy of the Sacred Image and, in his astonishment, came out spontaneously with these very words. Hence the frequent inscription attributing them to "Pope Benedict XIV."

The play between the genders works as well in Spanish as in Latin, but it becomes awkward in English. Also, the play works less happily in the second half of the verse than in the first. And finally, taken as a childlike expression of patriotism, the key words are fitting on Mexican lips, but elsewhere sound a bit odd. Better to highlight a phrase like Montúfar's "Blessed the eyes that see . . ."

Other Texts Prominent in the Guadalupan Liturgy

Other prominent texts in the Guadalupan liturgy are shared either with other Marian feasts, such as the Holy Rosary or the Visitation, and also by the Common for the Dedication of a Church: especially striking are those that speak of Our Lady's choice of Tepeyac in the same terms as Divine Wisdom's decision to "pitch her tent" in Jacob and Yahweh's choice of Zion as his dwelling-place. A stirring Latin melody gives great dignity to the following, as applied to Tepeyac: "I have chosen and hallowed this place, that my name be here forever, and my eyes and my heart dwell upon it for all days to come." (II Chroniclés 7:16).

While the great stress is thus put on the heavenly honor done in Our Lady's "visiting" our land, there are also minor themes of the land's blossoming into flowers and rainbows in response. Such passages are drawn from the Wisdom literature, and especially the Song of Songs.

The heavenly Woman of the Apocalypse is prominent too, and the traditional Gospel reading is that of the Visitation (Lk 1:39-56). This last is important for homilists concerned with social justice, for it enables them to juxtapose Our Lady's promises at Tepeyac with what she says in her *Magnificat* about the vindication of the poor.

How to Blend Guadalupan Devotion with a Modern Love for the Bible

We each have our own starting point for thinking about Guadalupe: a place to visit on pilgrimage; or an Image of Providence with feminine features and tones; or an astounding miracle, fit to refute the atheism of our times. Whatever our approach, the Bible can enrich it, but can also warn us of pitfalls ahead.

A pilgrimage to Tepeyac can borrow dignity from the memory of Jacob's march to Bethel or that of Moses or Elijah to Sinai

(Horeb) or David's and Solomon's triumphs on Mount Zion itself. But let us also hear little Amos of Teqoa's warnings about excesses at Bethel, and Jeremiah's about abuses in Jerusalem, and all the New Testament says against "temples built by human hands." A rich echo of all these themes is caught in an old title for Tepeyac: *"extramuros de Mexico,"* "a shrine reached by going *away from* the city, just *a little ways away,* but *far enough away* to escape our myopia and to regain perspective on Providence . . .."

Or perhaps the femininity, the motherliness of Guadalupe most captures our heart: the tenderness of her countenance, the gentleness of her words, the thrill of her healing hand upon someone near or dear to us. Then let us have as backdrop to her hand, the hand of her Son in the Gospel; let us see her motherly providence silhouetted in the fatherly love announced in the Sermon on the Mount. There is a mystery here: Providence personified as Mother, in terms of Mary the creature, and personified as Father in terms of the Divine Creator.

Our Lady has given us the tilma to enjoy, meaning it to be for us an earnest of further gifts to come. So long as we stay childlike and rejoice in her motherly gifts, we are in harmony both with her and with the Bible. Indeed, we are never more in harmony than when we make the most of the earliest of all Guadalupan biblical texts, cited so spontaneously by Archbishop Montúfar: "Blessed are the eyes that see what we have been granted to see . . ."

Links Between Scriptures and Tepeyac Revealed to Little Ones

The traditional links between the Scriptures and the Miracle at Tepeyac are so many clues to the mystery of Christ and Mary, of the New Adam and the New Eve, which the Miracle makes real, so easily understood, yet accessible only to the little ones who believe. Those who follow them and persevere in a living Faith will find all their hopes and desires for mercy and peace fulfilled, now and in the life to come, in the enjoyment of that heavenly beauty reflected in the Image on the tilma of Juan Diego.

—Fr. Peter Fehlner, F.F.I.

PART X

The Authenticity of Guadalupe

No apparitions of Our Lady have the approval of so many Popes as Guadalupe. The first two bishops in Mexico City gave their full support. Although there is little early documentation, this does not in any way warrant the questioning of its authenticity. The Miraculous Image itself is argument enough to answer the anti-apparitionists.

What the Church . . .
Has to Say about Guadalupe

Bro. Francis Mary, F.F.I.

*T*hey say that the weakest argument is the one based on authority. That may be true generally speaking, but when it comes to matters of Faith, Christians look to God as the final authority, and we Catholics look to the Church, the voice of Christ in our times, for our answers. When it comes to accepting an apparition of Our Lady as authentic and worthy of belief and devotion, we first look to the local bishop who has the authority of accepting or rejecting it. In the case of the apparitions of Our Lady of Guadalupe in Mexico City in 1531, that person was Bishop Juan Zumárraga. He was still to be consecrated a bishop when he was told by Our Lady, through her emissary, Juan Diego, to "build my house of God that I am asking for."

The sign he asked for turned out to be greater than he would ever have imagined in his wildest dreams. The evidence of the miraculous image on the tilma of Juan Diego was all he needed to go ahead and "build the Sacred Little House," which Our Lady had requested, in the short space of eight working days. This in itself was as good a sign of the approbation of the bishop as any written decree would be, which would come much later. But why didn't the Bishop follow up with an official letter of approval? There could be several reasons.

First, it would have been imprudent and an invitation to trouble and misunderstanding both by the secular and by the religious Spaniards at that time. Although the suppressive regime of the First Audiencia had been replaced by a more benign civil government, there were still powerful and violent adventurers ready to resist anything which could be interpreted as favoring the Indians over the Spanish administration. Being vocal in supporting an Indian devotion could have brought further persecution and ridicule on the

Bishop who had suffered much already, including threats on his life. Moreover, his Franciscan confreres were very cautious about supporting any devotion attributed to an Indian which might be misinterpreted as a carry-over from worship of one of their pagan deities. The prudence of Bishop Zumárraga is borne out in the subsequent opposition to his successor, Archbishop Alonso Montúfar, by the over-cautious Franciscans who openly contested his support of the Guadalupan devotion among the Indians. So bitter was the disagreement over the way the devotions to Our Lady of Guadalupe should be handled, that the Archbishop turned the sanctuary over to the diocesan clergy, and an official silence descended upon Guadalupe.

This too would explain the scarcity of documentation in those early years. Besides this, there was a scarcity of paper. In a letter to Emperor Charles V, Bishop Zumárraga had lamented that "little progress was made with his printing," due to an acute shortage of paper. In the twenty years he was bishop in Mexico there is but one signature of his to be found on an official document in Mexico. Bishop Zumárraga recognized the Hand of God in the Miraculous Image, and in founding the Sanctuary at Tepeyac, in allowing public worship there, he had done all that was required of him as the local bishop in showing his approval.

The second bishop of Mexico, Archbishop Alonso de Montúfar, who openly supported the devotion to Our Lady of Guadalupe, saw in it positive signs of conversion and piety, and a wonderful means of evangelizing the Indians. However, in doing so, he precipitated a vocal, public reaction from the Provincial Superior of the Franciscans, Francisco de Bustamante. The existence of his sermon, and the incident that it caused, did confirm the fact that there was already a widespread devotion to Mary of Guadalupe and her Miraculous Image by 1556. There are some who question the authenticity of this incident. They say that it is hoax perpetuated by 19th century anti-apparitionists, but it seems quite unlikely since in the end it actually supports the authenticity of Guadalupe. Stronger evidence of Archbishop Montófar's support, is the fact that he didn't hesitate to build a larger chapel to accommodate the many pilgrims coming to the shrine.

Approval from Rome, which never precedes that of the local diocesan Ordinary, was slow in coming. The first recognition of Guadalupe from Rome was a memorandum issued by Pope Gregory XIII in 1575, extending the indulgences granted by his predecessor to the Guadalupe Shrine. Several Popes after him also gave their blessing to the Tepeyac Shrine. Due to the lack of communications from Mexico about Guadalupe, support from the Holy See was understandably slow. Yet, of the 46 Popes who have reigned since the apparitions, 26 of them have issued decrees underlining their belief and approval, and practically all of the modern day Popes have been lavish in words and deeds in promoting devotion to Our Lady of Guadalupe.

In 1754, the Mexicans sent Fr. Juan López, S.J. to Rome to petition the Holy Father for further formal recognition of Guadalupe. When he unrolled the reproduction of the Sacred Image painted by the famous Mexican artist, Manuel Cabrera, before Pope Benedict XIV (1740-1758) the Pope fell on his knees and exclaimed, "To no other nation has this been done" (Psalm 147). He was from that moment on, one of the most ardent promoters of Our Lady of Guadalupe and authorized the crowning of the Sacred Image, which unfortunately, through a series of unanticipated events, was not carried out until 1895.

Upon viewing the painting of Our Lady of Guadalupe Pope Benedict XIV exclaimed "To no other nation has this been done" (Psalm 147).

Pope Benedict XIV decreed that Dec. 12th be a Holy Day of Obligation with an octave of the first class for the Mexican Church, and later extended it to all Spanish-speaking countries. He personally composed the Collect for the Mass and made the Sanctuary of Guadalupe equal in rank to the Lateran Basilica. He also issued a Bull approving Our Lady of Guadalupe as Patroness of Mexico. Besides Alexander VII and Benedict XIV, eighteen other popes have been liberal in granting indulgences and privileges to the Images, Churches, Chapters, Sodalities, etc., of Our Lady of Guadalupe. In 1805, Pope Pius VII attached the Sanctuary of Guadalupe permanently to the Basilica of St. John Lateran. To appreciate this honor, one must realize that the Lateran Basilica is the second most important Catholic church in the world after St. Peter's in Rome. The Guadalupe Sanctuary itself was raised to Basilica status in 1904 by St. Pius X.

In 1894, Pope Leo XIII approved the new Office and Mass of Our Lady of Guadalupe, and authorized the crowning of the Sacred Image, which took place the following year on October 12 (see

The Pontifical Coronation of the sacred Image of Our Lady of Guadalupe on October 12, 1895. Two Archbishops had the honor of crowning the Image amid loud cries of, "Viva la Virgin de Guadalupe." See story on page 125.

article on page 125; also above). On that occasion he composed a poem which was engraved on the marble beneath the Sacred Image:

> **"Happy in the possession of Thy Miraculous Image**
> **The Mexican people rejoice in Thy sway**
> **And firm in their Faith and Thy Patronage, Pray**
> **Thy Son's Will always govern their land."**

On August 24, 1910, at the request of seventy Latin American bishops, Pope Saint Pius X proclaimed Holy Mary of Guadalupe "Patroness of the whole of Latin America." Pope Pius XI confirmed this title again in 1933. Pius XII and three Popes since have continued to give much attention in honoring Mary of Guadalupe. Pope Pius XII established nine shrines in Italy dedicated to Our Lady of Guadalupe and ordered the image crowned again in his name on October 12, 1945, on the 50th anniversary of the coronation by Pope Leo XIII. It was Pope Pius XII who proclaimed Mary **Empress of All the Americas.** On that occasion, he broadcast a radio message to Mexicans and all Americans during which he recited a beautiful prayer to her. The following is the conclusion of that prayer he himself composed:

"Hail, O Virgin of Guadalupe! We to whom the admirable ordering of Providence has confided (not taking into account our unworthiness) the sacred treasure of Divine Wisdom on earth for the salvation of souls, place again upon your brow the crown that forever places under your powerful patronage the purity and integrity of the Mexican faith and of the entire American continent. *For we are certain that as long as you are recognized as Queen and Mother, Mexico and America will be safe."*

Pope John XXIII proclaimed a Marian Year from Dec. 12, 1960, to Dec. 12, 1961, and extolled her as the "Mother of the Americas." The last time he left the Vatican before his final illness, he dedicated a church in Rome to Our Lady of Guadalupe. To express his filial devotion to Mary on that occasion, he sought her intercession: ". . . From the sanctuary of Tepeyac, for more than four centuries you have been the Mother and Teacher of the Faith to the peoples of the Americas. Be also our protector and save us, O Immaculate Mary . . . "

Pope Paul VI reintroduced a beautiful custom of presenting a Golden Rose to an outstanding shrine of Our Lady, and authorized this singular honor to the Image of Our Lady of Guadalupe on March 25, 1966. He subsequently accorded the same honor to only two other Marian shrines, Lourdes and Fatima. On October 12, 1970, he made a Telestar appearance to the people of Mexico to commemorate the 75th anniversary, 1895-1970, of the crowning of Our Lady as Queen of Mexico and Empress of all the Americas.

In January of 1979, the newly elected Pope, John Paul II arrived at the Guadalupe shrine. It was the first of his many world-wide pilgrimages to Marian Shrines. His week-long visit to Mexico was to open and attend the Third General Conference of the Latin-American Episcopate. The day after he arrived in Mexico, January 27, he paid homage before a flower-decked image of Our Lady of Guadalupe on the outside balcony of the new Basilica. He declared:

"Ever since the time that the Indian Juan Diego spoke to the sweet Lady of Tepeyac, you, Mother of Guadalupe, have entered decisively into the Christian life of the people of Mexico." He concelebrated his opening Mass with 300 cardinals and bishops beneath the Miraculous Image.

There is a close bond between Poland, where the Icon of Our Lady of Czestochowa is the center of the country's national identity and history, and Mexico, uniting the two Catholic countries. They both claim Mary as their Queen and have consecrated their nation on a number of occasions to her. Both countries have experienced religious persecution. They both have had martyrs for the Faith. (Remember, this was in 1979 when both countries were still under anti-Catholic governments). So the Holy Father, from Poland had much to share with his Mexican flock. He couldn't help but be moved deeply. Manuel Ramirez of the NC News Service wrote on that occasion:

> **"Some 450 years after a man called Juan Diego talked with the Virgin Mary at Tepeyac Hill, another man called Juan Pablo prayed before the image which she left imprinted on the Indian Juan Diego's cloak. Both men called her 'Mother' and both had tears in their eyes as they pleaded for her help."**

On his second pilgrimage, he beatified Juan Diego on May 6, 1990, and raised to the altar three Tlaxcalan boy-martyrs and a Mexican priest. In his homily the Pope praised the Mexicans for their fidelity to Christ, under Mary:

> **"These five Blesseds are inscribed in an indelible way in the great epic of the evangelization of Mexico. The first four at the dawn of the sowing of the Word in these lands; the fifth in the story of his faithfulness to Christ amid the vicissitudes of the last century. All have lived and given witness to this Faith under the protection of the Virgin Mary. She, in fact, was and continues to be the 'Star of Evangelization,' who with her presence and protection continues nurturing the Faith and strengthening ecclesial communion."**

He touched upon how a layman, Juan Diego, whom the Mexicans had venerated over the centuries,

> **". . . assumes particular importance. It is a strong call to all the lay faithful of the nation to assume all their responsibilities in**

the transmission of the Gospel message and in the witness of a living and operative Faith in Mexican society. From this privileged place of Guadalupe, the heart of always faithful Mexico, I want to call all the Mexican laity to commit themselves more actively to the reevangelization of society."

Pope John Paul II made the first of his many worldwide pilgrimages to the Guadalupe shrine in January, 1979.

From these and other comments it would seem that the Holy Father may be preparing the way to declare Blessed Juan Diego the special patron of the lay apostolate. The theme of re-evangelizing society was stressed again in the summer of that same year when he sent a letter to all Religious in the Americas, on the eve of the fifth century of the evangelization of America:

" I entrust to Our Lady of Guadalupe, who is 'the first evangelizer of Latin America' the longings and hopes which I have confided to you in this letter. She is the real 'Star of Evangelization,' the evangelizer of your people. Her motherly closeness gave a decisive thrust to the preaching of the message of Christ and towards fellowship among Latin American nations and their inhabitants. Devotion to Mary has always been a guarantee of fidelity to the Catholic Faith during these five centuries. May she keep guiding your steps and making your evangelization efforts fruitful."

Perhaps no apparitions of Our Lady have received as much support from the Holy See as those of Our Lady of Guadalupe, especially in our day. What happened in Mexico on the morning of December 12, 1531, is perhaps more relevant and important in our times, as we prepare for the third millennium of Christianity, than that first time when she converted millions. Today she is reaching out to all mankind as the Star of Evangelization to bring them to the fullness of truth, found only in the Church founded by her Son upon the Rock, the Vicar of Christ.

What About the Name "Guadalupe?"

By the Editor

*A*mong a number of controversial issues pertaining to Guadalupe, perhaps the most heated and diverse involves the word "Guadalupe." The question is asked by scholars, "How did Our Lady identify herself to Juan Bernardino, and wish to be known?" The first and the most common is *Holy Mary of Guadalupe.* This interpretation, of the name by which Mary wished to be identified, is found in the earliest account on Guadalupe, the Nican Mopohua. However, it seems unlikely that she used the Spanish, *Santa Maria de Guadalupe,* since the Indians had a difficult time in pronouncing *g* and *d,* sounds which were unknown to them.

The elderly Juan Bernardino, whom Our Lady addressed in his native tongue, probably conveyed the Aztec name to the Spanish interpreter, Juan González. It may have sounded to him like the name associated with the famous Marian shrine in Extremadura, Spain. Moreover, the Image on the tilma, consistently referred to as the Immaculate Conception, is quite similar to the statue of the Immaculate Conception at that shrine. Juan González, coming from that area of Spain, would certainly have associated the Miraculous Icon with the Extremadura statue. Moreover, the Spanish were notorious in not being able to pronounce Nahuatl words. They would naturally change names of people, places etc. into Spanish words having a similar sound.

It wasn't until 1666, over a hundred years after Our Lady had appeared to Juan Bernardino, that anyone seriously questioned the word Guadalupe. At the first official inquiry to validate the Miracle of Tepeyac, the learned scholar, Becerra Tanco, devoted a long footnote on the meaning of Guadalupe, which showed that the word had aroused suspicion among scholars from the beginning. He gave several interpretations of Aztec names sounding similar to the Spanish, *Guadalupe*. The first is Tequatlanopeuh, "She who originated at the summit of the crags," the second Tequantlaxopeuh (pronounced Tequatlashope), which means, "She who saves us from the Devourers" which at that time would mean both Satan and their terrible pagan gods whom they believed demanded countless human sacrifices.

Another scholar, Fr. de Florencia, in his a work, *Estrella del Norte*, concurs with Becerra Tanco that Our Lady did not use the word Guadalupe but the word for the "one who saves us from the Devourer," in the Nahuatl language; again, pointing to the Immaculate Conception. Nothing of further note appeared until 1895, when Prof. D. Mariano Jacobo Rojas, head of the department of Nahuatl at the National Museum of Archeology, History and Ethnography, made a thorough study of the word Guadalupe and concluded that the word Our Lady used in speaking to Juan Bernardino was the Aztec word Coatlaxopeuh which means, "she who breaks, stamps or crushes the serpent," again referring to her Immaculate Conception.

In 1936, Ignacio Davila Garibi, an authority on the Miracle, wrote a tract on the etymology of the word Guadalupe, and in 1953, Fr. A. Montoya Quiralte also published a tract on the same topic. Both writers were in agreement with Professor Rojas. The Belgian Jesuit, Fr. Bernard Bergöend, who spent many years in Mexico researching Guadalupe wrote the book, *"La Nacionalidad Mexicana y la Virgen de Guadalupe."* First published in 1931 and a second edition in 1968, he makes some insightful observations on the name Guadalupe. Basically, Fr. Bergöend shows how unlikely it was that Our Lady used the Arabic name, Guadalupe, so hard to pronounce by the Indians, to identify herself.

Fr. Bergöend then ties in the Immaculate Conception with Guadalupe by showing that she gave the name shortly after the very feast day when the Franciscans were preaching on the Immaculate Conception and would have referred to Our Lady as "she who crushes the serpent," from Genesis 3:15. Among the pantheon of gods that the Aztecs worshiped was the stone serpent which is visible to this day among the many fearsome looking stone carvings decorating their pyramids. If Our Lady used the word Tecoatlaxopeuh, she could not have timed it better. They would understand

When Mary of Guadalupe appeared to Juan Bernardino and cured him, what name did she use to identify herself to him?

that the true God, whose emissary she was, would replace their pagan gods. He adds that the word she used would be the theological equivalent of the Immaculate Conception.

This evidence that Our Lady identified herself as the Immaculate Conception has been taken from a monograph by Dr. Charles Wahlig, "An Analysis of the Word Guadalupe." He concludes: " We must never lose sight of her true significance as the Mother of God and our Mother, she who crushes the head of the serpent, and all the other enemies who try to devour us." However, confusion arises over the name and identity of the stone serpent. In the 50's Helen Behrens, who was one of the first promoters of Guadalupe among the English speaking, accepted the traditional belief which held that Our Lady used the Aztec word Tecoatlaxopeuh in identifying herself as the Woman from Genesis 3:15, the Immaculate Conception. To this day it remains the commonly held interpretation in the United States. She went one step further by naming the Feathered Serpent, Quetzalcóatl whom she identified with the planet Venus which was supposed to have been at one time a comet circling the earth and causing every kind of catastrophe. She mistook this comet with a fiery tail, similar to a ferocious serpent of fire, to be the principal god to whom the Aztecs offered countless human sacrifices to head off disaster.

Dr. Wahlig accepted her interpretation of Quetzalcóatl to be the chief god that Our Lady came to stamp out, perhaps because of its similarity to the serpent in Genesis. However, most scholars today reject Behren's thesis. The name Quetzalcóatl also refers to a cultural-hero-king who taught his subjects to worship a Supreme Being who did not require human sacrifice and is regarded now as a "seed of the Gospel" (see reference to Religion on page 31).

Janet Barber points out that Fr. Mario Rojas Sánchez, who is one of the foremost living experts on the Nahuatl language and a Guadalupan scholar, gives another interpretation of the word Guadalupe, "Whatever name is suggested must be in character with the entire narration, which is consistently constructive and kind. . . . The drama uses only positive and legitimate elements of the former religion to give the new Message." Barber further points out that Rojas proposes, and Clodomiro Siller agrees with him, that "the Virgin Mary very likely gave the name Tlecuautlapcupeuh, which would mean "She who proceeds from the region of light like the fire eagle." Its cultural content would expand the meaning to 'She who comes flying from the region of light and music and singing a song, like the fire eagle." Rojas explains that to the Indians fire is the element that recalls the place where God lives and acts. The eagle is the symbol of the sun and divinity. The East was the region of Light, and also the region of music. The verb can mean to proceed from, to fly, to sing a song, among other possibilities.

"This interpretation, of course, does not deter other students of Guadalupe from insisting that she said 'Guadalupe' to Juan Bernardino, and that he passed it on to the Bishop correctly, either with divine help or with the Virgin's coaching. No one has managed to explain satisfactorily why she would have wanted the Indians to call her by the name so popular in Spain, but Becerra Tanco might have thought he was giving the last word on that question long, long ago, and I quote: 'The Virgin didn't say why her Image should be called Guadalupe, and consequently, no one knows why, until God should be pleased to clear up this mystery.'

"However, I would like to venture another idea. I believe that Mary of Guadalupe deliberately chose a meaningful name for the Indians which at the same time could sound like the name that the Spaniards already loved, so that those Spaniards who were hostile to the Indians could easily accept that the 'Spanish' Mother of God had appeared to them and consequently be well-disposed towards her Miraculous Image. Almighty God intended that Mary of

Guadalupe should be the catalyst in the formation and preservation of a new nation."

For us Catholics of the United States who have the Immaculate Conception as our special Patroness, the common consensus among devotees of Our Lady of Guadalupe is that Mary did indeed identify herself as the Immaculate, the One who is in constant battle against the forces of darkness and sin, especially Satan. As Fr. Peter Fehlner points out (see article on page 158), the fact that she is the Immaculate Conception at Tepeyac does not depend exclusively on the Indian name that she used to identify herself.

We recognize a close connection between the Virgin of Tepeyac and the Patroness of the United States. When twenty-two Bishops met on May 13, 1846, at the Sixth Provincial Council of Baltimore they unanimously petitioned Rome that Mary, "The Virgin Mother of God, conceived without sin," be hailed as our Patroness. Our Lady identified herself at Guadalupe in practically the same way, as the "perfect and perpetual Virgin, Mother of the true God." "Perfect" implies the Immaculate Conception, inasmuch as she was to be a fitting vessel to carry the Son of God.

In his book *Mary of the Americas,* Fr. Christopher Rengers, O.F.M. Cap., points out that, "On the tilma Mary folds her hands [in prayer]. The Bishops' Pastoral says that she will pray for us. On Tepeyac she asks us to call on her, to fear nothing, to have confidence . . . . The Bishops mention confident hope. They commend [others to her] in confidence. They are certain that a blessing will come to those who take care to fulfill the prediction that all generations will call her blessed." He concludes the chapter with these words:

"They [the Bishops] named as Patroness of the United States *the Virgin Mother of God, conceived without sin.* We would do well to use this title in speaking of our Patroness. The phrase, 'conceived without sin' sets this great privilege in clear focus, and brings an implicit and much needed reminder that the rest of us were conceived in original sin. The highest gifts of the Creator to the chosen woman of our race are recognized and honored in the main part of the title Virgin Mother of God. Therefore, there is good reason to use the Guadalupe Image as the ordinary representation of the National Patroness of the United States, and to use the full, official title in formally speaking of her: *The Virgin Mother of God, Conceived Without Sin.*"

The Guadalupan Apparitions:
Historical Fact?

Janet Barber, I.H.M.

There are some scholars, even in our day, who persist in questioning the authenticity of the apparitions, in spite of all the evidence which definitely points to their historical and scientific authenticity. Because there is little early written evidence, they look on the whole Guadalupe event as a legend, and on the Image as an ordinary painting. They are an invitation to "believers" to show their love of Our Lady by deepening their own knowledge of all that pertains to Guadalupe and sharing with others. We asked Janet Barber to write a response to some of the more recent "anti-apparitionist" literature. We hope it will dispel doubts about the historicity of the appearances of Mary of Guadalupe at Tepeyac in 1531. The recent discovery of "Codex 1548" is especially exciting. —Editor

If we insist on seeing Church documents of the 1530s which attest to Mary's appearances at Tepeyac in 1531, we are worse off than poor "doubting Thomas." We can neither see nor touch such documents, because if they exist, we do not know where they are.[1] There were no official archives yet, since Bishop-elect Zumárraga had not yet been consecrated, and there was barely an informal diocesan apparatus (Even the records of the Cathedral Chapter did not report his death in 1548!). Paper work was probably the last thing on the mind of this tired man of over 60 as he daily faced the almost overwhelming practical challenges of the political, social, and religious chaos that seethed around him. If he did manage to write a report about the marvelous event, it could well have been among the Archdiocesan papers which we know were stolen during a severe paper shortage before 1666. Then, what credible evidence is left to us?

The Indian Evidence

The highly respected and distinguished scholar and Canon of

the Basilica of Guadalupe, the late Dr. Angel Maria Garibay Kintana, gave some of his own reasons over the years for believing in the Apparitions of Mary in 1531. While his reasons may seem deceptively simple, they are all the more credible to me, because I am familiar with the depth of his knowledge and the rigorous tests he applied to all facets of Guadalupan matters. In an address given in 1945, he pointed out that nowadays, although we can falsify photographs and sound recordings (today with amazing ease, thanks to digitalization and the computer!), nevertheless, the word of eyewitnesses continues to be accepted as proof that something did in fact happen. Doctor Garibay points out:

"Those of us who saw Madero arrive in Mexico City can affirm. . . that he arrived, the day and hour that he arrived, the way he was received.[2] And those who hear us . . . believe us and repeat it. . . The written record that we leave is as valid as [our] spoken word. . . But, equally valid is the written word of the person who did not see it but heard us repeat the fact. It would be folly to reject that testimony. Otherwise, we deny the possibility of retaining any memory of past events."

Comparable to Written Word

The spoken and written word of the eyewitness, the spoken and written word repeating the testimony that was heard, and the written word describing what was heard from someone else, all have the value of an authenticating document, according to Garibay. At this point, it can be objected that what has not been seen or heard firsthand is called "hearsay," which is inadmissible in most of our courts. However, the prior question might be whether the person reporting an event is known to be reliable. And indeed, in most courts that ordinarily do not accept hearsay evidence, if the witness can be demonstrated to be reliable, it is possible for hearsay testimony to be admitted. As we search for the historicity of the Guadalupe apparitions, let us remember that integrity is integrity, no matter what the century or context. Garibay touches on this question of reliability as he continues:

"And this value increases if the nature [of the happening] is social rather than individual; . . . if it is from an educated person rather than an uneducated one. For certifying the reality of an event, the eyes and the ears of the ignorant are better than the 'mystified' eyes and ears of the worldly wise. [Garibay ministered for years among the Nahuatl-speaking Indians of Mexico, and must have developed great respect for their powers of observation.] . . . If the mysterious Lady appears to an Indian and sends a message to a bishop, one must ask the Indian and the bishop about the reality of the event. . . If [the bishop] left a written record, we do not know what he said. What the Indian told Indians; what the Indians repeated and what the Indians preserved for the future. . . we do know and have at hand. The various means of indigenous testimony about the real fact of the apparition of Mary are true historical proofs. These proofs speak in a way that is social rather than personal and they come from different places, from different hands, from different origins, with some minor errors, . . .but all are united in saying that Mary appeared at Tepeyac.[3]

The Oral Tradition

One of the most convincing documents in the recent successful Beatification Cause of Juan Diego was the transcription of the oral testimony in 1666 of very old Indians of Cuauhtitlán, where the *Nican Mopohua* suggests that Juan Diego and Juan Bernardino were living at the time of the Apparitions.[4] They knew the story from their immediate elders, five of whom had heard it directly from Blessed Juan Diego himself. In other words, *they were only one witness away from Juan Diego*. The elders of the other Indians who testified had received the story from contemporaries of Juan Diego and Juan Bernardino. The Indians, all of them illiterate, belonged to a highly developed oral tradition. They gave a wealth of details, and made it clear that what they testified under oath was common knowledge in Cuauhtitlán. Although there are some discrepancies in their testimonies, there can be absolutely no doubt about their basic veracity and their witness to the "ample, continuous, and uniform tradition" that Holy Mary of Guadalupe had appeared at Tepeyac and left her Image on Juan Diego's tilma.

Some of the authenticated Indian annals,[5] while affirming the apparitions, differ in regard to their date. Garibay and others have explained in detail that the various Indian calendric systems not only began and ended their years at different times, but even the most learned Indian historians had difficulty coordinating their systems with the European calendar. Several of these annals, though, specify either that Mary of Guadalupe "descended to Tepeyac" in the year that "a star smoked" (their way of saying "comet"; Halley's Comet was visible over Mexico City in December, 1531); or that she "appeared to an Indian named Juan Diego" when "a new President came to govern in Mexico." (Don Sebastian Ramirez de Fuenleal arrived on September 23, 1531, to assume the presidency of the Second Audiencia, before there was a Viceroy to govern); or that "our beloved

The Seville engraving which first appeared in Becerra Tanco's Felicidad de Mexico, published in Mexico in 1675. It would seem that this engraving and the "oldest portrait of Juan Diego" was derived from the 1548 codex.

Mother of Guadalupe appeared" in the year "when the chief of the priests came, a Bishop, his name was Fray Juan de Zumárraga, a priest of St. Francis." Actually, he had arrived three years earlier, but the discrepancy seems minor, given the calendric confusion.[6]

Over the centuries, many such authenticating annals and codices have been lost, even though some had been seen by reputable scholars. Rare is the student of Mexican history who does not hope that these and hitherto unknown ones can still come to light in Mexican or European archives or in private collections. Then imagine the feelings of a Mexican chemical engineer, Don Manuel Betancourt V, when he found what is currently being called "Codex 1548" in a private library![7] Painted on deer skin, it shows a woman easily recognizable as Mary of Guadalupe appearing from the southeast, which is consistent with the *Nican Mopohua,* and Juan Diego kneeling, looking up at her. The Virgin is not wearing a crown. The Nahuatl text has been deciphered by Fr. Mario Rojas Sanchez, and I am translating from his Spanish text. "Also in this year our Beloved Mother the Maiden Guadalupe appeared to Cuauhtlactoatzin (Juan Diego's pre-Christian name) in Mexico [City]." At the top of the fragment is written "1548," and at the bottom left, "Cuautlactoatzin died with dignity." According to the *Nican Motecpana,* Juan Diego died in 1548. At the upper left is a small representation of a man, presumably Juan Diego, and what appears to me to be a tiny representation of the Virgin within her aureole.

At the bottom right, clearly distinguishable, is the glyph or

The 1569 engraving by Antonio Castro, considered the oldest portrait of Juan Diego.

symbol of Don Antonio Valeriano (the previously-known glyph and the codex both give his name as "Juez [judge] Anton Vareliano," involving a common transposition of sounds known as "metathesis.") Father Rojas assumes that this glyph and two distinguishable letters of words no longer legible date the codex as having been painted during his governorship of the Indians of Mexico City. The signature is that of Fray Bernardino de Sahagun, who arrived in New Spain in 1529. His first assignments seem to have been in the Valley of Mexico, putting him not too far from the happenings at Tepeyac.

It would seem that this scene was the model for two engravings, one by Antonio Castro, which has been called by Mariano Cuevas "the oldest portrait of Juan Diego." The other was published in Seville. The first is very simple, and shows only the left side of the deerskin codex, including the small representations of Juan Diego and the Virgin in the upper left. The Seville engraving appears in Becerra Tanco's *Felicidad de Mexico*, published in Mexico in 1675, and includes virtually the complete scene of the codex, with the Virgin in the upper left much larger than in the codex, although Juan Diego is smaller. Oddly, it gives him a Spanish physiognomy, and replaces the Indian glyph of "Don Antonio Valeriano" with what Father Estrada identifies as the Capilla del Sagrario in Seville. Both engravings show Mary without a crown, just as in the codex, and Juan Diego barefoot, as he is in the codex and as was the case with the commoners (*macehualtin*) at the time of the apparitions. Pictures of the 17th century have Juan Diego in sandals.

While 1531 is not to be found in the Codex 1548, it is implied.[8] The sun is rising in the extreme southeastern position, as it does on the morning of the Winter Solstice, which occurred in 1531 on Tuesday, December 12 of the Julian Calendar, the day the *Nican Mopohua* gives for the miracle of the flowers and the appearance of the Image on the tilma.[9]

Our primary source of information about the Guadalupan

Event is the *Nican Mopohua* ["Here is told"], probably written between 1548 and 1560, presumably by Antonio Valeriano.[10] We know from Fray Bernardino de Sahagun that Valeriano was the most valuable member of the team of young Indians who helped him in his monumental ethnographic study of the Pre-Conquest Nahuatl culture. However, Dr. Garibay finds more than one style in the *Nican mopohua*, and suggests that it was a collaborative effort of several of Sahagun's team, which included Alonso Vegerano and Pedro de San Buenaventura, both from Cuauhtitlan. They, of all people, would have access to Juan Diego, a Cuauhtiteca, and would know the story from their own families. Siguenza y Gongora swears that the manuscript of the *Nican Mopohua* in his collection was in Valeriano's handwriting and that the latter was the author. That statement, however, would not preclude Valeriano's having headed the effort, edited the jointly produced account, and written it in final form. Garibay points out that something resulting from the collaborative efforts of a team can have more validity than if it were written by one person alone.[11]

But, the skeptic might ask, what can prove that Our Lady really appeared, that the "principals" in the story didn't simply conspire in the interests of a speedier evangelization of the Indians? In a seminal address to the Mariological Congress of 1960 in Mexico City, after a fine analysis of Mary's introduction of herself and her errand in Mexico to Juan Diego, Garibay continues,

"Either the person who writes this in the Indians' language and with so much harmony of style and manner and such a depth of theological meaning, has to be a genius, or what he wrote was said by someone who does know, even though [the writer] does not. The first is impossible for the people of the 16th century, not just Indians, but also Spaniards. The precision of terms, the division of the subject matter, the perfect inclusion of all the aspects require that the person who is saying this . . . knows what she is talking about. It is one more proof that it is not being invented, but transcribed. And it is one more indication that the person who is speaking is she who can be called a supreme "master" of the highest theology. In view of the tenor of this part of the message an extremely strong presumption [is justified] that Mary said it and that in it she declared herself to be a universal and true Mother, with all the functions that mothers have."[12]

To me, it is unbelievable that any member of the mixed society of New Spain at that time, including the learned Bishop Zumárraga and the highly educated friars, could have conceived or written the Marian theology expressed so succinctly in the *Nican Mopohua* and embedded in such a culturally accurate and meaningful sequence of events for the Indians. In a sense, Mary of Guadalupe left her own authentication of Juan Diego's story: the quality of the story itself.

A Sign to All Generations

But Mary left an even more convincing authentication of her apparitions: the sign itself, the Image which suddenly appeared before the Bishop's eyes on the white tilma of Juan Diego.[13] Those who believe that such things simply don't happen, that the Image had to have been painted by a human being beforehand, must not be aware of the reflections discovered in both eyes of the Image in 1929 and again in 1951.[14] The Guadalupan eyes have been examined many times since then by ocular experts from various countries, and none, to my knowledge, has denied the presence of the Purkinje-Sanson phenomenon, an effect which clearly constitutes an ongoing, constant miracle, not to be explained in any human terms.

And this without even mentioning all the other inexplicable qualities of the tilma and Image. In my opinion, no human painter could have created the extraordinarily beautiful gold designs on Our Lady's tunic, given the tilma's unsized material of maguey fibers.[15] And even if such a painter could have, I think it humanly impossible to combine so many indigenous glyphs so harmoniously, with such a quantity of Gospel meanings, many of which are not even mentioned in the short article referred to in note 14. As if all other pointers to the year of the Guadalupan Event were not enough, the Divine Tlacuilo even dates his Amoxtli, in the lower left corner of Our Lady's mantle and tunic: the year 13 Acatl, 13 Reed, 1531.

Conclusion

Mary of Guadalupe did appear in Mexico in December of 1531. The Bishop asked for a sign that she had appeared, and the sign was not only granted, but still remains as a witness to us of the event. Later, the Indians to whose representative she appeared, faithfully recorded the happening and Our Lady's carefully chosen words. Because there would be those who would not rely upon the Indians and mestizos and Spaniards of known integrity who passed the story down the generations, Almighty God infused both the event and the Miraculous Image with their own self-authentication.

Footnotes

1 There is no reason for doubting the word of two honorable men, one of whom reported seeing Zumárraga's report in a Franciscan house in Vitoria, Spain (presumably destroyed in a later fire); the other reported having found the Archbishop of Mexico reading the "autos y procesos" of the apparition around the beginning of the 17th century.

2 Francisco I. Madero was one of the principal leaders of the Mexican Revolution which began in 1910 and lasted more than a decade. He made a triumphal entry into Mexico City on June 7, 1911, eleven days before Garibay's 19th birthday, and was received with great joy by the people.

3 "Temas guadalupanos," *Abside,* 9, enero-marzo, 1945 (reprinted in *El alma y la palabra.* [Toluca: Ediciones del Gobierno del estado de Mexico, 1985], 363-397.

4 This Inquiry, known as the Informaciones de 1666, received oral testimony from seven Indians, one Mestizo and twelve Spaniards and Criollos, as well as a written document from Luis Becerra Tanco, probably the best informed Guadalupan scholar of that century. The integrity of the 21 witnesses is beyond question. The proceedings have not been translated into English. However, English-speaking readers will find excellent accounts of the Inquiry in *The Dark Virgin: The Book of Our Lady of Guadalupe,* by Donald Demarest and Coley Taylor, 1953. For those who read Spanish, facsimiles of the original handwritten records of their testimony are given in *Las Informaciones Juridicas de 1666 y el Beato Indio Juan Diego,* compiled and printed by Ana Maria Sada Lambreton, H.M.I.G. Mexico, 1991.

5 We may take "annals" to mean Indian records written after the Conquest in the Spanish alphabet, as opposed to pre-Conquest "codices," composed of stylized pictures and symbols. Annals can also be used as a general term that includes codices.

6 While there is no space to document all the statements in this article, I will say that these annals are respectively the *Anonymous A,* from the region of Mexico City; the *Anonymous C,* from the Puebla region; and the *Anonymous B,* from the region of Tlaxcala. All are from the collection of Gomez de Orozco and are known by other names as well. These three do not exhaust the number of extant Indian documents witnessing to the Apparitions of 1531.

7 The codex is reproduced enlarged, in full color, in Volume 3 of Fr. Javier Escalada's *Enciclopedia guadalupana,* Mexico, 1995, between pages 456 and 457. The deer skin was "scanned by computer and infrared photography, with no additions or touchups of any kind." It is currently being scrutinized for its authenticity.

8 "In this year" suggests to me that "1531" has either been obliterated by time or appears on another part of the codex which has yet to be found. One would think that if the codex were a hoax, "1531" would be included. The fact that it doesn't appear is an indication to me that the Codex 1548 is genuine.

9 Those who admit to apparitions but doubt that they occurred in 1531 point to the well-substantiated story of a miracle sometime between 1559 and 1563 (the month is not given), in which the Virgin appeared personally to take the bridle of a runaway horse that had dragged its rider half a league over hardpan and ravines. They seem not to take into account the fact that the Image had already been such an object of veneration and pilgrimage that when the second Archbishop of Mexico, Alonso de Montúfar, arrived from Spain in June of 1554 he realized he must build a larger chapel to accommodate the devotion. They also overlook that the *Nican Mopohua* specifies Juan de Zumárraga as the bishop of the apparitions.

10 See "The Author of the *Nican Mopohua,* Don Antonio Valeriano," page 51.

11 Angel Maria Garibay K, *Historia de la Literatura Nahuatl,* 2 (Mexico: Editorial Porrua, S.A., 1954), 256-266.

12 *"La maternidad espiritual de Maria,"* Tepeyac, July 1 and 15, 1977.

13 See "The Tilma and Its Image," page 56.

14 See "Our Lady's Eyes," page 89.

15 See "The Image as a Divine Codex, page 68.

Queen of All the Americas

For many years people in the United States thought of Our Lady of Guadalupe as a Mexican Madonna. Actually, the Mexican Nation did not exist at the time when Our Lady appeared on Tepeyac Hill near Mexico City. In 1531, there were no geographical boundaries between the various countries as exist today. Our Lady did not appear to a European, that the Spanish colonists might claim her for themselves. She appeared to one of the native Americans who were the original inhabitants of the New World. It was her desire that the people, who lived here for centuries, would come to understand that Christianity is not a foreign import, but a Religion that embraces all men, Native Americans, as well as Europeans. Yet, Mary never intended to be exclusively the Mother of just the people who lived in Mexico. She herself emphasized, "I am a merciful mother of *all* of you who live united in this land and of all mankind."

This is why Pope Pius XII called her the "Empress" or "Queen" of all the Americas. Cardinal Corripio at a public Mass in the Basilica of Our Lady of Guadalupe made the same statement, that Mexicans alone cannot claim Our Lady as their Madonna, but that they must realize she is the Madonna of *all* the American people. Our Lady of Guadalupe has a particular interest in each of the countries in this hemisphere. But, we in the United States have a particular need of her. We need the humility of Juan Diego, to come under Mary's mantle for protection from the pagan, materialistic and secular values we find rampant in the United States. God has allowed us to experience many natural disasters in recent years (hurricanes, fires, earthquakes), as well as terrorism etc., that we might realize the passing value of the things on which we have placed so much importance. We, thus, are given the opportunity to realize that there are greater values than those obtained through education, skills and hard work. All of these are worthless when they are not related to God.

Mary comes to us and pleads with us, "Why are you disturbed? Why are you troubled? Why are you afraid? Am I not your Mother?" So many people are fearful in this world today. They need a mother's care, a mother's concern, a mother's protection. Mary showed her compassion in healing the uncle of Juan Diego, Juan Bernardino, at Tulpetlac. We have many physical and spiritual ills that need to be cured. Let us ask her to pray to Almighty God that our bodies and our souls may be whole again.

Moreover, Mary is the model we need in the role she played at Cana of Galilee, at the foot of the Cross, and with the Apostles after Jesus' death. Mary is still the "Mother of the Church." If we are working toward the recognition of the Kingship of Christ, we must also work to have Mary recognized as Queen. We have a Queen that unfortunately many do not recognize. Yet, mankind will never succeed in overcoming the world and obtaining peace without recognizing the Queen of the Universe, Our Lady of Guadalupe.

The above is a condensation of an article that the late Bishop Jerome Hastrich, Founder of the Queen of the Americas Guild, wrote for the Handbook.

PART XI

Nican Mopohua: Original Account of Guadalupe

The following account of the Guadalupan apparitions by the editor, is based on several English translations of the Nican Mopohua, *the original account written by Antonio Valeriano in Nahuatl, the language spoken by Juan Diego and the Aztecs. The tender, motherly expressions and words of Our Lady to Juan Diego in the account are paraphrased from the literal translation done by Janet Barber, I.H.M., of the new Spanish version prepared by the renowned Natuatl scholar, Fr. Mario Rojas Sánchez.*

*H*ere follows a carefully ordered account of the marvelous manner in which the Ever Virgin Holy Mary, Mother of God, Our Queen, recently appeared on Tepeyac Hill, known as Guadalupe. She first appeared to a poor Indian, worthy of respect, Juan Diego; and afterwards her beautiful Image appeared [on his tilma] in the presence of the new bishop, Friar Don Juan de Zumárraga.

Ten years after the fall of the city of Mexico, when arrows and shields were put aside and there was peace in the villages, the faith and knowledge of the true God, Author of life, had begun to put forth shoots and blossom. At that time, in the year 1531, a few days after the beginning of December, there was a humble man of the people, Juan Diego, a native of Cauhtitlan, who worshipped at the chapel at Tlatilolco.

He was on his way to pursue the study of God and His Commandments at the small church in Tlatilolco. It was still dark on Saturday when he set out. Dawn was breaking as he arrived at the foot of Tepeyac Hill. He heard singing from the crest of the hill, which sounded like the song of many birds. When at times their voices quieted, the hillside seemed to echo in response. Their singing, very soft and pleasant, surpassed that of the coyoltototl and tzinizcan and other fine song birds. Juan Diego stopped to look and thought, "Could I be worthy of what I'm hearing? Am I dreaming?

Am I arising from sleep? Where am I? Perhaps in the earthly paradise of flowers and corn, about which our ancestors spoke? Maybe already in heaven?" He was looking toward the summit and to the dawning to the east of the foothill to see the source of the beautiful heavenly singing, when suddenly it stopped and silence fell, and he heard someone calling him from the top of the hill, saying, **"Juan, dearest Juan Diego."**

He then climbed the hill in the direction of the voice, not at all frightened, but rather, feeling extremely happy. Upon reaching the summit, he saw a lady standing there who told him to come closer. He was filled with awe and admiration by her splendor. Her clothing was radiant like the sun; the crag on which her foot was resting was giving off rays of light, and looked like a bracelet of precious stones; even the earth glistened like the mist of a rainbow. The mesquite bushes, prickly pears, and other lowly herbs and grasses which usually grow there seemed like emeralds, the foliage like fine turquoise, and the branches and thorns like shining gold.

He bowed before her, hearing her very gentle, polite words which were delivered as to someone very respected. She said: **"Listen, Juan, my dearest and youngest son, where are you going?"** He answered, "My Lady, my Queen and my little Girl, I am going to your house in Mexico-Tlatilolco to continue the study of the divine mysteries taught us by the images of Our Lord, our priests." She spoke then, revealing her blessed will, saying:

"Know, know for sure, my dearest, littlest, and youngest son, that I am the perfect and ever Virgin Holy Mary, Mother of the God of truth through Whom everything lives, the Lord of all things near us, the Lord of heaven and earth. I want very much to have a little house built here for me, in which I will show Him, I will exalt Him and make Him manifest. I will give Him to the people in all my personal love, in my compassion, in my help, in my protection: because I am truly your merciful Mother, yours and all the people who live united in this land and of all the other people of different ancestries, my lovers, who love me, those who seek me, those who trust in me. Here I will hear their weeping, their complaints and heal all their sorrows, hardships and sufferings. And to bring about what my compassionate and merciful concern is trying to achieve, you must go to the residence of the Bishop of Mexico and tell him that I sent you to show him how strongly I wish him to build me a temple here on the plain; you will report to him exactly all you have seen, admired and what you

Painter, Jorge Sánchez Hernández, portrays Our Lady of Guadalupe in her role as Mediatrix of All Graces. This, and the following color illustrations are by Hernández.

have heard.

Know for sure I will appreciate it very much, be grateful and reward you. And You? You will deserve very much the reward I will give you for your fatigue, the work and trouble that my mission will cause you. Now, my dearest son, you have heard my breath, my word; go now and put forth your best effort."

At this, he bowed low before her and said, "My Lady, I am going now to carry out your charge; for the present, I, your poor servant, take leave of you." He then descended the hill, intent on fulfilling her command, and continued on along the causeway which goes directly to Mexico City. Once inside the city, he went without delay to the residence of the bishop, a new prelate, who had only recently arrived. His name was Friar Don Juan de Zumárraga, a religious of St. Francis. As soon as he got there he tried to see him, begging the servants to announce him. After a long while they came to call him, the Bishop having ordered that he should enter.

Upon entering, he bowed and knelt before him and immediately gave him the message of the Lady from heaven, telling him everything he had admired and had seen and heard. After hearing the story and the message, the bishop didn't seem to believe him and said, "You will come again, my son, and I will hear what you have to say at greater leisure; I shall look into the matter carefully from the very beginning and give much thought and consideration to the request you have brought me." He left feeling sad, because the message entrusted to him was not immediately accepted. He returned that same day, heading directly to the crest of the hill and found the Lady from heaven waiting for him on the very spot where he first saw her. He fell to his knees before her saying,

"My dear little Mistress, Lady, and Queen, my littlest Daughter, my dear little Girl, I went where you sent me to carry out your order. Although it was difficult for me to enter the bishop's quarters, I saw him and explained your message exactly as instructed. He received me kindly and listened with attention; but as soon as he answered, it was apparent that he did not believe it; he said: 'You will come back some other time, and I shall listen to what you say at greater leisure; and I shall examine it from the very beginning and think about the request you have delivered.'

"The way he answered me I could clearly see that he thinks I may have made it up, about your wanting a little house built for you here, or that it is not from you. So I beg you, my Lady, Queen and

my little Girl, to send one of the nobles who are held in esteem and respected with the message, so that it will be believed; for I am a man of no importance, a backframe, a follower. You are sending me to a place that I am not used to spending my time, my little Virgin, my youngest Daughter, my Lady. Forgive me if I grieve you and you are angry with me."

The Most Holy Virgin, worthy of all honor and veneration answered:

"Listen to me, my youngest and dearest son, know for sure that I do not lack servants and messengers to whom I can give the task of carrying out my words, who will carry out my will. But it is very necessary that you plead my cause and, with your help and through your mediation, that my will be fulfilled. My youngest and dearest son, I urge and firmly order you to go to the bishop again tomorrow. Tell him in my name and make him fully understand my intention that he start work on the chapel I'm requesting. Tell him again that I am the ever Virgin, Holy Mary, the Mother of God, who is sending you."

Juan answered, "My Lady, Queen, my little Girl, I do not wish to give you anguish, pain or grieve your heart; I shall go very gladly as you command; I shall by no means give up, nor do I consider it any trouble. I shall go to fulfill your wish; but I may not be heard or, if heard, still not believed. Tomorrow afternoon, when the sun goes down, I shall return to give you an account of the Bishop's answer. I must now take leave of you, my youngest Daughter, little Maiden, my little Girl and Lady. Rest well in the meantime." Then he went to his home to rest.

The following day was Sunday and in the very early dawn he left his house going directly to Tlatilolco for religious instruction. He arrived just before ten o'clock and heard Mass, keeping his mission in mind. Once the crowd had dispersed, he set out for the bishop's residence. As soon as he got there, he insisted on seeing the bishop, and after many difficulties was allowed in. Kneeling down before him, he repeated sadly and tearfully the demand he brought from the Lady from heaven. He was extremely anxious to be believed and that the bishop comply with the wish of the Perfect Virgin that a place of worship be erected on the spot she had clearly indicated.

The bishop, in order to verify the matter, asked many questions. Where had he seen her? What was she like? He gave a full account of everything. But even though he recounted with great exactitude what she was like and all he had seen and marveled at, and the Bishop saw that it was the Perfect Virgin, Mother of the Savior, he was unable to act without further evidence. He said he could not carry out the order only on his word and request, but that it was necessary to give him a sign that the message had come from the Lady from heaven herself. As soon as he heard that, Juan Diego said, "Lord Bishop, what kind of sign do you require? I shall go and request it of the Lady from heaven who sent me."

When the bishop saw that he confirmed everything and did not hesitate or doubt in the slightest, he dismissed him. He had him followed by members of the household whom he trusted so that they could watch and see where he went, whom he saw and spoke to. This they did. When Juan Diego came directly to the causeway, those who were following him lost sight of him on the wooden bridge where the brook comes out near Tepeyac; and although they looked everywhere, there was no trace of him to be found. So they turned back, annoyed not only because he had slipped out of sight, but because he had frustrated their attempt in shadowing him. After telling the bishop what had happened, they urged him not to believe his story, that Juan was lying, making up a story, dreaming or imagining the whole thing.

They agreed that if he should ever come back, they would grab him and punish him severely so that he would never tell lies nor get the people all excited. In the meantime, Juan Diego was with the Most Holy Virgin giving her the bishop's reply. Upon hearing it, she said:

"That is fine, my youngest and dearest son; you will return here tomorrow so that you may take the sign he asked for. Then, he will believe and no longer doubt or be suspicious of you; and know, my dear son, I shall reward your care, work and fatigue in my behalf. Go now; tomorrow I shall be here waiting for you."

Upon arriving home Sunday, he found his uncle, Juan Bernardino, seriously ill and in danger of death. First, he went for the native healer who treated him, but he was too late. The next day, Monday, when Juan Diego was to take the sign to the bishop in order to be believed, he did not return. During the night, the uncle begged him to go to Tlatilolco to bring a priest to hear his confession and prepare him for dying, knowing that his time had arrived, and that he would never get well.

Early in the morning of Tuesday, in the middle of the night, Juan Diego was already on his way to Tlatilolco for a priest. As he approached the road that passes at the side of the foothill of Tepeyac toward the west, which was his usual route, he thought, "If I take the direct path, the Lady may see me and I must not be detained by the sign she wished to give me. I must hurry to get a priest first, since my poor uncle is anxiously waiting for him." So Juan Diego took another path around the hill which crosses toward the east side in order to reach Mexico more quickly, and not be detained by the Queen of Heaven. He thought this would prevent his being seen by her, but she was watching him from where she saw him before.

She came down the hill and blocked his way and said to him:

"What is happening, dearest and youngest of my sons? Where are you going? Where are you headed?"

And he, regretful, ashamed and fearful, prostrated himself before her and said in greeting:

"My little Maiden, my youngest Daughter, my Girl, I hope that you are happy. How are you this morning? Do you feel well? Although it grieves me, and may cause you anguish, I must tell you that one of your servants, my uncle, is very ill. A terrible sickness has struck him down and he will surely die soon.

"And now I hurry to your little house in Tlatilolco to call on the beloved ones of Our Lord, our priests, to hear his confession and prepare him for death. For we all are born for that and await the difficult day of our own death. Although I go, I shall return right away to take care of your message, my Lady and my little Maiden. I beg you to forgive me, be patient with me a little longer, because I am not deceiving you, my youngest Daughter, my little Girl. Tomorrow without fail, I will return as fast as possible." After hearing Juan Diego's words, the most merciful Virgin spoke:

"Listen, put it into your heart, my youngest and dearest son, that the thing that disturbs you, the thing that afflicts you, is nothing. Do not let your countenance, your heart be disturbed. Do not fear this sickness of your uncle or any other sickness, nor anything that is sharp or hurtful. Am I not here, I, who am your Mother? Are you not under my shadow and protection? Am I not the source of your joy? Are you not in the hollow of my mantle, in the crossing of my arms? Do you need anything more? Let nothing else worry you, disturb you. Do not let your uncle's illness worry you, because he will not die now. You may be certain that he is already well." [And at that moment the uncle was restored to health, as they were to learn later.]

When Juan Diego heard this from the Queen of Heaven, he felt better, was comforted and at peace. He begged her to send him to the bishop without delay with some sign that he would believe. The Lady from heaven then told him:

"Go up, my dearest son, to the top of the hill, to where you saw me and received my directions and you will find different kinds of flowers. Cut them, gather them, put them all together, then come down here and bring them before me."

Juan Diego went up the hill immediately, and upon reaching the crest was astonished to find so many beautiful, exotic varieties of fine, full-bloomed flowers since it was out of season, being the time of biting frost. They were very fragrant and covered with night dew which gleamed like precious pearls. He went around cutting and gathering them and placed them inside the fold of his tilma. The top of the hill was no place for flowers to grow; it was stony and full of nothing but thistles, thorns, prickly pears and mesquites. At times grass grew there, but this was the month of December when frost kills everything. He hurried down the hill taking the flowers to the heavenly Maiden. She took them into her precious hands and rearranged them in his tilma saying:

"My youngest and dearest son, these different kinds of flowers are the proof, the sign that you will take to the Bishop. You will tell him from me that he is to see in them my desire, and therefore he is to carry out my wish, my will. And you, who are my messenger, in you I place my absolute trust. I strictly order you not to unfold your tilma or reveal its contents until you are in his presence. You will relate to him everything very carefully: how I sent you to the top of the hill to cut and gather flowers, all you saw and marveled at in order to convince the Governing Priest so that he will then do what lies within his responsibility so that my house of God which I requested will be made, will be built."

After the Lady from heaven had finished her instructions, he set out along the causeway leading directly to Mexico City. Happy now, and feeling sure that this time everything would go well, he held his precious burden close to protect it and prevent any of its contents from falling out, while delighting in the fragrance of the various beautiful flowers. When he arrived at the residence of the Bishop, the doorkeeper and the other servants stepped out to meet him. He begged them to inform the Bishop how urgent it was that he see him, but they all refused pretending they did not hear him, either because it was still dark, or because they knew him from his other visits and felt he was giving them trouble with his repeated visits.

Also, they had already been informed by their companions of how he had slipped from their sight the time they had been ordered to follow him. When they saw him standing there a long time, head lowered, doing nothing in case he should be called; they noticed that he seemed to be carrying something. Out of curiosity, they went over to him and tried to see what it was he was carrying.

When Juan Diego saw that he couldn't hide what he carried, and fearing that they would continue to harrass him and possibly damage the flowers, he opened the folds of his tilma a bit to give them a peek. When they saw that it contained exquisite, different, blooming flowers out of season, they were awed. They were impressed how fresh they were, how open their corollas were, how good they smelled, and how beautiful. They dared to snatch some of them away from him three times but they could not succeed. They no longer saw real flowers, but flowers which seemed to be painted, embroidered or sewn on the tilma.

They went right away to tell the Bishop what they had seen and informed him about the humble Indian who had come before and was waiting a long time to see him. Hearing this, the Bishop realized that Juan had the proof he needed to convince him to carry out Our Lady's wish. He immediately ordered them to show him in. Upon entering, Juan Diego prostrated himself before the Bishop as he had done the other times, reporting everything he had seen and marveled at, and repeating her message. He said:

"Your Excellency, I did as you ordered, telling my Mistress, the Heavenly Maiden, Holy Mary, the Beloved Mother of God, that you were asking for proof so that you could believe me, so that you could build her sacred little house that she requested. I told her that I had promised to bring you some sign of proof just as you requested. She listened carefully to your word and was pleased to receive your request for a sign, so that her beloved will could be carried out. Today, while it was still night, she ordered me to see you again. I asked for the proof, so that I would be believed and she kept her promise immediately, sending me up the hill where I had seen her before to cut various roses and other flowers.

"Although I knew very well that the top of the hill wasn't the place where flowers grow, because it is full of craggy rocks, thorns, spiny acacias and mesquite bushes, I didn't doubt or hesitate one minute to do her bidding. When I arrived at the crest of the hill, it seemed as if I were in paradise, because there in one place was a great variety of different precious flowers, all exquisite and sparkling with dew, which I set about gathering. After I brought them down to her she took them in her holy hands and rearranged them in the hollow of my ayate for me to bring and present to you in person. She told me to give them to you from her so that you would recognize the sign you requested and comply with her wishes, and also to show you that I was truthful. Here they are, please receive them."

He then opened his white mantle which held the flowers, and as the different precious flowers fell to the floor, then and there the beloved Image of the Perfect Virgin, Holy Mary, Mother of God, suddenly appeared in the form and figure in which it remains to this day and is preserved in her chapel at Tepeyac called Guadalupe. Upon seeing it, the bishop and all those present fell to their knees full of awe and reverence, greatly affected and moved by what they saw. They then grew sad, they wept, and their hearts and minds were in ecstasy.

The Lord Bishop prayed in tears begging forgiveness for not having immediately carried out her will to do what she wanted. He rose to his feet, and untied the mantle from around Juan Diego's neck on which the heavenly Queen's Image was imprinted and took it to his private chapel. He detained Juan Diego, who remained another day at the Bishop's house. The following day he said, "Come, let us go to see the place where the Lady from heaven wants her temple to be built." People were immediately invited to build her "sacred little house." As soon as Juan Diego had pointed out where the Lady from heaven wanted her chapel to be built, he asked permission to leave. He wanted to see his uncle who had been gravely ill when he left for Tlatilolco to call the priest to confess him and prepare him for dying.

But they didn't let Juan Diego go alone; a number of people went with him to his house. Upon arriving, they saw the uncle was well and happy without ache or pain. He was surprised to see his nephew accompanied by so many people and inquired as to the cause for so much honor and attention. The nephew explained that when he had left to bring the priest to hear his confession and prepare him for dying, the Lady from heaven had appeared to him on Tepeyac, and that she had consoled him greatly by telling him not to worry because his uncle was already restored to health. She then had sent him to Mexico City to ask that a house be erected for her on Tepeyac.

The uncle then revealed that it was indeed at that same moment he was suddenly restored to health, when she appeared in much the same way as she had appeared to his nephew. She related too that she had sent Juan to see the bishop in Mexico. At the same time, the Lady told Juan Bernardino that as soon as he saw the bishop he must reveal to him the miraculous manner in which she had effected his cure and that he should convey to him the proper name for her blessed Image, The Perfect Virgin Holy Mary of Guadalupe.

Then they took Juan Bernardino before the bishop so he might speak to him and give his testimony. Both Juan Bernardino and his nephew stayed at the bishop's residence several days, until the chapel of the little Queen of Tepeyac was erected where she revealed herself to Juan Diego. The Reverend Bishop had the Holy Image of the beloved heavenly Maiden transferred from the oratory to the main church, so that all the people could see and admire it. Absolutely, the whole city came to see and admire her precious Image and pray before it. They marveled at the miraculous way it had appeared, since absolutely no one on earth could have painted her beloved Image.

The above is the original account of Guadalupe by Antonio Valeriano. The original was in Nahuatl, the language of the Aztecs, and was translated into Spanish, then into English. This version was edited from several English translations, keeping as close as possible to the poetic, tender words of Juan Diego and Our Lady of Guadalupe. In order to be more authentic, the words of Our Lady are a literal translation from the Spanish by Janet Barber who worked from the Spanish translation of the original Aztec language, by the renowned Nahuatl scholar, Fr. Mario Rojas Sánchez.

Our Lady's Submission to the Church

One aspect of Mary's apparitions which is unnoticed at first glance, is in reality, both strikingly and vitally important — the Perfect Virgin Mary, the Mother of God, submitted herself with reverence and humility to the authority of the Church. When she made her *request* for a church to be built, she *submitted* it to Bishop Zumárraga, who was a prudent and wise leader. He hesitated and required her to give a sign; the Mother of God obeyed without delay or question, sending Juan Diego to Tepeyac Hill to gather a wide assortment of beautiful flowers in frosty mid-December and then graced us with her heavenly Image on his tilma.

In so doing the Perfect Virgin teaches us by her example that total submission to the Church is indispensable. One has only to look at the sad divisions which struck the Church in Europe through proud, worldly and disobedient "Renaissance man." Reform was needed, but separation from the center of unity, the papacy, only made matters far worse. We see the sad results of foresaking Faith in the Catholic Church, which Christ Himself instituted, in the tragic divisions of Christianity today. Yet, it was precisely in this age of scandalous Popes and worldly Bishops, of the Protestant revolt that Mary, the Missionary of the Most High, intervened. She, the Mother of God, submitted to Church authority, and consequently brought about the conversion of nine million to the Faith in less than ten years, making up for the millions that left the Church in Europe.

—Fr. Maximilian, F.F.I.

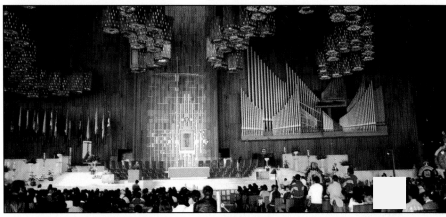

Top and center, the Basilica of Guadalupe, which is rich in Paschal Symbols. Above: The other churches at Guadalupe, left to right: the Basilica, where the sacred Image had been venerated for over 250 years, the parish church and, on the hill, the church where Our Lady first appeared to Juan Diego.

PART XII

Visiting Guadalupe Shrines

Our Lady's "Little House of God"

Janet Barber, I.H.M.

*M*ary of Guadalupe's request in 1531 for a "little house of God" at Tepeyac was answered with heroic speed: The Nican Mopohua tells us that Juan Diego and Juan Bernardino stayed with Bishop Zumárraga as his guests "a few days until the sacred little house of the Niña Queen was built." We have good reason to believe that the procession took place on December 26, 1531, and that the *ermita* was made of adobe with no mortar. After Bishop Zumárraga had ascertained the spot where Holy Mary wanted her house, only 11 days remained before the 26th, two of which were Sundays and a third was Christmas! It would have been impossible to finish in eight days if the workers had made the adobe bricks specially for the chapel. They undoubtedly used previously dried bricks. Don Pablo Juarez of Cuauhtitlan stated in 1666 that his grandmother, Justina Cananea, had watched while the foundations for the *ermita* were being excavated and then she worked on them! It was also testified in 1666 that after the installation of the Image, the Indians of Cuauhtitlan continued to work for weeks on the building.

As pilgrims and visitors increased over the centuries, Mary's "little house of God" had to be expanded and then replaced several times by ever larger churches. In 1709, the Image was placed in the fourth church, which was elevated to Basilica status in 1904 and was in constant use until 1976. By then, it was averaging 20,000 visitors a day. While it could hold 3,000 persons, only 1,000 of them could see the Image at one time. The grand old building finally had to be evacuated, because, like other buildings of the city originally built on a lake, it had sunk, was leaning precariously, and had dangerous fissures.

Monsignor Guillermo Schulenberg Prado, Abbot of the Basilica, said that in 1976 the new Basilica had already been under discussion for over fifty years. Studies were made and plans drawn up during the early 70's, and construction was begun in early 1975. Fund raisers, architects, engineers and builders worked with the love, zeal and speed of the first builders, so that the building was ready to be dedicated on October 11, 1976!

To assure that it will not sink as its predecessor did, this second Basilica was built on a magnificent system of 350 *"pilotes de control,"* control piles, designed by the renowned Mexican engineer Manuel González Flores. The *pilotes* support the Basilica's weight of more than 35,000 tons, and can be manipulated to allow the Basilica to remain evenly vertical at street level, regardless of how much the surrounding area may sink.

True to the architectural principle that form follows function, the new Basilica was designed to serve the needs of the people it will receive. The first and most obvious need was to handle the immense throngs of pilgrims and visitors gracefully. The whole atrium, or great plaza, was incorporated into the liturgical area, as was customary even in the early colonial years of evangelization. Some 10,000 persons are accommodated inside the Basilica, and when its nine doors are opened to the plaza 40,000 more can see the Mass celebrated at the main altar with the Image of Holy Mary of Guadalupe above it. True to the colonial tradition, there is an "open chapel" on the upper level of the Basilica facing the plaza. When Mass is celebrated there, 40,000 people can participate in it.

There are eight chapels on the Mezzanine level of the Basilica able to contain 250 persons, and on the lower level there are three more chapels. The chapel dedicated to the Blessed Sacrament has a beautiful mural depicting the Trinity on the wall behind a huge tabernacle. The other two chapels are of St. Joseph, and the Resurrection. So that pilgrims will not disturb the constant Masses in the main part of the Basilica, a ramp leads down behind and below the altar area, where four moving treadways carry the people, unseen by the worshipers, so that they can look up and see the Image at close range. The Basilica also has offices, a chapter room, library, and sacristy, as well as a small shop offering excellent reproductions of the Image and other items.

Mary of Guadalupe calls her people together to give them her Son through the liturgy. This second Basilica is above all a liturgical space, allowing the people to participate in union with their priests during the liturgy without any physical obstructions to their unity. The circular design and the massive off-center support of the Basilica roof provide freedom of sight and movement, and eliminate

The marble statue depicting the scene of Juan Diego giving Bishop Zumárraga the "sign." The statue is in the Guadalupe Museum.

columns which would block the view.

As the Benedictine architect, Fray Gabriel Chávez de la Mora has pointed out, all liturgy has a paschal sense, a meaning of passage from death to life in Jesus Christ, which is our most essential

The interior and exterior of the chapel of the "Little Hill" (see article on page 212). The Chapel on the hill where Our Lady first appeared to Juan Diego. The concrete sail is an ex–voto commemorating the miraculous intervention of Our Lady when she saved the crew of a ship that was sinking in a terrible storm.

liberation. The light filtered through more than 3,900 square feet of stained glass windows gives an atmosphere of Easter joy. The vertical roof support behind the altar has the Cross as its center, the sign of our Redemption. To its lower right is the miraculously conserved Image of Mary of Guadalupe. Fray Gabriel, who had the primary responsibility for planning the liturgical aspects of the Basilica, points out that from her Immaculate Conception all the way to her action in heaven and on earth with us now, Mary's life has had a profoundly paschal meaning, and that her apparitions at Tepeyac offer us several paschal signs.

The first of such signs is the healing of Juan Bernardino, Juan Diego's uncle. He symbolizes the entire Indian people, who by 1531 were near cultural death, but recovered their health through Mary's intervention, a "passage from death to life." The miraculous flowers were another paschal sign, because where there had been only thorns and thistles on a barren hill, Mary brought flowers, symbolizing the passage from death to life. The third sign, says Fray Gabriel, involves her Image on the tilma, where Mary of Guadalupe appears as the Woman of the Apocalypse (Rev 12). As such, she is temple, the Ark which contains the presence of God. At the same time, she is a sign of the Church, gathered as the people of God in community.

The second aspect of the tilma has to do with Bishop Zumárraga's passage from the inability to believe Juan Diego the first time he brought him the Virgin's message, to his belief as soon as he saw the flowers and her miraculous Image as it suddenly appeared on the tilma. A transforming step, points out Fray Gabriel, symbolizing passage from death to life.

The roof of the new Basilica is in the shape of a tent, reminding us that, like the Israelites of old, we are a people on pilgrimage - a pilgrim Church. The copper roof is gradually gaining its full patina, and recalls for us the Virgin's mantle, which has been described as the color of the ocean on a clear day. She said to Juan Diego, who represents all those who love and seek her, "Are you not in the hollow of my mantle, in the crossing of my arms?" How appropriate for visitors to remember this, as they worship her Son in this house of God where her portrait is venerated. Holy Mary of Guadalupe in her lovely Image is a "swarm" of salvific and paschal meanings. The Basilica roof is topped by a large cross rising from the letter M, a fitting high point for the glorious structure built for the Woman who said to Juan Diego, "Am I not the source of your joy?" Mary the source, Jesus our Joy.

Capilla del Cerrito

(Chapel of the "Little Hill")

Martin Kelly

*O*ne of the most hallowed spots in Christendom must be the tip of the little hill called Tepeyac on the northern fringe of Mexico City. There, in 1531, the Ever Virgin Holy Mary, Mother of the True God, appeared on earth in Her "perfect wonderfulness" and spoke on four different occasions over a four-day period to a fifty-seven year old Indian, Juan Diego.

The first time, in the pre-dawn darkness of Saturday morning, December 9, She called from the top of the hill for him to come close to her. There, radiantly resplendent amid a dazzling, transfigured landscape, she importuned him to go to the Bishop of Mexico City with her request that he build a sacred little house there for Her use.

The second time, toward evening of the same day, Juan Diego returned to the exact same spot where She had appeared to him the first time and reported the bishop's skepticism about the story. The third time, Sunday afternoon, December 10, Juan Diego returned to the hilltop to report the bishop's continuing disbelief and his statement that some sign of Her presence would be necessary.

The fourth time, on Tuesday morning, December 12, Juan Diego observed her coming down from atop the hill to intercept him. At her order, he climbed right away to the top of the hill and gathered a bouquet of flowers (albeit blooming out of season) to take to the bishop as a sign. The little hill *(el Cerrito)* where these marvelous episodes occurred quickly became a place of devotion. For reasons difficult to explain, this hallowed spot was marked for over a century with only a plain wooden cross held in place by a pile of large stones. Her sacred little house was build at the base.

Finally, in 1660, a devout couple donated funds for the construction of a little chapel *(capilla)* atop the hill to commemorate the apparitions. In 1694, a stone ramp was built up the east side of the hill to facilitate access. In 1745, the chapel was enlarged, stone steps up the west side were built and several rooms for lodging were added (reminiscent of the "booths" that Peter wanted to build on the Mount of the Transfiguration). Over the next fifty years, more additions were made to the chapel and new main and side altars constructed.

In 1831, a cemetery was built behind the chapel with dirt being hauled up in buckets to cover the bare rocks. In 1893, a convent of cloistered Discalced Carmelite nuns was founded in rooms on the east side of the chapel. This convent has thrived and celebrated its 100th anniversary in 1993. In the 1950's, the chapel was completely renovated, a new facade added, sculpted stone staircases constructed up both sides of the hill, snack and souvenir shops built below the chapel and four huge statues of the principal Archangels—Michael, Gabriel, Rafael and Uriel—erected in the forecourt.

In the 1980's, the entire hill was magnificently landscaped with lawns, trees, bushes, plants, flowers, shrubs, terraces and water falls. A monumental sculpted stone tableau was installed on the east slope. All the characters in the drama are depicted.

The scale of the chapel is intimate and the ambiance prayerful, the combination seeming to work a powerful transformative effect. No pews obstruct movement within. Pilgrims quietly constantly shuffle about gazing at six lovely frescoes which portray details of the Guadalupe story. Many kneel on the floor or at the altar rail, their eyes fixed in rapt contemplation before the Image of Our Lady positioned above the altar. Others seem lost in reverie sensing her presence or absorbed in deep spiritual communion with her. One can hear hymns being sung in her honor, as well as the the frequent recitation of Rosaries. It is an experience which tends to be intensely moving and uplifting.

An early visitor remarked, "In all the earth, I doubt if there be a calmer spot in which to still the vain emotions of the hour, or a sweeter spot in which to rest from life's fitful fever."

When You Go to Guadalupe—
Don't Forget Tulpetlac

Fr. Christopher Rengers, O.F.M.Cap.

*O*ver the four and half centuries since Our Lady came to Guadalupe and gave Juan Diego her motherly message and self-portrait, little attention has been given to Tulpetlac, eight miles to the north. Yet, it was here that Our Lady appeared on December 12, 1531 to Juan Bernardino, Juan Diego's uncle, curing him of a near-fatal illness. It was here too, that she gave him the name by which she wishes to be called (see article on page 179). Here, Juan Diego lived close to the shore of Lake Texcoco, sharing life with his cherished uncle. The Guadalupe event is wrapped in the touching story of Juan Diego's love for his uncle and Our Lady's special attention to Juan Bernardino.

Today, the centerpiece of the shrine of the Fifth Apparition at Tulpetlac, is a painting of Our Lady curing Juan Bernardino. Above it hangs a large crown, an indication of the papal coronation of the painting in 1979. In front of the painting, perhaps five or six feet below the level of the sanctuary floor, is a well. Its clear water is readily available to pilgrims. They may descend to the walk-around space which circles the well. The shrine of the Fifth Apparition is a cruciform chapel of medium size. On its plain white walls hang a number of large framed paintings. Several show the quiet scene from Juan Diego's life, weaving mats along the shores of Lake Texcoco. To one side, resting on the floor are seven clean-cut stone pieces, inscribed with the names of buildings planned for the *Mesa of Our Lady*. The *Mesa* is a flat stretch of land behind and a bit above the roof-level of the shrine.

In contrast to the quiet lapping of the waters of Lake Texcoco in 1531, today a superhighway toll-road carries its stream of noisy traffic past the front doors of the shrine. In fact, the highway bridges the road leading to the chapel. Tulpetlac is in the Diocese of Texcoco which is different from the where the Guadalupe Basilica is located. The Basilica is in the largest Catholic Diocese of the world, that of Mexico City, headed by Norberto Cardinal Rivera. It was Bishop Magin Torreblanca of the Texcoco Diocese who fervently asked for and obtained permission for a papal crowning of the painting of Our Lady curing Juan Bernardino. Father Enrique Amezcua commissioned and directed artist Don Luis Toral, on March 19, 1961, to paint *Our Lady of Guadalupe, Health of the Sick,* appearing to Juan Bernardino. It was finished and solemnly blessed on October 12, 1961. On the same day Pope John XXIII addressed those gathered in the Basilica of Our Lady of Guadalupe for the close of the Holy Year of Our Lady of Guadalupe. He spoke by radio from Vatican City and ended with his own prayer:

"Hail Mother of the Americas, Heavenly Missionary of the New World! From the sanctuary of Tepeyac you have been for more than four centuries the Mother and Teacher of the Faith to the peoples of the Americas. Be also our protection and save us, O Immaculate Mary. Aid our rulers; stir up a new zeal in our prelates; increase the virtues of our clergy, and preserve forever our Faith. In every home may the holiness of the family flourish, and in the shelter of the home may Catholic education, favored by your own benign glance, achieve wholesome growth. Amen."

At the ceremony of the crowning of *Our Lady of Guadalupe, Health of the Sick* in December, 1979, a ray of light came at a different slant from the more direct ray of the noonday sun and stopped at the edge of Our Lady's garment. Photos taken at the time plainly show this unusual ray. It began during Cardinal Corripio's homily and intensified as he and Bishop Torreblanca approached to crown the painting. In order to accommodate the crowds, the Mass and coronation ceremony took place in the village square next to the parish church of Cristo Rey and Our Lady of Guadalupe.

Fr. Enrique Amezcua, now deceased and buried under the front entrance of the Tulpetlac shrine, founded two communities. The men's community is dedicated to Christ the King. Priests of the men's community care for the parish church of Tulpetlac and the shrine of the Fifth Apparition. There is also a community of Sisters who have their novitiate immediately next to the Shrine, and accommodate visitors by offering prints of the papally crowned paint-ing, as well as containers for the water of the well in the sanctuary (The novices and their mistress came to our Mass in December, 1988. Twenty-five clear, young voices helped us say a fond farewell to Our Lady of Guadalupe, Health of the Sick, as they sang the sadly poignant *Adios O Maria*).

Various buildings are planned for the *Mesa of Our Lady,* near the entrance. Two are convents, one for "The Blue Sisters," the oth-er for Carmelites. You can walk from the shrine to the *Mesa* or take a circuitous auto and bus road to get there. Our 1988 bus treaded a careful, devious way over the then unpaved streets to the *Mesa.* The Carmelite Convent we visited offered handmade rosaries and scapulars to take home as a special remembrance. The Carmelite Convent also offers visitors a chance to relax in a small courtyard and adjoining porch.

Before there were any buildings on the *Mesa,* Bishop Jerome Hastrich of Gallup, NM and other officers of the *Queen of the Americas Guild,* buried St. Joseph Medals in the ground. Their spe-cial petition was to ask his help in founding an American *House of Hope and Healing* on the *Mesa.* Frank Smoczynski, the Guild Presi-dent, has color slides showing the *Mesa* in its pristine openness and the Cordi-Marian Sisters burying a medal. The idea of a *House of Hope and Healing* is to have a fairly large facility for people to come for healing in sickness, in some grave life problem, or direction in planning for the future. The half-hour ride to Guadalupe could be arranged on a daily basis.

Tulpetlac today is a busy town. You get a touch of contact here with the daily family life of the poor in Mexico. You pass by their houses, see the children trooping to church or school, or possibly crowding around you, eager for a holy card, or ready to present gleeful, laughing faces to your camera. The thought of a childless Juan Diego, devoted to Uncle Juan Bernardino, may recall a few ne-glected aunts and uncles or lonely grandparents. Perhaps pilgrims will remember to take a remembrance back to them of the special blessings of Our Lady, Health of the Sick, brought to Tulpetlac De-cember 12, 1531. She brought restored health and gave her name to Juan Bernardino. At the same time, and on the same day, she sent Juan Diego to gather flowers on Tepeyac Hill and used rose petals to paint her own lovely Image on Juan Diego's tilma. Would that more people might see the image of Christ in the aged and termi-nally ill.

Chronology of Notable Events

1325. The Tenochcas, a few thousand Aztecs, establish themselves on an island in Lake Texcoco. Here they had sighted their sign of destiny: "Perched on a cactus is an eagle devouring a snake." Today the eagle devouring a snake is the coat of arms of the nation and can be seen on the Mexican National Flag.

1505. Montezuma II is elected Emperor of Aztecs. Their capital is Tenochtitlan (Mexico City).

1519. March 12: Hernando Cortés anchors off the coast of what is now Vera Cruz, and makes friends with the rulers of Cempoala persuading them to imprison Montezuma's tax officers. Word spreads that the white gods will deliver the nations from slavery. Fifty soldiers destroy their idols and more allies join Cortés.

1519. November 8: Cortés arrives in Tenochtitlan. Montezuma, persuaded by various legends and his sister's vision, receives Cortés in peace and later acknowledges Charles V, King of Spain and Emperor, as his lord.

1520. June 20: Trouble breaks out, and Montezuma is deposed and dies. The new Emperor drives out the Spaniards.

1521. Cortés and allies lay seige to Tenochtitlan and after ninty-three days capture Emperor Cuauhtemoc (Fallen Eagle) near Tlaltelolco, the present day Center of Three Cultures

1527. Cuautlatohuac (he who speaks like an eagle) is baptized Juan Diego and his wife is baptized Maria Lucia.

1528. Bishop-elect Juan de Zumárraga, O.F.M., Protector of the Indians, arrives with the First Royal Audiencia (Governors) .

1531. The Indians were plotting to massacre the Spaniards because of the harsh and unjust rule of the First Royal Governors. At the end of 1531, the Second Royal Audiencia, a good one, is installed.

1531. December 9: First Apparition of Our Lady. At dawn, Juan Diego passes the barren hill of Tepeyac where he sees a beautiful Lady standing before a luminous cloud. She identifies herself as the Blessed Virgin Mary, and gives him a message for the Bishop. Juan hastens to the Bishop's house with the message. **Second Apparition of Our Lady:** That afternoon on his way home, he sees the Blessed Virgin again, and reports that he gave the message to Bishop Zumárraga, but the Bishop did not believe him. Our Lady tells him to return to the Bishop the next day.

1531. December 10: Third Appearance of Our Lady. After seeing the Bishop a second time, Juan Diego reports to Our Lady that the Bishop is willing to build her sanctuary if she will give him a sign. The Blessed Virgin agrees, and tells Juan to return the following morning when she will give him the sign. Continuing on to Tolpetlac, Juan finds his uncle, Juan Bernardino, near death.

1531. December 11: As his uncle's condition worsens, Juan Diego misses his appointment with the Blessed Virgin. That evening he asks Juan to go to Santiago de Tlaltelolco for a priest.

1531. December 12: Fourth Appearance of Our Lady. On his way to Tolpetlac for a priest to anoint his uncle, he meets the Blessed Virgin. He apologizes for not keeping his appointment the day before and explains why. She tells him his uncle is already well, and sends him to the top of Tepeyac hill to pick roses as a sign for the bishop. **The Appearance of the Image of Our Lady on the tilma of Juan Diego:** Later in the day, he carries the roses to the house of the Bishop. When he opens his mantle to display the roses; suddenly the image of the Blessed Virgin appears on his tilma - the very one we see in the Basilica of Guadalupe today.

1531. December 12. Fifth Appearance of Our Lady. In Tolpetlac, Juan Bernardino is cured by Our Lady, who appears to him in the same manner as she did to Juan Diego.

1531 December: The miraculous picture is exposed for veneration in the Bishop's chapel and later in the church while a sanctuary is being built. Fourteen days later, the Indians complete a small adobe sanctuary at Tepeyac.

1531. December 26. Solemn translation of the picture to the sanctuary, with great festivities, during which an Indian is accidentally shot in the throat and killed. This is the occasion for the first miracle.

1533. The Indians build a bigger adobe chapel (Second Hermitage) while Bishop Juan de Zumárraga is in Spain.

1539. In the seven years from the time our Lady appeared, eight million Indians are converted, as a direct result of her appearances and of her sacred picture.

1544. Plague, cocollixti, kills 12,000 in Mexico City alone, but ceases after the Franciscans lead children, six and seven years old, to the shrine to pray.

The transfer of the sacred Image of Our Lady of Guadalupe from the old basilica to the new one, drew large crowds. Many of the bishops of Mexico and other Latin American countries attended this momentous event.

1545. *Nican Mopohua,* written in 1540-1545, by Don Antonio Valeriano, is earliest extant account of the apparitions.

1548. Juan Diego dies at Tepeyac at the age of 74.

1556. D. Alonso de Montúfar, O.P., Second Archbishop of Mexico, builds the Third Hermitage (sometimes called The Second), which became known as The Old Church of the Indians.

1556-1557. Don Fray Alonso de Montúfar canonically establishes the truth of the appearances of Our Lady of Guadalupe.

1570. Archbishop Montúfar sends Philip II of Spain a complete inventory of the Archbishopric. The inventory mentions the Hermitage (Chapel) of Our Lady of Guadalupe at Tepeyac. This is important because the official record of the appearances is lost. He also sent the King a copy of the picture of Our Lady of Guadalupe done in oils and touched to the original, which later played an important role in the Battle of Lepanto (page 101).

1629. September 21: Beginning of the flood which drowned 30,000 Indians in Mexico City. 27,000 Indians flee. Of some 20,000 Spaniards, only 400 remain in the city. A boat procession transfers the Sacred Image to the cathedral. It remains there until she can return "on foot."

1634. May 14: In thanksgiving for the end of the flood, Our Lady's Image is returned in a great procession to Tepeyac. The flood had lasted over four years.

1647-1649. Bachiller Luis Lasso de la Vega, Vicar of Guadalupe, publishes *"Huei Tlama Huizoltica," (The Story of the Miracle of Guadalupe)*, copied from *Nican Mopohua* of Don Antonio Valeriano.

1666. A chapel is built on Tepeyac, where Our Lady first appeared and where the flowers were found on the morning of December 12.

1709. April 27: The great new sanctuary of Our Lady of Guadalupe is dedicated.

1736. The plague, cocollixti or typhus, again strikes an estimated seven hundred thousand persons who die in the course of eight months. Forty thousand die in Mexico City alone.

1737. April 27: Our Lady of Guadalupe is proclaimed Patron of the capital of New Spain, and the plague ceases immediately after she is declared patron. December twelfth is proclaimed both a holy day and a civil holiday.

1754. April 24: Sacred Congregation of Rites issues a decree approving the Office and Mass for Our Lady of Guadalupe, May 25. His Holiness Benedict XIV issues a Bulla approving Our Lady of Guadalupe as Patroness of Mexico. He quotes Psalm 147: "To no other nation has such a wonder been done."

1777. June 1: Chapel of the Well *(El Pocito)* begun by Archbishop Nunez de Haro y Peralto, completed in **1791.** It is one of the most beautiful chapels in the world, and is situated on the eastern side of the *Plaza de Mexico.*

1810. Father Miguel Hidalgo uses a painting of Our Lady of Guadalupe as the flag, at the beginning of the Mexican War of Independence from Spain.

1821. October 12: Emperor Augustin de Iturbide, first Mexican emperor and governor after independence, gives thanks and places the future of the nation in Our Lady's hands. He proclaims her Patroness of the nation and founds the Order of Guadalupe.

1887. March 12: Pope Leo XIII orders the crowning of the Sacred Image

1894. Pope Leo XIII approves new Office and Mass of Our Lady of Guadalupe.

1895. October 12: The crowning of the Image of Our Lady of

Guadalupe by two Archbishops of Mexico, one the personal delegate of Pope Leo XIII.

1910. August 24: Pope St. Pius X proclaims Holy Mary of Guadalupe Patroness of Latin America.

1921. November 14: At 10:30 in the morning, a bomb, concealed in a vase of roses, explodes beneath the picture. The Sacred Image miraculously preserved from harm.

1933. December 10: Coronation of Our Lady of Guadalupe in Rome itself. December 12: Solemn Pontifical Mass in St. Peter's in the presence of Pope Pius XI who proclaims her Patronage over Latin America which had also been declared by St. Pius X in 1910.

1945. October 12: Pope Pius XII broadcasts a radio message to Mexico and commemorates the golden anniversary of the crowning of Our Lady's picture.

1950. December 12: The Plaza of the Americas, facing the Basilica is begun and inaugurated on November 25. The Mexican Government donated the land and services.

1962. The boulevard, *Calzada de los Misterios*, which covers the original causeway on which Juan Diego walked from Tepeyac to the residence of the Bishop is restored by the government.

1966. May 31: Pope Paul VI sends a Golden Rose to Our Lady of Guadalupe.

1970. October 12: Pope Paul VI makes a Telestar appearance to the people of Mexico. He commemorates the 75th Anniversary, 1895-1970, of the Crowning of Our Lady as Queen of Mexico and Empress of All the Americas

1976. October 11: The new Basilica opens, and the Sacred Image is transferred from the Old Basilica to the new one.

1979. January 2: John Paul II, shortly after his election, makes the first of his many world-wide pilgrimages to Mexico and the shrine of Our Lady of Guadalupe. On the same trip he attends the Third General Conference of the Latin-American Episcopate.

1990. May 6: The Holy Father makes his second pilgrimage to the Shrine of Our Lady and beatifies Juan Diego, along with three other Mexicans.

—*By the late Fr. James T. Meehan, S.J., up to and including 1970.*

Bibliography

The first book on Guadalupe published in English, as far as we know, was "Our Lady of Guadalupe, Patroness of the Americas," *by Fr. George Lee. The fact that it came out just under a hundred years ago shows how late the interest in Guadalupe was in the English-speaking countries. The next major work on Guadalupe,* "The Grace of Guadalupe," *by the well known author Frances Parkenson Keyes, came out in 1941. These books are easy reading and very well researched; but, unfortunately, both are out of print. Another good resource book is the anthology,* "The Dark Virgin," *by Donald Demarest and Coley Taylor, a hardback no longer in print. Listed below are more recent books, most of which are still available.*

The Franciscans Came First: Franchón Royer (St. Anthony Guild Press, Paterson, NJ, 1951) Hand cover, 295 pp. ❖ Less known than the story of the Spanish conquest of the New World, but of equal import is the inspiring story of the early Franciscans' role in the conquest of pagan hearts for Christ. Inspiring reading, especially the lives of these saintly men.

The Queen's Portrait: Sr. Mary Amatora, O.S.F. (Exposition Press, New York, 1961 and 1972). Hard cover, 144 pp. ❖ Inspirational and easy reading with many black and white illustrations.

Our Lady of Guadalupe, Hope of America: Fr. Bede O'Leary, O.C.S.O. (Trappist Abbey of Our Lady of Guadalupe, Lafayette, OR, 1949). Paperback, 36 pp. in its 1974 printing.

Guadalupe from the Aztec: Fr. Martinus Cawley, O.C.S.O. (First translation of *Nican Mopohua* into English from the original language it was written. Guadalupe Translations, P.O.Box 97, Lafayette, OR 97127, 1968). 36 pp. ❖ Aims to convey the poetic and theological beauty of the original. Illustrated by Jean Charlot. Bulk rate to allow for distribution to groups.

Anthology of Early Guadalupan Literature: Fr. Martinus Cawley, O.C.S.O. 88 pp. same address

That Motherly Mother of Guadalupe: Rev. L.M. Dooley, S.V.D. (The Daughters of St. Paul, 1962, 1979. 50 St. Paul Ave., Jamaica Plain, Boston, MA 02130). 72 pp. ❖ Nicely done, with prayers to Mary of Guadalupe at the end of the book.

Am I Not Here?: Harold Rahm, S.J. (The Blue Army of Our Lady of Fatima, P.O. Box 976, Washington, NJ, 07882). 176 pp. with two appendices in 1974 reprint. ❖ By the former official promoter of Guadalupe devotions in the United States, this book is very readable and gives some updated details about the Guadalupe devotion in the States. The author is at present a missionary in Brazil.

Mother for a New World, Our Lady of Guadalupe: Herbert Leies, S.M. (Newman Press, Westminster, MD. Distributed in the U.S. by

Christian Classics, 205 Willis Street, Westminster, MD 21157). 425 pp. four appendices and two bibliographies. ❖ Covers many subjects pertaining to Guadalupe in an interesting and thorough way. The author has drawn from a rich store of literature in Spanish on Guadalupe in Mexico for a well researched work.

The Wonder of Guadalupe: Francis Johnston (Tan Books and Publishers, Inc., P.O. Box 424, Rockford, IL 61105, 1981). Paperback, 144 pp. ❖ Written by a journalist who did much research in the cultural, religious and political background of the Guadalupe apparitions. The well written, easy to read book also contains information on the modern scientific studies of the tilma.

Our Lady of Guadalupe and The Conquest of Darkness: Warren H. Carroll (Christendom Publications, Rt. 3, Box 87, Front Royal, VA 22630, 1983). Paperback, 119 pp. ❖ Covers the conquest of Mexico by Cortés in the first part, with many interesting details and comments by the author. The second part is on the spiritual conversion of the Mexicans through Our Lady of Guadalupe. The noted Catholic historian recreates this period of New World history in a very readable way, by his attention to and ability in making the main characters in this history come alive.

The Image of Guadalupe: Myth or Miracle?: Jody Brant Smith, revised edition (Image Books, a division of Doubleday & Co. New York, 1984). Paperback, 191 pp. ❖ The non-Catholic scholar has done a very valuable work, which brings to the fore the various proofs substantiating the authenticity of Guadalupe by modern science. He is the founder of the on-going Guadalupe Research Project. The revised edition is more accurate than the first edition, and has seven appendices.

Mary of the Americas, Our Lady of Guadalupe: Fr. Christopher Rengers, O.F.M. Cap. (Alba House, Society of St. Paul, 2187 Victory Blvd., Staten Island, New York 10314, 1990) Paperback, 154 pp. ❖ This book by a long-time apostle of Guadalupe, in addition to the story of Guadalupe and the tilma, has information that one does not find in other books on Guadalupe. A valuable addition to any Guadalupan library by one of the foremost authorities on Guadalupe. Fr. Rengers' book is both factual and devotional and sure to inspire a love for Our Lady.

Our Lady of Guadalupe and Her Missionary Image: Daniel J. Lynch (The Missionary Image of Our Lady of Guadalupe, Inc., 26 Lake Street, St. Albans, VT 05478, 1993). Paperback, 210 pp. ❖ Relates how the practice of human sacrifice, amounting to many thousands yearly in the Aztec Empire, was replaced by the one true and only Sacrifice of the Mass, and how Our Lady of Guadalupe brought an end to pagan worship in Mexico, converting millions. Lynch also explains his role in the "Apostolate of Our Lady of Guadalupe and Her Missionary Image" and the many fruits that are being realized through this pro-life movement.

Mother of the Americas: Robert Feeney (Aquinas Press, 207 Newhall Place, S.W., Leesburg, VA 22075, 1995). Paperback, 100 pp.

❖ This book is unique in two ways: First, it makes a strong appeal to the reader to follow the lead of Pope John Paul II by participating in the "new evangelization" in preparation for the third Millennium of Christianity, and second, it places Mary of Guadalupe, the "Star of Evangelization" central to the conversion of the world.

"Juan de Zumárraga, First Bishop of Mexico:" Rev. Daniel J. Mulvihill, C.S.B. (University of Michigan, unpublished Ph.D. Dissertation, 1954, available from U.M.I., 300 N. Zeeb Road, Ann Arbor, MI 48106, 1-800-521-0600). 324 pp. ❖ Probably the best biography of Bishop Zumárraga available in English. It shows the true stature of this great man, carefully chosen by heaven to be a primary player in the Guadalupe Event. Excellent for those who want the ecclesial and social context of Mary's appearances in Mexico.

Children's Books

Miracle in Mexico - The Story of Juan Diego: Lon Tinkle (Hawthorn Books, New York, 1965). Hard cover, 188 pp. ❖ Word glossary and index very helpful, written for teens, but worthwhile reading for adults.

The Lady of Guadalupe: Written and illustrated by Tomie de Paola (Holiday House, Inc. 18 East 53rd St., New York, NY 10022, 1980). Approx. 44pp. ❖ The story is charmingly told and illustrated; suitable for ages 6 to 80!

Our Lady of Guadalupe: Rev. Lawrence G. Lovasik, S.V.D. (St. Joseph Picture Book Series, Catholic Book Publishing Co. New York, NY, 1985). 31 pp. ❖ Well illustrated and suitable for elementary ages.

Guadalupe in Song and Video Tapes

Counted As Mine: An operetta score on Our Lady of Guadalupe; music written by well-known composer Fr. Joseph Roff and lyrics by Sr. Mary Francis, P.C.C. (Sr. Mary Francis, P.C.C., Our Lady of Guadalupe Monastery, 809 East 19th St. Rosewell, New Mexico 88201).

I Wait on Tepeyac: Marty Rotella, a young dedicated music composer who devotes his talent in singing the praises of Our Lady of Guadalupe. 13 original songs telling the story of Guadalupe on a CD.

Once on a Barren Hill: A video tape, on the Story of Our Lady of Guadalupe (from the Daughters of St. Paul, 50 St. Paul Avenue, Jamaica Plain, MA 02130). ❖ An inspirational 27-minute video dramatization of the story of Mary's several apparitions to Juan Diego in full color on VHS cassette.

The Cloak of Juan Diego: A documentary tape which takes you right to the shrine (Passionist Communications Inc., 19 Second Ave., P.O. Box 440, Peltham, NY 10803).

The Academy of the Immaculate Books

All Generations Shall Call Me Blessed *by Fr. Stefano Manelli, F.I.* A scholarly easy to read book tracing Mary's role in the Old Testament through prophecies, figures, and symbols to Mary's presence in the New Testament. A concise exposition which shows clearly Mary's place in the economy of Salvation.

Totus Tuus *by Msgr. Arthur Burton Calkins* Provides a thorough examination of the Holy Father's thoughts on total consecration or entrustment to Our Lady based on the historic, theological and scriptural evidence. Vital in clearing away some misunderstandings about entrustment and consecration.

Jesus Our Eucharistic Love *by Fr. Stefano Manelli, F.I.* A treasure of Eucharistic devotional writings and examples from the Saints showing their stirring Eucharistic love and devotion. A valuable aid for reading meditatively before the Blessed Sacrament.

Virgo Facta Ecclesia *by Franciscan Friars of the Immaculate* is made up of two parts: the first a biography on St. Francis of Assisi and the second part on the Marian character of the Franciscan Order based on its long Marian tradition, from St. Francis to St. Maximilian Kolbe.

Not Made by Hands *by Thomas Sennott* An excellent resource book covering the two most controversial images in existence: the Holy Image of Our Lady of Guadalupe on the tilma of Juan Diego and the Sacred Image of the Crucified on the Shroud of Turin, giving scientific evidence for their authenticity and exposing the fraudulent carbon 14 test.

For the Life of the World *by Jerzy Domanski, O.F.M. Conv.* The former international director of the Knights of the Immaculata and Guardian of the City of the Immaculate in Poland examines Fr. Kolbe's Eucharistic, spiritual life as a priest and adorer of the Eucharist all in the context of his love of the Immaculate.

Padre Pio of Pietrelcina *by Fr. Stefano Manelli, F.I.* This 144 page popular life of Padre Pio is packed with details about his life, spirituality, and charisms, by one who knew the Padre intimately. The author turned to Padre Pio for guidance in establishing a new Community, the Franciscans of the Immaculate.

Come Follow Me *by Fr. Stefano Manelli, F.I.* A book directed to any young person contemplating a Religious vocation. Informative, with many inspiring illustrations and words from the lives and writings of the Saints on the challenging vocation of total dedication in the following of Christ and His Immaculate Mother through the three vows of religion.

St. Thérèse: Doctor of the Little Way A compendium of 32 chapters covering many unique facets about the latest Doctor of the Church by 23 authors including the late Fr. John Hardon, S.J., Msgr. Vernon Johnson,

Sister Marie of the Trinity, O.C.D., and Stephanè Piat. The 174 page book is well illustrated.

Marian Shrines of France On the three major Marian shrines and apparitions of France during the 19th century: Our Lady at Rue du Bac (Paris), La Salette and Lourdes. Shows how already in the 19th century Our Lady checkmated our secular, godless 20th century introducing the present Age of Mary. Well illustrated.

Padre Pio—The Wonder Worker This book on the popular saint of our times includes the two inspirational homilies given by Pope John Paul II during the beatification celebration in Rome. The first part of the book is a short biography. The second is on his spirituality, charisms, apostolate of the confessional, and his great works of charity.

Marian Shrines of Italy One of the series of "Marian Saints and Shrines," with 36 pages of colorful illustrations on over thirty of the 1500 Marian shrines in Italy. The book covers that topic with an underlying theme of the intimate and vital relationship between Mary and the Church. This is especially apparent in Catholic Italy, where the center of the Catholic Faith is found in Rome.

Kolbe, Saint of the Immaculata The latest "Marian Saints and Shrines" books on St. Maximilian, missionary, theologian, publisher, founder of the Knights of the Immaculate Movement and martyr of charity, edited by Bro. Francis Mary, FI, with over ten different contributors. Foremost Mariologists contributing Fr. Peter Fehlner, F.I., Fr. James McCurry, O.F.M. Conv., Fr. Jerzy Domanski, O.F.M. Conv., and Marak Miravalle, S.T.D. Well researched, provocative, inspiring, life and ideals of one of the greatest Marian saints of all times. Over 100 illustrations, 270 pages.

Mail Orders to: Academy of the Immaculate
POB 667
Valatie, NY 12184
USA
FAX (518) 758-1584
Email:academy@nycap.rr.com